US Government and Politics

Books in the Politics Study Guides series

US Government and Politics

William Storey

Edinburgh University Press

Edinburgh University Press Ltd
22 George Square, Edinburgh

Typeset in 11/13pt Monotype Baskerville by
Servis Filmsetting Ltd, Manchester, and
printed and bound in Spain by
GraphyCems

A CIP record for this book is available from the British Library

ISBN 978 0 7486 2429 4 (paperback)

Contents

Part III: Testing the Limits of Federal Power – the Legislature and the Executive

Boxes

Tables

A Beacon on the Hill?

When the thirteen North American colonies broke away from Britain in 1776, they opened their Declaration of Independence with the words, 'We believe these truths to be self-evident, that all men are created equal, that they are endowed by their Creator with certain inalienable Rights, that among these are Life, Liberty and the pursuit of Happiness.'

The Constitution they drew up in 1787, after the War of Independence, was designed to ensure that no single person, or group of people, could acquire enough power to threaten the liberties of the new nation's citizens, or threaten their ability to freely pursue whatever goals would bring them happiness. The first ten amendments to the Constitution reinforced these safeguards by protecting specified rights against any threat, even the will of a majority of Americans. The political culture which then developed ensured that almost anyone with the power to influence people's way of life, from members of the local school board to Senators, were held accountable at frequent elections.

Many in the USA, and around the world, regard this political system as a model for liberal democracy, a 'beacon on the hill'. It is seen as providing liberty for Americans and the world's 'huddled masses, yearning to breathe free'. It is also seen as a framework for equality of opportunity, a genuine meritocracy in which anyone can develop their true potential if they try hard enough.

Yet, as this political culture was being moulded, even as the Declaration of Independence was setting out its high ideals and the Constitution was being written and debated, the USA permitted slavery and, later, legalised segregation. As a former slave, Frederick Douglass, put it, "liberty and slavery – opposite as heaven and hell – are both in the Constitution". With racism and oppression as much a feature of mainstream US politics as liberty and opportunity, questions have long been asked about whether the country is truly the meritocracy it is held up to be. Furthermore, the mechanisms for holding those in power to account, such as elections, have been criticised for becoming tools for the already powerful to reinforce their political, social and economic dominance.

This book challenges readers to examine both of these viewpoints and decide whether the US political system can be legitimately described as a 'beacon on the hill', the benchmark of liberal democracy. *Part 1* covers the framework of the US political system. Chapter 1 examines the Constitution, its aims, structure and development. Chapter 2 explores the suggestion, exemplified by the experience of African-Americans, that the USA has produced the appearance, but not the reality, of a meritocracy. It outlines the fierce debate over whether the government has a moral and constitutional responsibility to ensure that there is genuine equality of opportunity. Chapter 3 examines the role of the Supreme Court in enforcing the provisions of the Constitution, ensuring that the Constitution lives up to its ideals, and the political debate that has developed over the way that the Court has used its position as the guardian of the Constitution's aims and values.

Part 2 covers the mechanisms that the Founding Fathers expected would ensure that power would remain fragmented, preventing any group of people from becoming politically dominant and using their power oppressively. Chapter 4 examines the role of Federalism and considers whether it provides local control and accountability that would be impossible for the national government in a country as large and diverse as the USA or, conversely, whether the national government is the most effective defender of constitutional liberties when a dominant group in any region of the country uses its political power to oppress minorities. Similarly, Chapter 5 examines whether the sheer number and frequency of elections ensures that the powerful are held effectively to account or whether the cost of elections, together with their frequency, ensures that representatives are more concerned with the interests of their financial donors than the interests of the humble voter. Chapters 6 and 7 evaluate whether the organisations that represent the interests of all sections of society, political parties and pressure groups, are effective vehicles for ensuring that the concerns of all groups are properly considered when policies are being developed or whether they promote the interests of a wealthy, influential minority.

Having considered the purpose of the political system and the methods used to achieve its aims, *Part 3* examines whether the framework, and the systems to prevent concentrations of power, are having the desired effect at the Federal level in the modern USA. Chapter 8 explains the constitutional responsibilities of the two houses of Congress and analyses how effectively it fulfils them. Chapters 9 and 10 explore the development of the President's powers in domestic and foreign affairs, and evaluate how this institution's powers have developed since the Constitution came into operation in 1789.

Does the US political system provide its 300 million diverse citizens the liberty and equality of opportunity that the Founding Fathers aimed to guarantee? This book outlines the arguments and offers the evidence to help its readers decide.

PART I: THE FRAMEWORK OF US POLITICS

CHAPTER 1

The Constitution – History and Key Features

Contents

Overview

On 11 September 2001, airliners were flown into the World Trade Center in New York City and the Pentagon in Washington DC, with the loss of over 3,000 lives. Forty-five days later, President George W. Bush signed into law the PATRIOT Act which, among many other measures, allowed the FBI to seize 'any tangible thing', including books, letters, diaries, library records, medical and psychiatric records, financial information, membership lists of religious institutions, and even genetic information.

For many Americans, this represented the right balance between their country's cherished traditions of personal liberty and the government's need to be able to effectively resist the greatest threat of the modern era – terrorism. For others, it did not go far enough in providing the government with the tools it needed. For a third group, it went too far in sacrificing freedom in the name of security.

When, on 25 May 1787, fifty-five men gathered in Philadelphia for a convention that would produce the Constitution of the United States of America, they faced the same challenge in finding the right balance between the great threat of their age, tyranny, and the ability of government to effectively manage the country.

This chapter examines what conclusions they reached, how they reached them and raises questions as to whether the Constitution has succeeded in its goal of providing a framework for effective government that guarantees freedom and equality of opportunity for all.

Key issues to be covered in this chapter

- The importance of freedom and equality of opportunity, and the process of creating a document in which these values were protected
- The political arrangements designed to ensure that government could be effective without jeopardising liberty
- The debates on whether the Constitution successfully strikes the intended balance between freedom and effective government

The origins of the Constitution

A haven for refugees

The fifty-five men who attended the Constitutional Convention in May 1787 represented all of the thirteen states, except Rhode Island, which had fought for and won independence from Britain. All of them were descendents of early European settlers who had made the long, dangerous journey across the Atlantic for two main reasons:

1. Economic freedom. In 1607, the first English settlement was formed at Jamestown, Virginia. At that time, in England, people's social positions and opportunities to build wealth depended on the family they were born into, rather than their ability, hard work and ambition. In the new settlement there were no such restrictions and, in contrast to Britain, fertile land was freely available. Even convicts brought over to provide cheap labour were able to become wealthy land-owners once they had served their sentence. These new freedoms, however, created new challenges. How should this community, not based on privilege, be governed? And with all settlers having the option of becoming land-owners, who would provide the labour needed on farms? Within twelve years, Jamestown had set up a legislature with an upper and lower house and had imported its first group of slaves.

2. Religious freedom. In 1620, the *Mayflower* landed in Massachusetts, bringing Pilgrims from England. These uncompromising Protestants not only wanted to practise their faith without being persecuted by the authorities but also believed that a new Christian community, free of the 'evil' influences they had left behind, would serve as a model, 'a beacon on the hill', to Europeans. The kind of religious tolerance they wanted, however, created some difficulties. Were they prepared to be tolerant towards people of other faiths, such as Roman Catholics, whom they fundamentally disagreed with? If not, would they be guilty of the kind of religious intolerance from which they themselves had fled? Even before reaching the coast of North America, the Pilgrims agreed to, and signed, a written set of rules known as the Mayflower Compact, which included the election of officers to administer their community and to wrestle with these difficult questions. In 1639, the

new colony of Connecticut went one step further, drawing up the Fundamental Orders of Connecticut, the first written constitution.

By the time they became independent from Britain, therefore, the people of this new nation already had firmly established political traditions. At the heart of them was a commitment to personal liberty and a determination that government would never be able to oppress them in the way that the British monarch had done.

Fighting for freedom

Having risked their lives crossing the Atlantic to find a level of freedom not available in Europe, the early settlers set up local government that would not become as oppressive as the one they had left behind. By 1700, they had created a pattern across the thirteen colonies, as follows:

- The **executive branch** of government: A governor, responsible for the day-to-day running of the colony, appointed or approved by the monarch.
- The **legislative branch** of government: A parliament, with an upper and lower house. The upper house, appointed or approved by the monarch, played a role similar to the House of Lords in England, with advisory and court of appeal functions. The lower house, elected by citizens, passed the laws the Executive branch was responsible for administering.
- Written constitutions: A document defining the structure of government and the powers and duties of each branch of government.

In contrast to representative forms of government in North America, the monarch could issue Royal Proclamations and the British Parliament could pass laws, without consultation, which each colony had to obey. After the seven years war (1756–63), Britain gained land from France and Spain which seemed to provide new opportunities for expansion by the thirteen colonies. However, Parliament expected the colonies to contribute towards the cost of the war, which meant higher taxes, and the King issued a proclamation reserving the new territories for Native Americans. These two steps, as well as simmering discontent with other decisions taken in London, led to demands for self-government for America.

The Declaration of Independence, issued on 4 July 1776, marked the start of the War of Independence, which lasted for five years. In simple terms, it did two things:

1. Identified the rights to which all people were entitled and the purpose of government. The experience of representative democracy had drawn the support of philosophers who challenged the traditional belief that monarchs were chosen by God and should never be questioned. The political thinker John Locke argued that God distinguished people from animals by giving them 'natural rights' that no one, not even monarchs, could infringe. The Declaration of Independence asserted that:

   We hold these truths to be self-evident, that all men are created equal, and that they are endowed by their Creator with certain inalienable Rights, that among these are Life, Liberty and the pursuit of Happiness.

   That to secure these rights, Governments are instituted among Men, deriving their just powers from the consent of the governed.

   That whenever any Form of Government becomes destructive of these ends, it is the Right of the People to alter or to abolish it, and to institute new Government . . .

2. Listed twenty-seven examples of the British government, especially the King, abusing its power, which, in turn, justified the revolution. These included many concerns that were still evident at the Constitutional Convention, eleven years later, including:

   - He has made Judges dependent on his Will alone.
   - He has kept among us, in times of peace, Standing armies without the Consent of our legislatures.
   - He has affected to render the Military independent of and superior to the Civil power.
   - Imposing taxes on us without our consent.
   - Suspending our own Legislatures.

A shared political culture
Having arrived in North America seeking personal freedom, set up forms of government to protect that freedom and having fought to retain it, by 1787 the leaders of the thirteen states had developed a shared political culture. Although each state had its own distinctive

lifestyles and traditions, there was general agreement in the following areas:

- There should be minimal government interference in business/commerce.
- There should be freedom of speech and religion.
- Each state should retain its separate traditions and sense of identity.
- The people should decide, at elections, who has political power and should have regular opportunities to remove them from power.
- No one, not even people of the highest integrity, should have too much power.
  - Therefore, the three branches of government should be separate and their powers clearly defined.
  - Therefore, each branch of government should be responsible for ensuring that the others did not, over time, accumulate power.
  - Therefore, political education, public participation and general debate on political issues should be encouraged.

Taken together, with the role of government being severely restricted and business being encouraged, it was understood that the USA would have a low-tax economy, based on robust individualism.

How the Constitution was written

Had the pendulum swung too far?

After the War of Independence, the leaders of this new nation were so determined not to replace one tyrannical government (in London) with another (in the USA) that they set up a weak central government, mainly to conduct foreign affairs. It had no executive branch to propose and co-ordinate policies and no **judicial branch** to enforce laws. These Articles of **Confederation** certainly ensured that the government could not interfere in the affairs of the thirteen states, or oppress the citizens, but they also ensured that the government could do little to resolve problems facing the country.

A border dispute between Maryland and Virginia in 1785 illustrated the need for greater co-ordination between the States. The dispute was resolved by a successful convention held at Annapolis, in

Maryland. However, to ensure that there was a more effective mechanism for dealing with such disputes, it was decided to review the system of government at a Constitutional Convention, to be held in Philadelphia.

The Constitutional Convention began with 'the sole and express purpose of revising the Articles of Confederation' The delegates elected George Washington as Chairman of the Convention and agreed a simple set of rules:

- Delegates from at least seven of the thirteen states had to be present for each meeting.
- Discussions would be secret, to enable the delegates to speak freely without coming under pressure from their states.
- Each state had one vote.
- A simple majority was required for all decisions.
- When the process was complete, all thirteen states would be bound by the outcome once nine of them had ratified it.

They started work on 25 May 1787.

Bitter disputes

Despite their shared political culture, there were two main areas of disagreement between the delegates that caused intense and bitter debate:

1. Big states *vs* small states. At the start of the Convention, the largest state, Virginia, proposed a strong central government based on three principles:
   - A two-chamber legislature, elected by the people, with wide-ranging powers.
   - A strong executive, chosen by the legislature.
   - A national judiciary, appointed by the legislature.
   Because such a legislature, making all the important decisions, would be dominated by representatives of the states with the largest populations, this plan was unacceptable to states with smaller populations. One of them, New Jersey, put forward a counter-plan, also based on three principles:
   - A single-chamber legislature, with one vote for each state and strictly limited powers.

- A weak executive, consisting of more than one person, chosen by the legislature.
- A limited national judiciary, appointed by the executive.

Debate on these plans resulted in deadlock for much of the summer of 1787.

2. Slavery. At the time of the Convention, almost one-third of the people of the southern states were enslaved Africans. Three northern states – Connecticut, Pennsylvania and Rhode Island – had put an end to slavery. Two others – Massachusetts and Delaware – had ended the importation of slaves. Delegates from these and other northern states wanted all slaves to be counted for taxation purposes (effectively increasing the cost of slavery) but not for representation in the legislature. Delegates from the southern states, whose prosperity depended on slavery, wanted the opposite, fearing that slavery would not last unless they were well-represented. In addition, they wanted to ensure that no law could be passed interfering with the slave trade, which provided additional slaves from overseas. They made it clear that they were not prepared to accept a constitution that restricted slavery.

Compromises

1. The deadlock between supporters of the Virginia Plan and the New Jersey Plan was resolved by the Connecticut Compromise. This adopted features from both plans for each branch of government but the key element was an agreement that the legislative branch would consist of two chambers, the lower based on population and the upper having two members from each state.

2. The deadlock on slavery was resolved by the **three-fifths compromise** which gave the southern states most of what they wanted. Slaves were counted as three-fifths of a person for the purposes of both taxation and representation. Although the word 'slave' does not occur in the Constitution, a clause was also included which protected the slave trade until at least 1808.

The 'miracle of Philadelphia'

It was comparatively straightforward to recognise that, under the Articles of Confederation, the pendulum had swung too far in

the direction of protecting the people from tyrannical government. It was far more difficult, potentially even impossible, for
people with conflicting interests to agree on how far it should swing
back.

The compromises reached meant that when the Convention
ended, on 17 September 1787, it had been able to find a balance
between effective government and personal freedom that a majority
could accept. None of the delegates found the outcome ideal but,
as the imperial European nations were growing in strength and
territorial ambition, all recognised that the only way for their newly
independent nation to survive was to find a way to work together.
As Benjamin Franklin said at the start of the War of Independence,
'we must all hang together or, most assuredly, we shall all hang
separately'. The fact that the Constitution it produced has
remained largely unaltered for over 200 years means that the
Constitutional Convention is now seen as an immense political
achievement.

The ratification debate: its advantages and disadvantages

A ferment of ideas

The arguments on the best balance between liberty and effective government did not end when the Constitutional Convention completed
its work. Before the Constitution could become law, nine of the thirteen states had to ratify it and this provided an opportunity for
renewed debate on its advantages and disadvantages. With the
general population to persuade, supporters and opponents of the
Constitution launched a massive propaganda campaign in newspapers and pamphlets in every state.

Three views dominated the debate, written by the leading
statesmen of the era under pseudonyms of ancient philosophers to
demonstrate that their arguments were based not only on their
personal opinions but on a solid understanding of political debates
through the ages. The involvement of the public became a form
of political education. The people became familiar with their
Constitution and understood it, a feature of American politics to this
day.

Thomas Jefferson and the anti-Federalists

Thomas Jefferson, who wrote the original draft of the Declaration of Independence and went on to become the 3rd President of the United States, was a leading member of the **anti-Federalists**, who opposed the Constitution mainly on the grounds that it created a national government that was too powerful and that would, ultimately, become oppressive.

As a group, they were not very unified but, between them, they expressed the following five arguments:

1. A strong executive, even with checks and balances, could develop into a tyrant, like the king they had fought against.
2. A strong legislature, with the power to raise an army and impose taxes, was being given the tools of oppression that the British had used.
3. Separation of powers was not strict enough. In particular, the Senate's role in ratifying the President's appointments might make it reluctant to fulfil its role of closely scrutinising the people it had helped appoint.
4. Representation could only be effective if the government was close to the people and understood the people. This would be difficult in a country as large and diverse as the United States, and especially for the President, who represented the entire country.
5. States' rights would erode over time as a strong national government would inevitably accumulate power at the expense of the states.

At the very least, therefore, they argued that the Constitution should be strengthened to protect liberty in the following ways:

1. Representatives should have shorter terms of office, a limit to the number of terms they could serve and there should be a system for recalling (sacking) representatives failing to meet the wishes of their constituents.
2. A Bill of Rights should be added to the Constitution to reinforce the checks and balances already included to protect individuals' freedoms.

Alexander Hamilton and the Federalists

Another of the Founding Fathers, Alexander Hamilton, was the principal author of a series of newspaper articles, known as the Federalist Papers, which outlined the arguments in favour of the Constitution. He took the opposite view to Jefferson and was a leading member of the **Federalists**, who supported a stronger national government.

The arguments of the Federalists were simple: the nation would not be able to survive without a national government and that that government had to be given sufficient power to be effective. It is not possible to govern through powerlessness.

Many Federalists opposed the addition of a Bill of Rights because, as one put it, 'if we list a set of rights, some fools in the future are going to claim that people are entitled only to those rights enumerated, and no others'.

James Madison and the Federalists

James Madison, who went on to become the 4th President of the United States, was a co-author of the Federalist Papers but held views that lay somewhere between those of Jefferson and Hamilton. He is principally associated with support for the mechanisms to ensure that the national government can have enough power to be effective but face restrictions that stop it from becoming tyrannical. These mechanisms are:

- **Federalism**, which ensures that power is not concentrated in the national government.
- Separation of powers, which allocates specific tasks to each branch of government and defines the limit of its powers.
- Checks and balances, in which each branch of government ensures that the others fully meet their responsibilities and do not encroach on the powers of any other branch.

The result, Madison believed, would be competition for power and competition between branches of government. This would promote diversity of ideas and beliefs, which, in turn, would generate debate, understanding of political issues and political participation, which are all beneficial to an active democracy, based on freedom.

The Bill of Rights

This ferment of ideas influenced the final document. As the debate raged through the winter of 1787–88, it became clear that **ratification** would not be possible unless a Bill of Rights was added, and it was agreed that once the Constitution came into effect, the first act of the legislature would be to draft the necessary amendments.

The key features of the Constitution

The purpose of the Constitution

The aims of the Constitution are clearly laid out in its Preamble. Its goal is to:

– Form a closer union between the states.
– Establish justice.
– Provide effective defence.
– Ensure liberty.

'Ambition counter-acting ambition'

The final document reflected the Founding Fathers' belief that anyone, even a person of the highest integrity, could be tempted to increase the amount of power they had and to use it for their own benefit or that of their friends and family. Once this happened, people would suffer. Therefore, the core principle of the Constitution was that people in government should have enough power to rule effectively but find it very difficult to accumulate and abuse power. Accordingly, the Constitution was based on James Madison's principles of:

- Federalism, which limited the power of central government as a whole
- **Separation of powers** between the three branches of the national government
- **Checks and balances**, which recognised that ambitious politicians would almost certainly attempt to increase their power but would be restrained by other, equally ambitious, politicians determined not to lose power.

Federalism was intended to ensure that the majority of decisions affecting daily life would be taken by people from the local community, who could best appreciate the needs and wishes of that community and would be accountable to that community. The central government would only make decisions that affected the whole country, with the Constitution outlining which exclusive powers were needed to do this and providing reserved powers for the states to take all other decisions. For many Americans, this is the greatest constitutional protection from the accumulation of power in few hands.

Separation of powers was intended to ensure that the three main roles of central government – passing laws, carrying out laws and ruling on the application of laws – would be carried out by different groups of people, again to avoid the concentration of power. The Constitution, therefore, outlined the specific responsibilities of each branch of government (see below).

Checks and balances were built into the Constitution to ensure that the powers of the three branches of government did not drift from one to another. With each branch having responsibility to monitor the powers of the other two, and to ensure that those powers were used appropriately, the relationships designed by the Founding Fathers would be maintained (see below).

Protecting the people from their Government

The first three articles of the Constitution outline the structure of government, giving each branch clearly defined powers that would enable it to govern effectively and strict limitations on the use of those powers.

Article I: The most important branch of government was to be the legislature, Congress. It would be bicameral, consisting of two houses or chambers. The lower chamber, the House of Representatives, was to be the voice of the people, with each state represented in proportion to its population. The upper chamber, the Senate, was to protect the interests of the states (especially the smaller ones), with each having two Senators. Between them, the two chambers would have responsibility for:

* Passing laws.
* Deciding on taxation and how taxes should be spent.
* Scrutinising the day-to-day work of the President.

- Agreeing to any appointments made by the President.
- Agreeing to any treaties signed by the President.
- Removing any officials who abused their power.

Checks and balances: virtually all actions of the President would be subject to Congressional oversight. 'Power of the purse' (control over the budget) is arguably the most powerful tool Congress has in relation to the executive branch of government. Appointments to the Supreme Court, although initiated by the President, would be subject to the advice and consent of the Senate. Congress's performance would, in turn, be reviewed on a regular basis. All members of the lower chamber, the House of Representatives, would serve for two years and then face an election. Senators would serve for six years before facing re-appointment by their state legislature. To ensure that the legislature itself did not become too powerful, its responsibilities were clearly defined in a long list in Section 8 of Article 1.

Article II: In defining the powers of the President, the Founding Fathers were determined to ensure that this position did not become similar to that of a monarch. Use of the powers given to this position required agreement from another branch of Government, usually the legislature. The main exception to this principle was the President's role as Commander-in-Chief of the armed forces but, with over 3,000 miles of ocean between the USA and its potential enemies, it was not expected that this would be a significant role.

Checks and balances: the principal powers of the President in relation to the other branches of government would be the ability to veto Congressional legislation and to nominate justices to the Supreme Court. Because of the growth of the USA as a world power, beyond the expectations of the Founding Fathers, checks and balances on the President in the field of foreign affairs has arguably been of limited effectiveness.

The president's term of office would last for four years, and his performance would then be reviewed by the voters.

Article III: There would be a national judiciary, headed by the Supreme Court, which would pass judgement on cases in which a state, a foreign diplomat or another branch of the national government was involved. It would also be the final court of appeal. With the fewest powers, the Supreme Court was expected to be the least significant branch of the national government.

Checks and balances: the Supreme Court was given few constitutional powers and provided with no constitutional checks on other branches. However, once it acquired the power of judicial review, enabling it to declare laws and presidential decisions unconstitutional, the judiciary gained one of the most powerful checks available to any of the branches of government.

Judges, with this formidable power, are appointed for life and it is argued by some that this is the greatest weakness in the system of checks and balances.

Protecting the people from themselves

It was possible that voters could be persuaded to elect one political group to both the legislature and the executive branches of government, who would then appoint their supporters to the judiciary, which would undermine the system of checks and balances. To prevent this, the Founding Fathers organised:

- Indirect elections. The upper chamber would consist of Senators appointed by state legislatures. The President would be elected by the people but their views would be filtered through an electoral college.
- Staggered elections. There would never be a time when everyone in the national government would be elected simultaneously. Members of the lower chamber would be elected every two years. The President would be elected every four years. Senators would hold office for six years but only one-third of them would be appointed at each election cycle.
- Defined election dates. To ensure that those in power could not use a crisis, or create a crisis, to extend their time in office, elections would be held on set dates regardless of circumstances.

Protecting the interests of the States

Article IV: The states would continue to have responsibility for most issues within their own borders. They would have to recognise the laws of other states and, together with Congress, be responsible for deciding if any new territory would be admitted into the United States.

Protecting the Constitution

Article V: There would be two mechanisms for changing the Constitution. To ensure that no group changed it to increase their own power or to reduce the protection of personal freedoms, both would be slow, complicated processes and would require the support not of a slim majority of the people but a 'super-majority'.

- The first method required a two-thirds majority in both houses of Congress to propose an amendment and at least three-quarters of the states to agree to the amendment for it to become law.
- The second method required at least two-thirds of the states to call a national convention, similar to the Convention at Philadelphia that wrote the Constitution, to propose and agree to an amendment. This method has never been used.

More than 5,000 amendments have been proposed but only twenty-seven amendments have ever been passed, of which the first ten are generally considered to be a part of the original constitution (see Bill of Rights, below).

The Equal Rights Amendment (ERA) illustrates the difficulty in amending the Constitution. Providing a constitutional guarantee of equal rights for women, this amendment was passed by Congress in March 1972 with a seven-year deadline for it to be ratified by three-quarters of the states. Twenty-two of the necessary thirty-eight state ratifications were achieved in the first year but the pace slowed as opposition began to organise. There were only eight ratifications in 1973, three in 1974, one in 1975, and none in 1976. In 1977, Indiana became the thirty-fifth and last state to ratify the ERA. A demonstration of 100,000 supporters of the amendment in Washington DC led to Congress granting an extension until 30 June 1982, but with no further support from the states the deadline passed, leaving it three short of the required threshold.

Even clearing the first hurdle is a considerable achievement. Recent examples of proposed amendments that opinion polls demonstrated had considerable popular support but failed to gain the necessary two-thirds support from Congress include:

- Balanced budget amendment.
- Flag desecration amendment.
- School prayer amendment.
- Tax limitation amendment.
- Defence of marriage amendment.

Persistence may pay off, however. The 19th Amendment (granting the vote to women) was introduced in Congress 118 times before its passage, and the 27th Amendment (restricting the ability of members of Congress to give themselves pay rises) was passed more than 200 years after it was originally introduced.

Protecting specific rights: the Bill of Rights
The first ten amendments, which make up the Bill of Rights, came into force on 15 December 1791. There is a distinct pattern to these amendments:

- Amendments I and II protect individual freedoms from the government, including freedom of religion, freedom of speech and freedom of assembly. Freedom of the press is also guaranteed.
- Amendments III and IV protect private property from government intrusion.
- Amendments V, VI, VII and VIII ensure proper treatment of people who have been arrested through custody, trial and sentencing.
- Amendment IX guarantees rights not covered in the previous eight.
- Amendment X reinforces the principle of Federalism.

Keeping the Constitution up to date: Amendments 11–27
As with the Bill of Rights, there is a distinct pattern to these amendments:

- The 11th, 12th, 16th, 17th, 20th, 22nd, 25th and 27th Amendments all clarify or revise the work of the three branches of government, for example:
  - Senators have been elected since the 17th Amendment was passed in 1913
  - The 22nd Amendment, passed in 1951, limited the number of terms a President can serve to two

- If the President is temporarily unable to serve, the 25th Amendment, passed in 1967, sets out the replacement procedure
- The 13th, 14th and 15th Amendments are generally known as the Civil Rights Amendments. After the Civil War, the three amendments abolished slavery (1865), extended the protections of the Bill of Rights to African-Americans (1868) and gave African-Americans the right to vote (1870). By the 1960s, these rights still did not apply to African-Americans and the poll tax, one of the methods to stop them from voting, was abolished by the 24th Amendment, passed in 1964.
- The 19th, 23rd and 26th Amendments expanded the range of people entitled to vote. Women gained the right to vote in 1920, people living in Washington DC gained the right to vote in presidential elections in 1961 (but are still not represented in Congress) and the voting age was lowered from twenty-one to eighteen in 1971.
- The 18th Amendment, passed in 1919, prohibiting alcoholic beverages, proved to be a disastrous failure and had to be repealed by the 21st Amendment passed in 1933.

Prohibition is the only example to date of a constitutional amendment being passed which defined how Americans should lead their lives. The remaining, successful, amendments have served to 'tidy up' the political process, or to extend rights previously denied.

Viewpoints on the effectiveness of the Constitution

American Exceptionalism
In 1832, just over forty years after the Constitution of the USA came into force, a French aristocrat, Alexis de Tocqueville, wrote: 'I saw in America more than America . . . it was the shape of democracy itself . . . its inclinations, character, prejudices and passions . . . I wanted to understand it so as at least to know what we have to fear or hope from there.'

The Founding Fathers, like the their ancestors from England who had originally colonised North America, aimed to create a 'beacon on the hill', a nation based on a set of ideals – democracy, political and legal equality and individual freedom – that would serve Americans and be a model for the rest of the world.

The sense, shared by Americans and foreigners alike, that they created a framework for a nation which is like no other is known as American Exceptionalism. It remains evident today. During the 2004 Presidential election campaign, a poll was conducted in which voters were asked two questions:

1. Is the USA basically a fair and decent country, or not?
2. Would the world be better off if more countries were more like America, or not?

About two-thirds of voters answered yes to both questions. But are they justified in this belief? And why might a third of voters question whether their country provides a model for the world?

Clear principles, flexible details

People who believe in American Exceptionalism argue that it is underpinned by the founding fathers achieving a remarkable balance between the conflicting demands on government. A century after the Constitution was written, another foreign observer, Lord Bryce from Britain, wrote that it was 'a judicious mixture of definiteness in principle with elasticity of details'. According to this view, the Constitution, only about 7,000 words long, combines a fundamental commitment to the protection of the nation and to the liberties of its people without going into a great deal of detail as to how these are to be achieved.

Consequently, even in times of crisis, governments have been able to respond effectively without infringing the liberties of the citizens. Or, on the rare occasions that the core principles of freedom and liberty have been breached, such as President Lincoln suspending constitutional freedoms during the Civil War or Japanese-Americans being denied their constitutional rights during World War II, the balance has been restored once the crisis passed. In short, the Constitution of the USA has always succeeded in providing a frame-work for effective government while protecting personal freedom and liberty and can be relied upon to continue to do so in the post-9/11 era. Evidence of this would be the Supreme Court decisions since 2001 restricting presidential action, outside the scope of the Constitution, in relation to terrorist suspects (see Chapter 3 for more details).

Too flexible, undermining core principles

Even as the Constitution was being written, it was argued by the anti-Federalists that personal liberty could only be effectively protected if the central government had strictly limited powers. Otherwise, over time, it would come to dominate the states, which are closer to the people and understand their needs and wishes.

Some critics of the Constitution argue that this concern has been shown to be valid by developments over the past 200 years. The Constitution contains what is known as the 'elastic clause', which authorises Congress 'to make all laws which shall be necessary and proper' to effectively govern the country. Furthermore, the 'commerce clause' entitles Congress to take action on any issue relating, even loosely, to inter-state commerce and has been used to pass laws relating to the exploitation of labour and racial discrimination. This level of flexibility, critics argue, encroaches on the responsibilities of the states and undermines Federalism, one of the key mechanisms to protect citizens from the power of the national government. The result is that the balance between effective government and personal freedom has tilted dangerously away from liberty, undermining the core principle of the Constitution.

Clear universal principles, not universally applied

During the Constitutional Convention, delegates were fully aware of the contradiction between their aim of creating a framework for liberty and the maintenance of slavery, which they attempted to resolve with the 'three-fifths compromise' (see above). For African-Americans, not represented at the Convention, the result was anything but satisfactory. Designed to 'establish Justice . . . and secure the Blessings of Liberty', the Constitution, in the case of African-Americans, took a clear decision to maintain injustice and exploitation. Indeed, some would go further and argue that slavery underpinned the wealth of the first European settlers and that their descendents, at the Constitutional Convention, created a framework to protect their interests.

From this viewpoint, the USA, far from being a basically fair and decent country, began as institutionally racist and has done too little since to eliminate racism from society. To some, racism is so dyed into the fabric of American society that the values that it claims to stand for cannot be realised until the full impact of racial discrimination is recognised and atoned for.

Conclusion

Clearly, the Constitution has stood the test of time. While other countries have responded to emergencies by ignoring or abolishing their constitutions, the structure of the US Constitution has remained intact, with separation of powers and fundamental rights effectively limiting the actions of people in power.

Despite this, the viewpoint that the Constitution has failed to provided genuine freedom and equality of opportunity for all has been the focus of the most intense conflicts in US political history. Efforts to ensure that the Constitution lives up to its own ideals have led to a Civil War and a Civil Rights movement, both of which have transformed the political landscape.

The debate over whether the goal of securing freedom and equality for all has finally been achieved continues to be fiercely argued. This fundamental challenge to the Constitution continues to be of such political significance today that the next chapter is devoted to an evaluation of whether freedom and equality of opportunity is a reality for all US citizens.

Box 1.1 Comparing the Constitution of the USA with the British Constitution

The importance of rights

The overriding purpose of the Constitution of the USA is to provide those in government with just enough power to meet the needs of society, while denying them any opportunity to infringe fundamental individual rights. The Constitution, in effect, says that it is prepared to accept that the effectiveness of government may be limited by the high priority placed on rights. For those who approve of this balance between rights and effective government, the **codified Constitution** of the USA has the following advantages:

- Rights are entrenched. Only in exceptional circumstances, when there is a 'super-majority' in favour of change, will the rights laid down by the Founding Fathers be changed. In most cases, such as the 13th Amendment which outlawed slavery, this will lead to a strengthening of rights rather than their dilution.

- People have a high level of awareness of their rights. In the USA, even those with few formal qualifications are likely to be aware of their rights to free speech (1st Amendment), to bear arms (2nd Amendment) and if arrested (4th Amendment). Some constitutional rights have even filtered into everyday language, such as 'taking the fifth'.
- Governments, while having to take account of individual rights, are still able to be effective. Within the restrictions under which the US branches of government have to operate, they generally find enough room for manoeuvre to implement their policies.

In Britain, by comparison, which does not have a written constitution, governments are able to ignore or alter any rights they find to be inconvenient. The Human Rights Act became law in 2000. Just one year later, in the fearful atmosphere that followed the terrorist attacks of 9/11, laws were passed that conflicted with some of the rights the Act was supposed to protect. In 2005, following suicide bombs in London, the Prime Minister announced that further anti-terrorism legislation would not be hindered by the Human Rights Act and, if necessary, parts of it would be repealed.

The importance of democracy
Critics of a codified constitution, with such an emphasis on rights, argue that it can be undemocratic for the following reasons:

- Although US governments have managed to find ways to implement their policies much of the time, there have been periods when the strict separation of powers has led to 'gridlock', with different branches of government at odds with each other and unable to act. This cannot be in keeping with the wishes of the voters.
- Decisions taken by the President and laws passed by Congress, both elected, can be overruled as unconstitutional by unelected Supreme Court judges.

British governments, working within an uncodified constitution, have neither of these problems. Rather they are seen as responsive to the needs of the electorate, able to act swiftly and effectively to address problems as they arise, in a framework that is flexible enough to adapt over time.

Which is more valuable – the protection of rights or a flexible framework for government – has been, and continues to be, a matter of dispute.

What you should have learnt from reading this chapter

- The Founding Fathers, determined to secure liberty for future generations regardless of how the country (and the wider world) might change, designed the Constitution to ensure that no individual or faction could accumulate sufficient power to become tyrannical.

- By creating a national government that would have specified powers (with the rest being held at local level) **and** ensuring those powers were distributed between the executive, legislative and judicial branches **and** keeping people from holding office in more than one branch at the same time **and** giving each branch responsibility for ensuring that their (potentially power-hungry) rivals in the other branches did not breach their designated boundaries **and** making people in power accountable to the general public in staggered elections, the delegates at the Constitutional Convention were satisfied that they had found the right formula for effective government while protecting the 'unalienable Rights' to 'Life, Liberty and the pursuit of Happiness'.

- Citizens with a political voice, however, were sceptical. During the public debate that accompanied the ratification process, it became clear the Constitution would only be adopted if a Bill of Rights was added to provide an additional layer of protection for citizens against their own government, in case the Founding Fathers' formula failed.

- To foreign observers – especially in Britain, which does not have a written constitution – the result was a system that appears inflexible, limiting governmental ability to respond rapidly to the wishes of the electorate and effectively to address problems as they arise.

- In the USA, however, this has rarely been the focus of debate. While the national Government may find itself operating within tight constraints, there is general agreement in the USA that this is preferable to a situation in which it may be able to infringe fundamental individual rights (probably at times of crisis, when the electorate might be willing to sacrifice them in the name of security). Rather the concern, expressed during the ratification debate and since, is that the Constitution is too flexible, with the powers of the states being steadily undermined and power being concentrated at the Federal level, especially in the hands of judges, leading to the kind of accumulation of power that the Founding Fathers feared.

- For those who did not have a voice when the Constitution was being written, the main concern has been the contrast between the high ideals of the Founding Fathers and the reality for groups on the margins of US society. In practice, the system protected the rights of white, male, able-bodied heterosexuals and enabled them to aggressively dominate anyone who did not share these characteristics. As one of the leaders of the movement to abolish slavery put it, 'liberty and slavery – opposite as heaven and hell – are both in the Constitution'. For African-Americans, explicitly excluded from the protections of the Constitution, and for others implicitly excluded, the greatest challenge of US politics has been to ensure that society meets the high ideals of genuine freedom and equality for all.

Glossary of key terms

Anti-Federalist A term applied to the people who opposed the adoption of the US Constitution because they feared that it gave too much power to the central government.

Checks and balances A system of providing each branch of government with the means of limiting the powers of the other branches, so that none of them exceed the powers assigned to them in the Constitution.

Codified constitution A document that sets out the powers and duties of Government, as well as the relationship between the people and the Government.

Confederation A league of independent states that co-operate with each other through a government they have set up to deal with matters of common concern. That government may only make decisions that have the unanimous support of all the member states.

Executive branch (of government) The arm of government with constitutional responsibility for ensuring that the laws of the land are implemented (as set out in Article 2).

Federalism A system of government in which the constitution provides both central government and individual states with powers that cannot be removed.

Federalist A term applied to the people who supported the adoption of the US Constitution and would, in many cases, have been prepared to increase the power it gave to the central government.

Judicial branch (of government) The arm of government with constitutional responsibility for interpreting the laws of the land (as set out in Article 3) and, later, for interpreting the constitution.

Legislative branch (of government) The arm of government with constitutional responsibility for passing laws and for close scrutiny of the executive branch to ensure that it does not develop into an institution resembling a monarchy (as set out in Article 1).

Ratification The process by which the Constitution, after it had been written, was debated and agreed by the thirteen original states, enabling it to come into force in 1789.

Separation of powers The distribution of power between the three branches of government to ensure that no single person, or group, is able to make, enforce, interpret and enforce the law.

'Three-fifths compromise' The compromise of the Constitutional Convention between opponents and supporters of slavery, which resulted in slaves being counted as three-fifths of a person for the purposes of both taxation and representation.

❓ Likely examination questions

Issues examiners may expect students to be able to effectively analyse include:

- The adaptability/flexibility of the Constitution
- Whether the checks and balances written into the Constitution still work today
- How well freedoms are protected by the Constitution
- Whether the Constitution is an aid or obstacle to effective government in the twenty-first century
- The means of achieving constitutional change and why it is so difficult

Thus, examples of the kind of questions that could be asked include:
'The US system of checks and balances is ineffective.' Discuss.
Explain, with examples, why it is so difficult to amend the US Constitution.

Where the question compares the US system with Britain's, issues may include:

- The arguments for and against codified constitutions
- The extent of the flexibility of the British and US constitutions
- The extent to which each constitution provides for effective government
- The extent to which each constitution safeguards rights and liberties

Thus, an example of the kind of question that could be asked is:
How successfully are civil liberties upheld in the UK and USA?

Helpful websites

www.constitutionalcenter.org – the museum in Philadelphia (where the Constitutional Convention took place) dedicated to the Constitution and related issues. Detailed, in-depth but very accessible.

www.justicelearning.org – accessible material on the constitutional implications of the main political issues today, produced by two highly respected news organisations, National Public Radio and *The New York Times*.

www.billofrightsinstitute.org – site dedicated to 'educate young people about the words and ideas of America's founders'. Particularly useful to teachers/lecturers.

Suggestions for further reading

For a more in-depth understanding of the passionate debates surrounding the writing and ratifying of the Constitution, read all or parts of *The Federalist Papers* by Alexander Hamilton, James Madison and John Jay. Their articles not only capture the flavour of their time but raise questions that continue to be debated today.

A modern version of writings that attempt to capture the spirit of the Constitution is *A Patriot's Handbook* by Caroline Kennedy. A collection of songs, poems, stories and speeches, it offers a perspective on America from a wide variety of angles expressed in a diverse range of voices.

CHAPTER 2

Evaluating the Constitution – Race and US Politics

Contents

Overview

On 29 August 2005, Hurricane Katrina hit the city of New Orleans, Louisiana, causing floods that killed 1,836 residents. Overwhelmingly, the victims were African Americans living in poverty-stricken neighbourhoods, built below sea level, which were known to be vulnerable if the flood defences failed. Without the means to escape, they discovered that the authorities had no rescue plan.

Outraged African American leaders and commentators argued that the deaths were a direct consequence of decades of discrimination which pushed 'minorities' to the margins of society. Slavery and racial segregation, they argued, had played such a major role in shaping modern society that they continued to make an impact. Katrina illustrated the historical failure of the USA to live up to the values of the Constitution and reminded the country that the great challenge of US politics is to ensure that society finally provides genuine freedom and equality for all.

This analysis was strongly resisted by many other political leaders. Acknowledging that not all people have been treated equally, they argued that the inclusive language of the Constitution has provided openings for previously excluded groups to play a full role in the mainstream of society.

This chapter examines inequalities permitted by the Constitution, measures taken to address them and considers views on whether it now ensures that freedom and equality of opportunity are available to all.

Key issues to be covered in this chapter

- The USA's history of legalised racism is considered in relation to the constitutional promise of freedom and equality of opportunity for all
- The political strategies to overcome racial segregation are outlined
- The debate on whether the government has a constitutional responsibility to redress the consequences of centuries of racial exclusion
- The prospects for the future are considered

The impact of slavery and segregation

Tyranny and Terrorism

The great fear of the Founding Fathers was tyranny and loss of freedom, so when designing the Constitution they aimed to create a framework that would make tyranny impossible. The great threat faced by American leaders today is terrorism, the use of violence to influence political decisions and the values of the nation. Even as the Constitution was being written, however, for the people brought from Africa to be slaves on American plantations, tyranny and terrorism were part of their everyday routine.

In order to ensure that people work productively for minimal reward and with little likelihood of improving their prospects, the following were necessary:

- Physical limitations: while slaves had to be able to move around plantations to work, they were not allowed to leave without the supervision or permission of their owners.
- Physical intimidation: slaves who demonstrated any signs of independence of mind (expressions or tone of voice), or who did not work hard enough, would be severely punished in front of other slaves to teach all the consequences of such behaviour. Attempted escape received greater punishment, including amputation of a foot, castration or death, depending on the number of escape attempts.
- Psychological intimidation: slaves played a similar role on plantations to that of farm animals and were treated in much the same way. Even the terminology used to describe slaves mirrored the language used for animals: men were 'bucks' had to be 'broken' to be productive. They were denied any sense of their African identity, not being allowed to use their local languages, religions, music, or even their own names. They were denied families, a nurturing, bonding environment, as slave-owners chose which of their slaves should 'breed' together to produce the biggest, strongest field-hands. They were denied an education: it was illegal for slaves to be taught to read and write, giving them access to ideas beyond those their owners thought suitable for them.
- Sexual intimidation: plantation-owners and overseers regularly used female slaves for their own sexual pleasure, making rape a

routine part of slavery. Again, the message sent to all slaves was that their inevitable destiny was to do whatever their owner needed them to do. The mixed-race children who resulted also became slaves.

Reconciling freedom and slavery

The obvious contradiction between the idea of America as a land of freedom and opportunity and the idea of America allowing slavery was widely recognised. Ensuring that the USA would be strong enough to resist the expansionist ambitions of European monarchs, which would mean the loss of freedom for all, was the primary motivation for holding the Constitutional Convention in 1787. It was evident that the southern states would never have joined the Union if slavery had been outlawed, undermining this goal. Despite this, much was done to ensure an end to slavery as soon as possible, as follows:

- The three-fifths compromise: The delegates from the Northern states attempted to undermine slavery by arguing that slaves should be counted when working out how much tax each state had to pay towards the costs of the national government, but they should not be counted when calculating how many seats each state should have in the House of Representatives. The Southern states, recognising that this was an attempt to make slavery uneconomic, and that they would be out-voted on any laws introduced to restrict slavery, resisted the proposal. The result was a compromise in which slaves were counted as three-fifths of a person for both taxation and representation.
- The Southern states were also able to include a clause in the Constitution that ensured that the trade in slaves from Africa would continue until 1808. As soon as this clause expired, however, the Northern states ensured a law was passed ended the trade.
- Abolitionist societies were formed in the 1820s. Strangely, none of them allowed black people to become members until the American Anti-Slavery Society was formed, open to all people, in 1833.
- A network of secret safe houses, known as the Underground Railroad, helped slaves to escape to the North, bringing stories of their experiences with them. The abolition movement used these

experiences to publicise the nature of slavery, and they were the basis for the best-selling novel, *Uncle Tom's Cabin* by Harriet Beecher Stowe.

Civil War and Reconstruction

Ultimately, compromises and campaigns proved inadequate to end slavery. It took a Civil War, lasting from 1861 to 1865, in which some 600,000 white men lost their lives, for the constitutional protections to be extended to all races.

Reconstruction: this is a term given to the period between the end of the Civil War in 1865 and the withdrawal of Union troops from the South in 1877. In the five years after the end of the Civil War, three amendments were made to the United States Constitution. Collectively known as the **Civil Rights** amendments, they were intended to guarantee to African-Americans the constitutional rights that other races had enjoyed since independence:

- the 13th Amendment incorporated the abolition of slavery into the Constitution.
- the 14th Amendment guaranteed full rights to all, regardless of race.
- the 15th Amendment guaranteed the right to vote, regardless of race.

Just as ex-slaves were granted the vote, many of their white neighbours were disenfranchised as a punishment for their involvement in the war. As a result, African-Americans won elected office all across the former Confederacy, from town councils to the United States Senate. A top priority for many of these politicians was to provide education to those who had been previously denied it, a policy which stood to benefit poor whites as well as former slaves. In this they were aided by the Freedmen's Bureau, an institution set up by the Federal government in 1865, which funded schools for ex-slaves in the South and helped set up a number of black universities, such as Fisk and Howard, which are the most significant legacy of this period.

'Jim Crow'

All of these measures can be seen as evidence that there has always been a determination, by many, to ensure that the values of the

Constitution be applied to all Americans. None of these initiatives, however, led to the integration of former slaves into the mainstream of American society. Newly-liberated slaves, in an area devastated by the war, had no land, shelter or money, and despite demands for 'forty acres and a mule' the Federal government felt itself under no obligation to compensate Africans for the effects of slavery. Foreshadowing current political debates in America, many argued that slavery was in the past and that there was no case for 'preferential treatment' for the freedmen. As Frederick Douglass, a former slave, put it, 'When the Russian serfs had their chains broken and given their liberty, the government of Russia gave to those poor emancipated serfs a few acres of land on which they could live and earn their bread. But when you turned us loose, you turned us loose to the sky, to the storm, to the whirlwind, and worst of all, you turned us loose to our infuriated masters.'

When Union troops left the South in 1877, the response of the 'infuriated masters' was to introduce laws designed to assert white supremacy and to deny black civil rights, collectively referred to as the **Jim Crow** laws. Most African-Americans lost the right to vote and any facilities offering the opportunity for the races to mingle were strictly segregated, from schools, hospitals and libraries to public transport, restaurants, hotels and swimming pools. The law-makers of the South were particularly concerned about inter-racial intimacy, so dating, sex and marriage between the races were made illegal.

Segregation was not only about the law, however; it was also about a social code, that was enforced with extreme violence, in which white superiority was expressed in the form of subjecting African-Americans to daily humiliation. Before trying on a hat, for example, which might later be bought by a white customer, it was expected that a prospective black customer would first line the band of the hat with tissue paper. And, as so effectively depicted by Harper Lee in *To Kill a Mockingbird*, any suggestion that a black person had harmed someone white would result in a lynch mob.

Plessy v. Ferguson

The legal dimension of Jim Crow would not have been possible without the complicity of all branches of the federal government. Neither the executive nor legislative branches took steps to outlaw racial discrimination, and in a series of decisions the Supreme Court provided constitutional justifications for Jim Crow. In *Plessy* v. *Ferguson* (1896) the Court ruled that separate facilities were acceptable provided that they did not infringe the equality clause of the Constitution, ignoring the self-evident reality that separate facilities were intended to reinforce unequal treatment of races.

Responding to exclusion from society

Political strategies to win freedom

Once segregation was firmly established, and endorsed as constitutional by the Supreme Court, it was apparent to African-American leaders that the commitment of mainstream politicians to fight for full equal rights for all was inadequate. There were divisions among African-Americans, however, on the most effective method to ensure that the constitutional protections available to other Americans would become available to them.

Campaigning for integration

The leader of the movement to campaign for Civil Rights in the early twentieth century was W. E. B. DuBois, the first African-American to receive a PhD from Harvard University. In 1909, with a group of whites and other African-Americans, Du Bois set up an organisation, the National Association for the Advancement of Colored People (NAACP). The NAACP's strategy was as follows:

- With white Anglo-Saxon Protestants controlling most of the key positions of economic and political power and, in the South, out-numbering and more heavily-armed than African-Americans, violent confrontation was never likely to bring about change. It was more likely to reinforce racist stereotypes of Africans as sinister and threatening, while giving weight to claims that different races could not live together.
- Rather, if the right political climate could be created, illustrating the clear injustice of Jim Crow, white leaders could be persuaded or shamed into changing their ways and laws.
- Alternatively, if it could be demonstrated to the Federal government that the Constitution was not being respected, and that

America's status in the world as the beacon of democracy was being undermined, Washington had the power to impose its will on the supporters of Jim Crow.

- Then, as the black community began to see real improvement in their lives, the organisation's membership would grow, contributing financially to the expensive process of bringing cases to Federal courts, leading, in turn, to further improvement.
- It was obvious that trying to put pressure on local politicians to change was not likely to yield results. In the South, segregation enjoyed high levels of support among white voters and very few African-Americans were able to vote. To win presidential elections, or to gain a majority in Congress, both of the main parties needed to win the Southern vote – and even the Republican Party, which had come into existence to oppose slavery, was reluctant to antagonise Southern voters. The primary method of the NAACP, therefore, was to bring legal cases before the Supreme Court, challenging segregation as unconstitutional.

Creating economic self-sufficiency.

Initially, proposals for black self-sufficiency were associated with Booker T. Washington, a former slave who became the headteacher of a black school in Tuskegee, Alabama. His approach was as follows:

- If black people did more to help themselves by developing basic agricultural skills, followed by a strong work ethic and finally their own businesses, white people would find African-Americans less threatening.
- This would reduce friction between the races and, over time, the issue of civil rights would take care of itself.
- Accordingly, he was in the forefront of a movement to set up black colleges that would provide African-Americans with the skills needed to be able to leave the plantations, on which most still lived, and become independent farmers. Many of these colleges, some of which have developed into prestigious universities, carry the designations A&M (agricultural and mechanical) or A&T (agricultural and technical).

Booker T. Washington was challenged by other black leaders who argued that this was providing white race-supremacists with exactly what they wanted: a black population content to toil away in menial positions, never challenging their status as second-class citizens. However, his ideas were taken forward by Black Nationalist groups, led most notably by Marcus Garvey, and given a more radical edge. Garvey founded the Universal Negro Improvement Association in his native Jamaica in 1914, based on the following strategy:

- Equality for Africans around the world could only be achieved on the basis of economic independence.
- This meant setting up industries, businesses and trading arrangements that could operate on equal terms with whites.
- Self-help needed, he believed, to be matched by the kind of pride and self-worth that had been systematically beaten out of Africans during slavery.
- Consequently, he promoted rallies, featuring pomp and ceremony, and refused to accept advertisements in his newspaper for 'race-degrading' products such as hair-straighteners.

Garvey brought his movement to the United States in 1916, and by 1920 it had more than two million members worldwide, including more than half a million in America. In the period between the two World Wars, this strategy enjoyed considerably more support among African-Americans than did the campaign for integration.

The struggle for integration

Brown v. *Board of Education*
While African-Americans were working to ensure that they were granted the rights they were entitled to under the Constitution, or to ensure that they were not dependent on the Constitution to secure their well-being, the mainstream of American society largely ignored the denial of freedom and equality of opportunity for 12 per cent of their population. This changed on 17 May 1954, when the Supreme Court ruled, in the case of *Brown* v. *Board of Education, Topeka, Kansas*, that segregation was 'inherently' unequal and therefore unconstitutional.

Although the Founding Fathers had designed the Constitution to protect people from oppressive government, since 1896 the Supreme Court had interpreted the Constitution to mean that any political authority could discriminate on the grounds of race. Once the Supreme Court changed its interpretation, it became the responsibility of the Federal government in Washington DC to ensure that all discriminatory laws were abolished and that political authorities treated everyone fairly.

Challenging the President to enforce the 'Brown' decision

The President in 1954, Dwight D. Eisenhower, was conservative and cautious. He did not publicly support the decision and privately criticised the Chief Justice of the Supreme Court, Earl Warren. He favoured gradual change that would minimise conflict and, in particular, would not provide the Soviet Union with propaganda material that could be used against the United States during the Cold War.

It fell, therefore, to the African-American population and their allies to conduct a series of campaigns to embarrass their own government into enforcing the constitutional rights to which they were entitled.

Desegregating education: Little Rock Central High School

In August1956, the Governor of Texas used police to prevent school integration in the town of Mansfield. But appeals to the Federal government to do its constitutional duty to enforce decisions of the Supreme Court (which has no enforcement arm of its own) were ignored, as the campaign failed to generate nationwide publicity. In September 1957, the local chapter of the NAACP led an attempt by the African-American community in Little Rock, Arkansas, to send nine of their students to the local high school. The Governor of Arkansas, a state considered moderate by Southern standards, used the National Guard to stop the students from entering the school. These troops were backed up by crowds of white parents, seen on camera with their faces contorted with hate, spitting on children who wanted nothing more than a decent education, threatening to lynch them and attacking black journalists.

President Eisenhower's response was telling. Sending Federal troops to protect the children, he announced, 'Our enemies are gloating over this incident and using it everywhere to misrepresent our whole nation.' The lesson was not lost on Civil Rights leaders. For non-violent protest to bring about change, it had to provoke a response that would generate either a wave of sympathic support across the country or, preferably, Federal intervention. Unfortunately, the latter usually occurred only after violent attacks on peaceful protesters, as a new generation of African-Americans were about to discover.

Desegregating restaurants: Lunch-counter Sit-ins

In February 1960, in Greensboro, North Carolina, African-American students began entering town-centre department stores, making their purchases and, like white customers, taking a break and some refreshment at the lunch counter. But, because lunch counters across the South were segregated, they were refused service. Sometimes they were simply ignored, sometimes the counter was closed and the lights turned off until they went away, and sometimes the whole store was closed.

Often, however, the response was violent. Police arresting students for breaking city laws were often rough and, in the cells, away from prying eyes, brutal. White customers were also often violent, pouring hot coffee over the protesters, stubbing out cigarettes on them, spitting and dragging them off their seats and assaulting them. In smaller establishments, store-owners and managers could also be violent. Lester Maddox, who later became Governor of Georgia, first came to prominence by threatening to attack with an axe-handle any African-American who tried to eat in his diner. The students, meanwhile, sat patiently, often working on their studies, waiting to be served. When the store closed, or when they felt they had made their point by disrupting business, they left.

If arrested, they refused bail and refused to pay fines, demonstrating that they were not prepared to respect laws that denied them the same rights as their fellow citizens. And regardless of the numbers arrested, there were always more to take their place as the student movement mushroomed. The scale of the protests developed so rapidly that it soon became clear that organisation would be needed. To ensure that events were effectively organised, and that protesters knew how to respond to the intimidation they would face, the Student Nonviolent Coordinating Committee (SNCC) was set up to apply the lessons of Little Rock, that effective leadership, dignity and courage in the face of violence and national publicity were all essential ingredients to a successful campaign.

Desegregating public transport: Freedom Riders

The next crusade to come to American television screens was prompted by a Supreme Court decision, *Boynton* v. *Virginia*, which ordered the desegregation of inter-state public transport. Passengers on buses travelling from the North, for example New York, were allowed to sit anywhere they wished and could share the same facilities at rest stops. When the bus was about to enter the South, however, passengers had to segregate and use segregated facilities at any further rest stops. It was this practice the Supreme Court banned but, as with the Brown decision, Southern states simply ignored it.

To force change, a Civil Rights organisation had been founded during the Second World War, the Congress for Racial Equality (CORE), which organised teams of black and white volunteers to travel as groups, disregarding expectations to segregate on the journey. The prominent role of whites marked a significant departure from previous campaigns but they maintained the approach of non-violence, publicising their intentions in order to provoke a response from the Southern authorities for all to see.

The response was every bit as violent as might have been anticipated. The first two buses carrying Freedom Riders from Washington DC to Alabama and Mississippi, in May 1961, were attacked in Anniston, Alabama, by mobs wielding sticks, stones and metal bars. The lead bus was then pursued by the mob in forty cars until it was forced to stop, and then it was fire-bombed. The second bus managed to reach Birmingham, Alabama, where it was met by another mob. In both cases the local police were conspicuously absent and the white volunteers, seen as race-traitors by the mobs, were subject to especially vicious attacks. The riders who managed to reach Mississippi were all arrested for 'inflammatory riding' and suffered beatings in jail away from the television cameras.

The publicity had the desired effect of demonstrating the brutality of segregation and galvanised young people from all over the country to join the campaign and become Freedom Riders. It also had a similar effect on the Federal government as did the event in Little Rock in 1957. Initially, the new President, J. F. Kennedy, was reluctant to intervene, calling for a 'cooling off' period because he was concerned that the protests would damage America's image abroad. However, in September, with the campaign in its fifth month, the

President increased pressure on Southern states to respect the law, and by the end of the year CORE was able to announce that the Boynton decision had been generally implemented.

The fruits of success

The need for these campaigns was finally addressed by the passage of two landmark Acts of Congress, which had the effect of ensuring that the Federal government would take full responsibility for enforcing desegregation. The Acts in question were:

- Civil Rights Act 1964: Partly because of the prominence of the Civil Rights movement, and partly because of the assassination of President Kennedy in November 1963, this powerful new Civil Rights Act was passed. President Kennedy's death at first appeared to be bad news for the movement. Although he had been half-hearted in his practical support for Civil Rights demonstrators under attack in the South, Kennedy had often expressed public support for the movement and was identified with its objectives. The new President, Lyndon Johnson, by comparison, was from Texas, a state with Jim Crow laws, and did not have a reputation for supporting Civil Rights. Once in power, however, Johnson was determined to demonstrate that he was the President of *all* Americans and, as a former Senator of considerable experience, knew how to get legislation through the complicated processes of Congress. The 1964 Civil Rights Act was not the first legislation to ban racial discrimination but, crucially, it was the first to use the power of the Federal government to enforce the law. Under the act, the Department of Justice could initiate legal action against a state, city or town to ensure equal treatment or, alternatively, the government could withhold Federal funds, which many communities were dependent on. In the face of these threats, Southern leaders began to end segregation without local campaigns being necessary.
- Voting Rights Act 1965: A campaign in Dallas County, Alabama, in early 1965 exposed one major flaw in the Civil Rights Act. Although segregation was being grudgingly abandoned, the Act did not contain provisions for ensuring that African-Americans were able to vote. Of the 29,000 residents of the town of Selma and the surrounding communities that made up the county, over

15,000 were black but only 335 had been allowed to register to vote. A voter-registration campaign in early 1965 was met with the type of resistance and violence with which the Civil Rights movement had become familiar. Within a month, 3,000 demonstrators were in jail (ten times the number of African-Americans entitled to vote), the county sheriff was seen on television assaulting demonstrators with his baton and a demonstrator was killed by a policeman. On 7 March, known as Bloody Sunday, the movement attempted to begin a march to the state capital, Montgomery, to petition for the right to vote. In front of television cameras, the march was attacked by the police, using clubs, tear gas and dogs, with white residents cheering them on. The vivid television pictures spurred the passing of a Voting Rights Act. It abolished the devices used to deny the vote to African-Americans, such as literacy tests, and required states to get clearance from the Federal government before they introduced any new electoral regulations, making sure that new devices did not replace the old ones. It also gave the Department of Justice the power to send Federal voter registrars to any area to ensure that no one was being denied the right to register for the vote.

Constitutional issues raised by the end of legalised segregation

Questioning the success of the Civil Rights movement

The campaigns between 1955 and 1965, together with the Civil Rights Act and Voting Rights Act, effectively ended segregation. Finally, the 14th and 15th Amendments to the Constitution were being applied. Did this mean that the Constitution, belatedly, provided freedom and equality of opportunity for all?

A range of voices in the African-American community expressed a sense that the denial of freedom and rights over a period of almost 200 years since the Constitution had been written could not meaningfully be rectified by the passage of two pieces of legislation.

Malcolm X

In the 1950s and 1960s, during the height of the Civil Rights movement, Malcolm X was the standard-bearer amongst those who argued that black liberation could only come about as a result of economic self-sufficiency. He had no doubt that American society was racist beyond redemption, making campaigns for racial integration pointless. Why else, he asked, would African-Americans find themselves, 300 years after being transported to the country, having to ask for fundamental human rights? Why did they have to publicly suffer at the hands of Southern communities before the Federal government would act?

In response to Martin Luther King Jnr's famous 'I Have a Dream' speech, Malcolm X said 'the black masses were, and are, having a nightmare', adding 'who ever heard of angry revolutionists swinging their bare feet together with their oppressor in lily-pad pools, with gospels and guitars?' When accused of being an extremist, he had a ready response: 'The black race here in North America is in extremely bad condition. You show me a black man who isn't an extremist and I'll show you one who needs psychiatric attention.'

Watts and Chicago

In August 1965, a riot erupted in the Watts neighbourhood of Los Angeles, California, a state where slavery had never existed and where there had never been legal segregation. An incident between the police and a young black man swiftly escalated into violence that lasted for six days. By the time the riot ended, the police and 14,000 National Guardsmen had been deployed, 34 people had been killed, 900 had been injured and 4,000 had been arrested. Over the next year, another thirty-eight ghettoes across America erupted into violence, watched by a confused white population who could grasp why Jim Crow led to anger and frustration but found it far more difficult to understand the fury of those entitled to vote and not subject to formal segregation.

Demonstrating urban problems in a way that would touch the conscience of Americans was more difficult than with segregation. However, Martin Luther King Jnr was determined to try and in January 1966, with coverage by the media, he moved with his family into an apartment in Chicago. The experience was as much an education for Dr King as anyone else, living with the powerful smell of urine from the hall, heaters that barely worked and an immediate change in his children's behaviour as their tempers flared in the absence of creative recreation. The atmosphere was one of hopelessness and powerlessness on a scale he had never encountered in the South. Nevertheless, while the brutality of segregation could be captured by television cameras, the oppressive atmosphere of the ghettoes could not be conveyed in the same way. By the end of his campaign, most Americans still had a very limited understanding of the conditions in urban slums.

Black Panthers

The Black Panther Party for Self-Defense was set up in 1966 in Oakland, California, to monitor police brutality by mounting patrols to observe and record encounters between African-Americans and the police. Although this was an exercise in ensuring that constitutional rights were not violated, what struck the general public was the Panthers' paramilitary appearance, wearing black leather jackets, black berets, dark glasses and carrying rifles, an image in stark contrast to the gentle, unthreatening determination of the campaigns to end desegregation in the South.

Black Power

By the mid-1960s, weary of having to endure violence and hardship in order achieve their political goals, many of the younger activists in the Civil Rights groups SNCC and CORE rejected the strategies that had previously brought them success when fighting segregation in the South. Influenced by intellectuals such as the black psychologist Franz Fanon, who argued that political liberation could only be achieved through fighting for freedom, and the experience of the ghettoes, which demonstrated that those in power took notice when confronted by violence, they adopted a more aggressive posture. They came to believe that the Civil Rights campaigns demonstrated that African-Americans would never enjoy full constitutional rights unless they became more assertive. Accordingly, they emphasised progress through black leadership, racial pride and solidarity, the kind of approaches that had worked for other ethnic groups in America such as the Italians and Irish. The slogan that captured this new approach was 'Black Power'.

Fundamental challenges to the Constitution

Collectively, these voices expressed a view that freedom and equality, guaranteed by the Constitution, was an illusion for the overwhelming majority of African-Americans even after the formal abolition of segregation. Furthermore, they pointed out, having been deliberately and systematically marginalised throughout US history, a high proportion of African-Americans were locked into a cycle of poverty as a direct result of being denied freedom and opportunity. Therefore, they argued, there was a constitutional obligation on government to rectify these injustices and take active steps to ensure that African-Americans were, belatedly, properly included in the mainstream of society. This was, however, a distinctly different interpretation of the Constitution to any that had been publicly discussed since the Reconstruction era following the Civil War, and the response to this view has largely shaped public debate about the extent and scope of the obligations on government to ensure genuine freedom and equality of opportunity for all.

The development of Affirmative Action programmes

After Jim Crow: what next?

In June 1965, the month that the Voting Rights Act was passed, effectively ending legalised racial discrimination, President Johnson made a speech at Howard University in which he made the following famous statement:

> You do not wipe away the scars of centuries by saying: Now you are free to go where you want, do as you desire, choose the leaders you please. You do not take a person who, for years, has been hobbled by chains and liberate him, bring him to the starting line and then say, 'You are free to compete with all the others,' and still justly believe that you have been completely fair. Thus it is not enough just to open the gates of opportunity. All our citizens must have the ability to walk through those gates. This is the next and the more profound stage of the battle for civil rights. We seek not just freedom but opportunity – not just equality as a right and a theory but equality as a fact and as a result.

In making it clear that ending segregation was not enough to ensure full and fair participation in society, the President was giving his support to the idea that the scars of racism could only be healed by programmes that compensated African-Americans for the harm they had suffered. These programmes concentrated mainly on education, housing, employment and political representation.

Affirmative Action in education

Affirmative Action was swiftly applied to education. In 1966, the Department for Housing, Education and Welfare (HEW) tightened the regulations for integrating schools, which in many areas remained segregated despite the Supreme Court's *Brown* v. *Board* ruling of 1954. Using powers given to it by the 1964 Civil Rights Act, HEW threatened to withhold funds from school districts that had failed to desegregate.

By 1970, with school desegregation continuing to make only slow progress in some parts of the country, in *Swann* v. *Charlotte-Mecklenburg* the Supreme Court not only demanded a rapid end to segregated schooling but specified the means of achieving it by bussing white and black children to each other's schools. In 1974, another Federal judge, Arthur Garrity, ordered the same remedy for the schools of Boston, Massachusetts.

Meanwhile, spurred on by the demands of the Civil Rights movement, which pointed out the poor record of elite educational institutions in offering places to minority applicants, universities began to set aside places to ensure that all groups would have an equal chance of achieving top degrees.

Affirmative Action in housing

The Johnson administration managed to push though Congress (aided by a wave of sympathy following the assassination of Martin Luther King Jnr) two bills to improve urban housing and combat housing discrimination.

- Housing and Urban Development Act (1968), which provided funds for increased construction of public housing and provided subsidies for the private construction of homes for low-income and middle-income families in cities.
- Fair Housing Act (1968), which prohibited racial discrimination in the sale or rental of housing and required the Department of Housing and Urban Development (HUD) 'affirmatively to further the purposes' of fair housing.

Affirmative Action in employment

Affirmative Action in employment did not gain momentum until the presidency of Richard Nixon, when he launched the Philadelphia

Plan in 1969. The Equal Employment Opportunity Commission (EEOC), a government agency, had been arguing for three years that if an industry demonstrated a clear pattern of racial discrimination, the Commission could force a change in hiring practices, through the courts if necessary. In 1969, Nixon gave his approval for the EEOC to force the construction industry, dominated by whites-only unions, to employ more African-Americans. The plan required all contractors doing business with the Federal government to establish 'goals and timetables' for the hiring of minorities and to draw up plans to demonstrate that they were taking active steps to meet their targets.

This plan is seen by many as the single greatest development of Affirmative Action, in that it directly improved job prospects for African-Americans in the construction industry and improved black employment prospects in other businesses that introduced Affirmative Action plans, using the 'Philadelphia' model, to avoid similar pressure from the government.

Affirmative Action in representation
In 1976, the Supreme Court ruled in *Beer* v. *United States* that any plan to redraw district boundaries should not leave ethnic minorities worse off in terms of political representation. In the spirit of increasing political representation for minorities, some states created race-conscious districts in which voters of the same race were grouped together.

These districts have been notable for two reasons. The first is their shape, which, in order to achieve their goals, can be strange. One Chicago district aimed at increasing Latino representation, for example, was nicknamed the 'earmuff' district because it consisted of two separate neighbourhoods connected by a narrow road. The second is their effect on Congress, which, in the words of the prominent African-American politician, Reverend Jesse Jackson, is to have 'made the US Congress look more like America, it's white, it's black, it's Hispanic, it's Asian, it's Native American'.

Resistance to Affirmative Action

An assault on the Constitution
Some sections of society welcomed Affirmative Action as an essential step towards making the constitutional values of equality and freedom

meaningful. Other sections of society, however, saw this development as a full-scale assault on the Constitution. From this point of view, Affirmative Action raised five main points of concern:

1. The American Constitution, laws and customs protect the rights of individuals, not groups, but programmes to make up for the historic discrimination against African-Americans are inevitably targeted at the whole group.
2. Affirmative Action appeared to make white Americans accept limitations on their opportunities to make up for the limitations imposed by their forefathers on previous generations of African-Americans. This can be described as using one form of discrimination to combat another or, simply, reverse discrimination. Therefore, far from promoting the constitutional principle of equality, Affirmative Action undermines it.
3. Since Affirmative Action can only be effectively monitored by measuring outcomes, it shifts the emphasis from the capitalist principle of equal opportunity, embodied in the Constitution, to the socialist principle of equal results.
4. The American colonies had been established by people relying on their own hard work, determination and creativity. The Founding Fathers, when writing the Constitution, had created a framework that promoted this kind of rugged individualism and the USA had flourished as a result. Taking away the incentive to use these qualities was, in the view of opponents of Affirmative Action, damaging to society as a whole, and to the poor in particular, who would never learn how to compete or tap their own inner resources.
5. Most damaging of all was the perception that Affirmative Action rewarded people for undermining the most fundamental of all constitutional protections, the right of people and property to be safe from attack. Just as Affirmative Action programmes were being established, between 1965 and 1968, violence swept through black districts in cities. Civil Rights leaders attempted to communicate to the American people the level of anger, frustration and cynicism fostered by slum conditions while the government responded with programmes to improve housing, education, job prospects and to end discrimination. Other voices, however, were unsympathetic. Senior Republican Gerald Ford, who later

went on to become President, asked, 'How long are we going to abdicate law and order – the backbone of civilisation – in favour of a soft social theory that the man who heaves a brick through your window or tosses a firebomb into your car is simply the misunderstood and underprivileged product of a broken home?' Ronald Reagan, who also went on to become President, explained the rioters in the simplest of terms: they were 'lawbreakers' and 'mad dogs'.

Although Affirmative Action had only been announced by President Johnson in 1965, as a response to nearly 200 years of constitutional rights having been denied to African-Americans, by 1968 there was already evidence of a white backlash. During the presidential election of that year, Governor Wallace of Alabama, a staunch defender of white supremacy, had run as an independent and won 13.5 per cent of the national vote, more than any other independent candidate since the Second World War, winning the states of Alabama, Arkansas, Georgia, Louisiana and Mississippi.

Restricting the scope of Affirmative Action
In response to these signs of resistance to Affirmative Action, decision-makers at all levels began to restrict the scope and effectiveness of the programmes from the mid-1970s. The tide appeared first to turn in 1974, with the first of a series of decisions by the Supreme Court to restrict the terms of Affirmative Action.

Restricting Affirmative Action in education
In 1974, the Supreme Court ruled, in *Milken* v. *Bradley*, that a bussing plan that included the overwhelmingly black schools of the city of Detroit and the overwhelmingly white schools of the surrounding suburbs was illegal on the grounds that the suburbs, which fell into different education districts, were not responsible for creating all-black schools in the city and therefore were not responsible for remedying the situation. The effect of the *Milken* case was to ensure that schools in and around Detroit remained, in practice, segregated.

In the area of higher education, the Supreme Court made a landmark decision on the use of Affirmative Action in 1978. In the case of *Regents of the University of California* v. *Bakke*, the court was split down the middle, with four justices arguing that race could be used to 'remedy disadvantage cast on minorities by past racial prejudice' and four justices arguing that the university's programme to set aside sixteen places for minorities at its medical school was illegal. The final judge, Justice Powell, was able to produce a judgement that found a measure of support from both sides but did not gain complete agreement from any of the others. His ruling rejected the use of Affirmative Action as a remedy for past discrimination and allowed its use only to achieve 'wide exposure to the ideas and mores of students as diverse as this Nation'. Even then, to achieve diversity, a range of characteristics could be taken into account, of which race was an important one but not of overriding importance.

Restricting Affirmative Action in employment
In the case of *City of Richmond* v. *J. A. Croson Co*, which was about ensuring that a minimum of 30 per cent of the value of city contracts went to minority-owned firms, the Supreme Court ruled against the city council on the grounds that Affirmative Action could not be used to remedy past discrimination in general.

Restricting Affirmative Action in representation
Cases were also brought before the Supreme Court that challenged attempts to increase ethnic-minority political representation through the creation of race-conscious districts in which voters of the same race were grouped together. In the cases of *Shaw* v. *Reno* (1993) and *Miller* v. *Johnson* (1995), the court rejected re-districting plans in which race was the 'predominant factor'.

Restricting Affirmative Action at state level
In 1997, a campaign was started in California to give voters the opportunity to ban Affirmative Action in state-supported programmes. Known as Proposition 209, it was passed by 54 per cent to 46 per cent. Two years later, a similar initiative was passed in the state of Washington and others were proposed in Colorado, Florida and Ohio.

The current political debate on Affirmative Action

A fundamental divide

For much of the 1960s and 1970s the debate on Affirmative Action centred on whether American values obliged governments, at both state and Federal levels, to remedy the effects of seventy-five years of segregation and two centuries of slavery. Was it enough to outlaw these practices or should the continuing consequences of racial discrimination be addressed?

Those in favour of Affirmative Action argued that, despite the brutality of slavery, physically, emotionally, psychologically and sexually, little was done and no compensation was offered to support its victims. Jim Crow, which followed, was almost as brutal. It was never realistic to expect African-Americans to emerge from this 'nightmare' ready and able to succeed in a highly competitive society. When the mass protests of the Civil Rights movement ended, the process of making American society live up to the ideals of the Constitution was incomplete. Active steps, or Affirmative Action, were needed to ensure that momentum towards genuine equality of opportunity was not lost. The alternative, they believed, was that the USA could slip back towards the tendency to pay lip service to the ideals of the Constitution, while doing little to achieve them.

Opponents of Affirmative Action adopted a simpler line. The spirit of the Founding Fathers, they argued, was expressed through the rule of law, self-reliance and limited government. Further, the Constitution provided equal protection for individuals, not groups. They saw Affirmative Action as coming about, in part, as a result of riots and the programmes as having the effect of reducing self-reliance while expanding governmental interference in day-to-day activities.

So what is the current state of the debate; and what is the constitutional position?

Regents of the University of California v. *Bakke* (1978)

This case changed the terms of the debate. The Supreme Court ruled that while Affirmative Action continued to be constitutional, it could not be used to remedy past wrongs. This went to the heart of the

Affirmative Action policies then in place and drew powerful dissent from the only African-American on the Court. Thurgood Marshall pointed out that, in the very week that the Court announced its decision, a report entitled 'Who Runs America' had listed the eighty-three most influential people in the country, none of them black. This 'vast gulf', he argued, 'was brought about by centuries of slavery and then by another century in which, with the approval of this Court, states were permitted to treat Negroes 'specially'. Measured by any benchmark of comfort or achievement, meaningful equality remains a distant dream. Now, when a State acts to remedy the effects of that legacy of discrimination, I cannot believe that this Constitution stands as a barrier.'

Once this argument had been rejected, however, arguments for and against Affirmative Action became limited to the need for it in today's society, and whether, excluding considerations of the past, it is constitutional.

Types of arguments against Affirmative Action

There are two strands to criticism of Affirmative Action. The first is that Affirmative Action is, and always has been, fundamentally at odds with the principles of the Constitution. The second is that there may have been a compelling case for Affirmative Action in the past but developments over the past forty years have demonstrated that the programmes are either no longer necessary or are counterproductive.

The argument that Affirmative Action is unfair

- The central American values are fairness and equality for everyone. Policies that appear to favour one group over others are out of step with American values.
- It uses one form of discrimination to compensate for another. All discrimination causes fear and anxiety. African-Americans continue to experience the fear of discrimination, now Affirmative Action has extended that fear to white Americans, making the overall situation worse rather than better.
- Affirmative Action is a form of compensation by whites for slavery and Jim Crow. But why should today's white Americans pay for the sins of their forefathers, especially as their forefathers may

have had nothing to do with slavery and Jim Crow? And what about the role of African-Americans themselves in slavery? Some free blacks were themselves slave-owners, so why should their descendents benefit from Affirmative Action?

- Affirmative Action is an industry in its own right, with some African-Americans making a handsome living out of the past victimisation of their own people.

The argument that Affirmative Action is no longer necessary

- Affirmative Action was justified for a time, when the Civil Rights movement exposed the depth of racism in America, but American society has done a great deal to compensate African-Americans and now it is time for them to depend on themselves.
- A significant number of African-Americans have prospered over the past thirty years yet they, and their families, can still benefit from Affirmative Action programmes, often at the expense of families of other races who are struggling to get by. Some of the 'victims' of Affirmative Action may even be from families that supported the Civil Rights movement.
- Affirmative Action claims to help integrate society but, in reality, even when races rub shoulders they tend not to be at ease with one another. The past forty years has demonstrated that the inescapable reality of America is that races tend to segregate by choice. Over the past thirty years, as black families moved into established suburbs just outside cities, white families that had, in previous generations, moved there to avoid having black neighbours moved on to other suburbs further away from the city. Affirmative Action may have done something to change the pattern of segregation, creating wealthy black suburbs, but it has done little to affect the fact of segregation.

The argument that Affirmative Action is counter-productive

- Affirmative Action encourages some African-Americans to have unrealistic expectations of their prospects. For example, black students who gain entry to elite colleges despite weak grades may be ill-equipped to cope with the academic demands.

- Affirmative Action encourages some African-Americans to be lazy. Why work hard if Affirmative Action programmes virtually guarantee progress?
- Because Affirmative Action programmes have been in place for decades, and have the appearance of becoming permanent, they send a message to African-Americans that they cannot, and never will, compete with other races on equal terms, which is bad for their self-esteem and self-confidence.
- Equally damaging is the message they send to other races – that African-Americans success is not really due to ability, determination and hard work but due to 'preferential treatment'.

These arguments were given a boost in 2003 with the publication of *No Excuses* by Abigail and Stephen Thernstrom, which provided an in-depth study of the racial gap in educational achievement. The authors argue that people who have equal skills and knowledge will have roughly equal earnings, which suggests that racism is no longer a major barrier to equality of opportunity, and that inequality of races can be erased if unequal educational achievement can be addressed. This, they claim, can be achieved by understanding the 'culture' of each race and, in the case of African-Americans, changing their culture. Although they acknowledge that black academic under-achievement has deep historical roots, they also contend that contemporary factors, which can be changed, are responsible for an educational gap that has not closed since 1988. These factors include:

- African-American children are far more likely to be born into a single-parent household, and to a very young mother, which provides a poor basis for educational support.
- African-American households, on average, contain relatively few books and children are allowed to watch far more television than children of other races, therefore having less educational stimulation around them.
- African-American children, perhaps as a result of the two previous factors, are much more likely to be disruptive in class while being less likely than children of other races to be eager to learn new things or persist at tasks.
- In contrast, Asian students from China and India, are likely to out-perform students of other races because they follow parental

orders to obey their teachers and do their schoolwork, even when they are from impoverished homes and study at inferior inner-city schools.

The solution to racial inequality, the Thernstroms believe, is not Affirmative Action but cultural change in which all racial groups, whether newly-arrived or long-term residents, conform more closely to American 'mainstream cultural norms'.

Types of arguments for Affirmative Action

There are also two distinct strands of support for Affirmative Action. The first argues that Affirmative Action has done much to make the USA a more integrated and fairer society but that much remains to be done and that subtle attempts to turn back the clock need to be resisted with official support. Since the terms of debate were changed by the Bakke decision, this line of argument has tended to be defensive, fending off attempts to take the logic of the decision one step further and have all Affirmative Action programmes declared unconstitutional.

The second type of argument rejects the basis of the Bakke decision, arguing that the legacies of slavery and Jim Crow have not been properly dealt with by Affirmative Action and that far more radical measures are needed.

The argument that Affirmative Action has made the USA a fairer, more integrated society

- In 1960, an NAACP investigation revealed that only 15 per cent of African-Americans were employed in white-collar jobs such as clerical or sales positions, compared to 44 per cent of whites. Black workers were virtually excluded from apprenticeships for skilled trades such as plumbers and electricians. Consequently, average income for black families was only 55 per cent of the average for white families, while unemployment was about twice that of whites. By 2002, with the assistance of Affirmative Action programmes such as the Philadelphia Plan (see above), the proportion of African-Americans in white-collar and service jobs had risen to almost 70 per cent, with almost one-fifth in management and professional positions.

- Even those who managed to overcome the hurdles to success were unable to move outside of black districts into more affluent suburbs because of housing discrimination. Since the passing of the Fair Housing Act (1968) there has been a steady flow of African-Americans out of the cities into the suburbs from which they were previously excluded.
- In 1970, there were ten African-American representatives in Congress. After the 2006 elections, there were forty African-American representatives, all Democrats, but only one Senator (only the sixth in US history). The lack of African-Americans in the Senate reflects the difficulty of winning state-wide elections in an environment where voting tends to be on ethnic lines and no state has a black majority. Despite this, African-Americans have managed to secure enough support from whites or other ethnic groups to win some state-wide elections and the number appears to be growing. Doug Wilder was elected Governor of Virginia in 1990 and early in the twenty-first century there are African-Americans holding state-wide elected positions in Colorado, Connecticut, Georgia, Massachusetts, New York, North Carolina, Oregon, Tennessee and Texas.
- In education, the percentage of African-Americans who had completed high school rose from 39 per cent in 1960, before the introduction of Affirmative Action, to 86.8 per cent in 2000. The number of African-Americans with a university degree was 15.5 per cent, an increase of 43 per cent since the 1970s.

The argument that Affirmative Action is still needed to ensure that the USA lives up to its constitutional ideals

Given the arguments outlined above that Affirmative Action has made the USA a fairer, more integrated society, people may ask: is it still needed? If it is not still needed, isn't it clear that Affirmative Action doesn't really work and should therefore be abandoned? Supporters of Affirmative Action believe that programmes will be needed for a considerable time to come. Their reasons are as follows:

- The advances made by African-Americans in employment are precarious and, compared to the rest of the population, limited. When African-Americans lose their jobs, they often suffer a dramatic decline in their standard of living, as one of the legacies of slavery and Jim Crow is that the black community was not allowed to build up capital such as land and homes, which can serve as a cushion in difficult times. Furthermore, like the passengers in the last carriage of a train, they benefit when the economy picks up speed but do not get any closer to the front, and so the proportion of unemployed African-Americans has remained stubbornly around twice the national average. Carefully crafted Affirmative Action programmes are needed to address these issues.

- In housing, the movement of African-Americans to the suburbs has, in some respects, produced more segregation rather than less. In the past, the black middle class were forced by housing discrimination to share the same schools, churches and shops as the less successful of their race. Their departure, together with the local taxes they pay, has led to ghettoes becoming even poorer than before, indeed becoming islands of concentrated deprivation, with poorer education and increased violence. Again, Affirmative Action is needed to help families break out of the destructive vicious cycle in which they are trapped.
- While the educational achievement of African-Americans has improved dramatically since the 1960s, it has not been evenly spread. Women are earning twice as many university degrees as men and in the areas of most concentrated deprivation there are now more black men aged under thirty in prison, on parole or on probation than there are in higher education. Factors that influence this statistic are considered in the following section.

The argument that Affirmative Action is needed to ensure that the USA does not lose momentum towards social justice

Supporters of Affirmative Action argue that if America takes its eyes off the prize of genuine equality of opportunity for all, not only will a historical opportunity be lost but even the gains of the past four decades could be squandered. Civil Rights groups have had to fight a variety of measures that combined to push African-Americans to the margins of society in ways that hark back to the days of Jim Crow. Of particular concern in recent years have been the following:

- Racial profiling: In a practice mockingly referred to as 'driving while black', the police use traffic enforcement as a justification to investigate African-Americans and other minorities in numbers far out of proportion to their presence on the road. Even prominent African-Americans such as actors Will Smith and Wesley Snipes, as well as lawyer Johnnie Cochran, have suffered the indignity of being questioned and sometimes handcuffed in full view of the general public. In Maryland, for instance, the state police admitted in 1992 that on Interstate 95 approximately 17 per cent of drivers were African-American while 77 per cent of those stopped and searched were African-American. Studies revealed similar patterns in areas as diverse as Ohio, North Carolina and Texas. In 1999, the Governor of New Jersey admitted that the state police had practised racial profiling for many years and promised to take action against it.
- Mandatory minimums: Sentencing laws, established by Congress in 1986, penalised users of crack cocaine, who are overwhelmingly black, more harshly than users of powder cocaine, who are overwhelmingly white. Defendants convicted of selling 500 g of powder cocaine or 5 g of crack cocaine receive 5-year sentences. For 5 kg of powder cocaine and 50 g of crack, the penalty is 10 years. Thus there is a 100:1 ratio.
- Disenfranchisement: Thirteen states take away the vote, for life, of people who have committed a felony (serious crime such as selling drugs). Forty years after the passing of the Voting Rights Act, to ensure that African-Americans could no longer be denied the right to vote, the combination of racial profiling and racial disparities in sentencing means that an estimated 13 per cent of all African-American men have lost the right to vote.

The reparations argument
Challenging the decision made in the Bakke case, that providing a remedy for the effects of racial discrimination is unconstitutional, a movement of law-makers, academics and grassroots activists has gathered momentum in recent years. Pointing out that **reparations** for human rights abuses, often made to the descendents of the victims, is firmly rooted in international law (supported by the USA), they say that:

- Affirmative Action can be likened to using a mild painkiller to treat a serious illness: it's just enough to take the patient's mind off the pain and make everyone feel that something is being done. According to this way of thinking, there needs to be recognition of the scale of the *Maafa* (meaning disaster) that befell African-Americans. This means recognising slavery, and to a lesser extent Jim Crow, as a crime against humanity. It then becomes appropriate to pay compensation to the victims.

- This is no different to the response to other crimes against humanity. In the past fifty years, apologies and financial compensation have been given to a wide range of groups, including survivors of the Jewish holocaust (as well as descendents of the victims), Japanese-Americans who were imprisoned during the Second World War as suspected enemy sympathisers, and Native Americans who had had their land illegally seized in the USA and Canada.

- African-Americans have been demanding compensation for slavery since the end of the American Civil War. Immediately after the abolition of slavery, the demand was for forty acres and a mule to ensure they would not be dependent on their former slave-owners. Then, between 1890 and 1917, there was a movement to lobby the government for pensions to compensate for their unpaid labour under slavery. Since 1989, Congressman John Conyers Jnr (Michigan) has introduced a bill every year to study the case for reparations. Each of these initiatives has been largely ignored by the political establishment.

- Reparations would ensure full recognition of the scale of the *Maafa* and, at the same time, undermine those who claim that there is no further need for Affirmative Action. They would also compensate for slavery, provide psychological relief for black anger and white guilt resulting from centuries of racial oppression and, as a result, build a more united nation based on a common understanding of American history.

- To those who argue that it would be impossible to determine who should pay, how much should be paid and who should receive, supporters of reparations argue that the principle should be established first and the details can be worked out later. A range of suggestions have been put forward, such as programmes that would benefit all African-Americans, for example free health care and college education, but a final decision should await the study proposed in Congressman Conyers' bill.

Freedom and equality of opportunity for all?

When attempting to understand the Constitution of the USA, one thing is clear. Even simple and clear terms, such as freedom and opportunity, mean very different things to different people. It is impossible, therefore, to reach a definitive judgement as to whether the Constitution lives up to its ideals. Consequently, much of US politics is about the battle between rival groups to have their viewpoint adopted by the Supreme Court as the official judgement of what is meant by the Constitution.

The prospects for Affirmative Action were defined by the Supreme Court in the 2003 case of *Grutter* v. *Bollinger*. The case (one of a series of cases sponsored by a conservative pressure group, the Center for Individual Rights) saw a rejected white applicant for a place at the University of Michigan Law School, Barbara Grutter, suing the college and claiming that her rejection had been due to the Law School using race as a 'predominant' factor, giving applicants from certain minority groups 'a significantly greater chance of admission'. The university's defence, filed in the name of the Dean of the Law School, Lee Bollinger, was that they had taken careful account of the Supreme Court's ruling in the Bakke case and considered race only insofar as it helped to achieve 'that diversity which has the potential to enrich everyone's education and thus make a law school's class stronger than the sum of its parts'. The Supreme Court ruled in favour of the university, arguing that:

- Elite institutions such as the University of Michigan produced many of America's leaders and 'it is necessary that the path to leadership be visibly open to talented and qualified individuals of every race and ethnicity'.
- There could be no racial quotas and race and ethnicity could only be considered as part of a flexible admissions policy that carefully weighed up all factors in relation to each applicant.
- The Court nevertheless expected that the need to use race as a factor, to achieve this goal, would last no longer than another twenty-five years.

It appeared, therefore, as if the matter had been resolved for the next generation. However, the Court was divided on the issue, with five Justices ruling in favour of maintaining Affirmative Action and four ruling against. In 2005, one of the Justices in favour, Sandra Day O'Connor, retired and was replaced by a much more conservative judge, Samuel Alito. With the balance of opinion appearing to have tilted against Affirmative Action, it is almost certain that another challenge will be brought before the Court within the next five years.

To complete our understanding of how the Constitution operates on a day-to-day basis, the next chapter will look at how the Supreme Court reaches its judgements of what is meant by the Constitution.

What you should have learnt from reading this chapter

- For much of the history of the USA, the benchmark of whether its political system delivers the constitutional promise of freedom and equality of opportunity for all has been the extent of constitutional protection of the interests of all Americans regardless of race, especially African-Americans, who were explicitly denied constitutional rights when the Constitution document was written. This debate, the focus of intense, even violent dispute, continues to rage today.

- After the Constitution came into effect in 1789, it took seventy-six years for constitutional equality to be extended to African-Americans, and even this limited advance was achieved only after a Civil War and three constitutional amendments. It took a further eighty-nine years for the Supreme Court to acknowledge that the 14th and 15th Amendments were being systematically ignored in large parts of the USA, that constitutional equality was a myth for most African-Americans and to instruct the South to desegregate. It took a Civil Rights campaign lasting a further eleven years, in the face of violent resistance, to force the Federal government to act decisively to ensure no elected officials could place obstacles in the way of full participation in US society, with the passage of the 1964 Civil Rights Act and the 1965 Voting Rights Act.

- These advances raised as many questions as they answered. For example, what of other forms of exclusion, such as continued discrimination in the workplace or in housing? What of the legacy of discrimination that had left African-Americans less qualified and less wealthy than other groups in society? Were they to be left to overcome these, less visible, obstacles on their own while the rest of US society returned to its pattern of quietly ignoring their plight? Or did the government have a continuing obligation to create a genuinely level playing field? In the view of President Johnson, the answer to these questions was clear: 'It is not enough just to open the gates of opportunity. All our citizens must have the ability to walk through those gates.' The government, in his view, had to take Affirmative Action to provide those who had been previously excluded with that ability.

- The movement to extend civil rights had invoked the spirit of the constitution in support of its aims. Resistance to the extension of civil rights had also been justified with reference to the constitution, arguing that race relations were a local issue and that the interference in state affairs was part of a dangerous process that undermined Federalism and concentrated far more power in Washington DC than the Founding Fathers had ever considered acceptable. Affirmative Action was a further assault on the Constitution, which protects the rights of individuals, not groups; provides for equality of opportunity, not equal results; promotes self-reliance, not government intervention; and, ultimately, cannot support using one form of discrimination to combat another.

- These two irreconcilable viewpoints make it impossible to reach a definitive judgement as to whether the Constitution lives up to its ideals. Yet both sides continue to struggle to have their views adopted as the official interpretation of the Constitution by working to persuade the Supreme Court to adopt their position. How the Supreme Court reaches such decisions is the focus of the next chapter.

🔎 Glossary of key terms

Affirmative Action Programmes to remedy the effects of past discrimination and prevent future discrimination.
Civil Rights The legal protection of personal liberties to which all citizens are entitled.
'Jim Crow' Term for laws requiring the segregation of races, primarily in Southern states.
Reconstruction Term applied to the period between the end of the Civil War in 1865 and the withdrawal of Union troops from the South in 1877, when most of the constitutional rights enjoyed by other races were extended to African-Americans.
Reparations Compensation, making amends, to the victims of crimes against humanity, or their descendents.

❓ Likely examination questions

Issues examiners may expect students to be able to effectively analyse include:

- Issues that are held up as evidence that racial divisions continue to play a major role in US society, such as disenfranchisement
- Arguments in favour of and against Affirmative Action
- Assessments of the impact of Affirmative Action
- Alternative proposals for ending racial disparities, such as reparations and examining African-American culture

Thus, an example of the type of question that could be asked is:
Discuss the impact of Affirmative Action and why it has attracted growing criticism.

 ## Helpful websites

www.naacp.org and www.nul.org – the websites of the two largest Civil Rights groups, the NAACP and the National Urban League.

www.jointcenter.org and www.civilrightsproject.harvard.edu – the websites of two academic organisations sympathetic to Affirmative Action: the Joint Center for Political and Economic Studies and Harvard University's Civil Rights Project.

www.heritage.org and www.cato.org – the websites for two leading conservative think-tanks, which have produced articles and books setting out the case against Affirmative Action: the Heritage Foundation and the Cato Institute.

 ## Suggestions for further reading

To capture the flavour of the American South during the era of segregation, and the effect it had on both whites and African-Americans, read either of two classic children's novels, *To Kill A Mockingbird* by Harper Lee or *Roll of Thunder, Hear My Cry* by Mildred Taylor.

The National Urban League publishes a magazine, *Opportunity*, which can be ordered through their website. They also publish an annual survey entitled *The State of Black America*.

The two books that are currently the most influential on each side of the debate are *No Excuses* by Abigail and Stephen Thernstrom and *Should America Pay?*, a series of essays edited by Raymond A. Winbush.

CHAPTER 3

Interpreting the Constitution – the Supreme Court

Contents

Overview

On 28 July 2003, the Supreme Court declared unconstitutional a Texas law, which made it illegal for two people of the same sex 'to engage in certain intimate sexual conduct'. The ruling, in *Texas* v. *Lawrence*, asserted that political authorities could not treat gays and lesbians in ways which 'demean their existence'.

For many Americans, this ruling was an example of the constitutional principles of freedom and equality of opportunity being universally applied. Elected officials, concerned with their popularity, cannot be relied upon to protect the rights of people despised by the majority. Consequently, it has fallen to the Supreme Court to provide constitutional protection for vulnerable groups. As the *Texas* v. *Lawrence* ruling stated, the Constitution enables every generation to 'invoke its principles in their own search for greater freedom'.

Many other Americans, however, were outraged at the ruling. Ensuring equal rights for homosexuals meant, logically, that gays and lesbians would in due course be entitled to marry. Critics argued that, far from applying constitutional principles, the Supreme Court was undermining the Constitution which made Congress responsible for making such important policy decisions.

This chapter examines the role of judiciary in interpreting the Constitution and why this process is becoming increasingly controversial.

Key issues to be covered in this chapter

- Why, and how, the power of the judicial branch has grown
- The limitations on the use of that power
- The ways in which judicial power has shaped American society
- The battle for political control of judicial power
- The prospects for the Roberts Court

The constitutional powers of the judicial branch of government

Sowing the seeds of controversy

The Founding Fathers were determined to ensure that neither the executive branch of government (the President) nor the legislative branch (Congress) became too powerful. Therefore, they devised a system of separation of powers, with clearly defined responsibilities for each branch, and checks and balances, which gave each branch responsibility for monitoring the others. However, in reaching these decisions, the Convention which drew up the Constitution gave very little thought, and there was very little debate on, the third branch of government, the Judiciary. As a result, they reached some decisions on the judicial branch but also left unresolved some important issues that dominate political debate today.

Constitutional powers given to the judiciary

- There would be a separate, independent judicial branch of government, with clearly defined powers and a role in the system of checks and balances.
- The national judiciary should be 'Supreme'.
- This 'Supreme Court' should be responsible for hearing certain types of cases. These **original jurisdiction** cases were defined as those involving the states or foreign diplomats.
- Because it would be the highest court in the land, it would also be the final court of appeal.
- To ensure that the Court would be independent of the other branches of government and political pressures, the judges would not be elected (as was the case in some states) but appointed.
- To ensure that the judges had a significant level of independence from the people who appointed them, the appointment process was split. The President would be responsible for nominating Supreme Court judges but the support of a majority of the Senate was required.
- To ensure that judges' decisions were based entirely on the merits of the case they were hearing, without concern about political pressure, they were provided with the following protections:

- They could not be removed from office for political reasons. Once appointed, they would serve for life or until they retired.
- Their income could not be reduced, which would have been another way of putting them under pressure.
- The only reason they could be removed would be if their personal conduct were inappropriate for a judge.

- This meant that judges could reach any decisions they thought appropriate, although some aspects of justice were still to be regulated:
  - Jury trials were to be guaranteed.
  - The crime of treason, and punishment if convicted, was strictly defined.

Constitutional powers not given to the judiciary

- Apart from the Supreme Court, should there be other Federal courts? Some people felt, strongly, that lower Federal courts would be too similar to the highest courts of the states, causing confusion and conflict. The Convention decided not to set up lower Federal courts, but gave Congress the right to do so at a later date.
- Should the Supreme Court be given the right of judicial review That is, should they have the right to decide whether another branch of government had passed a law or taken action that was not allowed by the Constitution? This issue had already caused controversy in some states before the Constitutional Convention. The experience of the states suggested that it was logical that the Supreme Court would have the power of judicial review. There were two views, however, on whether this should be the case at Federal level:
  - Some argued that the limitations on the power of government in the Constitution would be meaningless unless they were enforced by the Supreme Court.
  - Others argued that the power of judicial review would make unelected judges more powerful than both the elected legislature and elected executive.

Ultimately, the Constitutional Convention failed to resolve this argument and made no reference at all to judicial review in the final document.

The organisation of the judiciary

Structure of the court system

- Federal court jurisdiction: Since the Supreme Court was established by the Constitution, its workload has expanded enormously.
  As a result, Congress has established lower Federal courts, which
  hear cases involving Federal laws. The Supreme Court is the
  highest court of appeal for these cases.

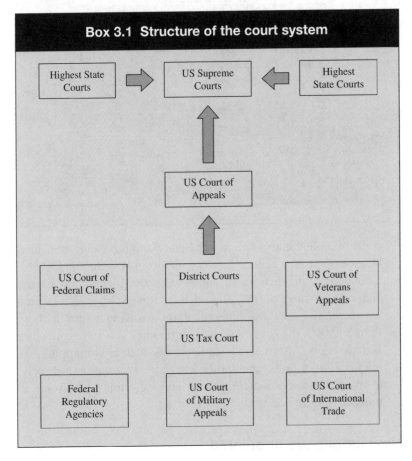

Box 3.1 Structure of the court system

- State courts jurisdiction: Each of the fifty states has its own court
  system to hear cases arising from state laws, such as the New York
  state system illustrated below. Cases which have reached the highest

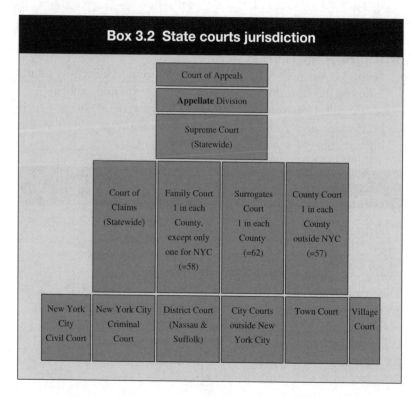

Box 3.2 State courts jurisdiction

| Court of Appeals |
| Appellate Division |
| Supreme Court (Statewide) |

| Court of Claims (Statewide) | Family Court 1 in each County, except only one for NYC (=58) | Surrogates Court 1 in each County (=62) | County Court 1 in each County outside NYC (=57) |

| New York City Civil Court | New York City Criminal Court | District Court (Nassau & Suffolk) | City Courts outside New York City | Town Court | Village Court |

court of appeal in this system, the State Supreme Court, may then be appealed to the Federal Supreme Court in Washington DC.

- Concurrent jurisdiction: In some cases the jurisdiction of the Federal and state courts overlap. For example, if there is a dispute between citizens of two different states involving a sum of more than $50,000, the case could be heard either in a state court or a Federal court. Alternatively, some crimes, such as kidnapping, are offences under both state and Federal laws. It comes as a surprise to many, however, that there is no Federal crime of murder: all murder cases are heard by state courts.

How judges are appointed

How Federal judges are nominated
At all levels, including appointments to district courts, judges are chosen by the President and then confirmed by the Senate. On the

Supreme Court there are nine Justices, led by the Chief Justice. There are a range of factors to consider when a candidate is being chosen:

- The American Bar Association – since 1952, the Association's Committee on the Federal Judiciary has been consulted concerning almost every Federal judicial appointment, rating each nominee as 'exceptionally well qualified', 'well qualified', 'qualified' or 'not qualified'.
- Other pressure groups – some nominees attract strong support or opposition, leading to pressure groups campaigning for/against their **nomination**.
- Balance – throughout the history of the judiciary, most judges have been white Anglo-Saxon men. On the Supreme Court, the first Jewish Justice, Louis Brandeis, was appointed in 1916; the first African-American, Thurgood Marshall, in 1967; the first woman, Sandra Day O'Connor, in 1981; and the first Italian-American, Antonin Scalia, in 1986.
- Geography – Since its earliest days, Presidents have done their best to ensure that all regions of the United States have been represented on the Court. In 1932, the principal objection to the strongest candidate, Justice Cardozo, arose from the fact that he was from New York and there were already two justices from that state on the bench. One of the other Justices from New York generously offered to resign so that Justice Cardozo could be appointed.
- Payment of political debts – although not a common reason, on occasion Justices have been chosen to reward them for past service. Chief Justice Earl Warren was promised a position on the Court in return for not running against Eisenhower in the 1952 presidential election.

How Federal Justices are confirmed

The **confirmation** of Federal judges requires a vote by a majority of the Senate. Historically, this has not proved difficult to achieve. In the early days of the Supreme Court, before it developed the status and authority with which it is now associated, the main challenge was to find suitable candidates who would not resign as soon as a more attractive position became available. Until 1967, most confirmations did not even require a formal vote. In recent decades, however, the President and the person who has been nominated have had to devote considerable time and effort preparing for the confirmation process.

- Pressure groups, which take a special interest in the work of the courts, keep files on all potential nominees. As soon as an announcement is made, they will issue press releases and produce television adverts supporting or opposing the nominee, with a view to putting pressure on the Senators.
- Nominees are expected to meet with Senators of both parties to discuss any issues or concerns they may have.
- Nominees are expected to fill out a questionnaire, prepared by the Senate Judiciary Committee, explaining their approach to making judgements and indicating their views on the major issues of the day. If a candidate has failed to make a positive impression by this stage, it may be unwise to face the grilling of the confirmation hearings. President George W. Bush's nominee, Harriet Miers, withdrew at this stage in 2005.
- Nominees have to testify at hearings held by the Judiciary Committee, at which other interested groups also have the opportunity to attempt the influence the committee's decision.
- If the Judiciary Committee supports a nominee, the whole Senate votes on whether to confirm the appointment.

As the Constitution requires a simple majority to confirm a nomination, fifty-one votes should be enough for an appointment to be made. However, the Senate has a procedure that allows a minority to block anything they feel very strongly about. This is called a filibuster. This blocking mechanism can only be overcome if sixty Senators vote to end the filibuster. Between 2002 and 2005, ten of President George W. Bush's more controversial nominees were filibustered by the minority Democratic Party in the Senate.

The ill-feeling generated by the Democrats' use of this tactic, which is traditionally saved for controversial legislation, was so intense that the majority Republican Party threatened to change the rules of the Senate to remove the right to filibuster confirmation hearings. The Democrats, in response, threatened to withdraw all of the cross-party co-operation that is essential for the Senate to operate smoothly. This confrontation, referred to by the media as the nuclear option, was averted when a group of fourteen moderate Senators (seven from each party) agreed that the filibuster would only be used in 'exceptional circumstances'. It has not been used since the deal was agreed in June 2005, but exactly what is meant by exceptional circumstances is unclear.

Why judicial appointments have become increasingly controversial

Since its 1954 ruling in *Brown* v. *Board of Education*, when it declared racial segregation to be unconstitutional, the Supreme Court's role in extending rights to marginalised groups has generated high emotion across the United States.

As the President can serve a maximum of two terms (eight years), but judges are appointed 'during good behaviour' until they retire, the President can use their choices' power to influence policy for many years after leaving office. They can nominate judges who, they believe, will continue the process of extending constitutional rights. In general, Democrat Presidents tend to be more liberal and prefer to appoint this kind of 'activist' judge. Alternatively, they can nominate judges who believe that it is the role of the legislature, not the courts, to pass laws which govern people's daily lives, according to the will of the electorate as expressed at the most recent election. In general, Republican Presidents tend to be more conservative and prefer to appoint this kind of 'restrained' judge who is reluctant to use the powers available to the courts to shape US society.

For liberal groups, a Federal judiciary made up of people who do not share their commitment to defending hard-won rights threatens the core American constitutional values of liberty and equality of opportunity. They are prepared to spend millions of dollars on advertising campaigns to convey their concerns to the Senate and the public when a conservative judge is nominated, and they are committed to the use of the filibuster to resist the confirmation of judges who might reverse any of the Civil Rights gains made in the past.

For conservative groups, the Court's tendency to invent new rights not found in the text of the Constitution amounts to a **krytocracy**, a government of judges. The USA, in their view, is ruled not by elected representatives but unelected judges, a situation fundamentally at odds with the core principle of the Constitution – that people in government should have enough power to rule effectively, but find it very difficult for anyone to accumulate and abuse power. They are also prepared to spend millions of dollars supporting nominees who will restore the courts to their proper role of interpreting, not making, laws.

The consequent public scrutiny of nominees is made even more intense by the fact that judges, once appointed, do not always act as expected. Conservatives, especially, have been dismayed that a significant proportion of Supreme Court Justices have proved to be far less conservative than the Presidents who nominated them expected. In the 1950s, President Eisenhower described his appointment of Earl Warren to Chief Justice as 'the biggest damn fool mistake I ever made'. Of the justices currently on the Supreme Court, two of the more liberal members – Justices Stevens and Souter – were appointed by Republican Presidents.

This has happened despite steps taken by President Reagan and his successors to vet potential nominees very carefully. A committee was set up to analyse all the court judgements, published writings and statements of people being considered and to interview them on their views on politically controversial issues. Conservatives have been determined to ensure that President George W. Bush does not make similar mistakes. Liberals, acutely aware that life expectancy is rising and that Justices may serve for as long as forty years, are equally determined that conservatives will not be allowed to re-make the Federal courts in their own image.

As well as the conviction, on both sides, that judicial appointments are of crucial importance, both are also mindful of the potential impact of a public battle during confirmation hearings. In 1987, the Senate refused to confirm Robert Bork, nominated by President Reagan, as a result of twelve days of public hearings in which liberals set out to discredit his record. Famously, Senator Edward Kennedy declared that 'Robert Bork's America is a land in which women would be forced into back-alley abortions, blacks would sit at segregated lunch counters, rogue police could break down citizens' doors at midnight'. Four years later, in 1991, the public was transfixed by live television coverage of the confirmation hearings of Clarence Thomas, who was accused of sexual harassment. Added to the suggestion that he harboured extreme right-wing views and was inadequately qualified to sit on the Supreme Court, he polarised opinion in the Senate and in society at large. Eventually, he was confirmed by a vote of 52–48, the narrowest margin of victory in the twentieth century. No subsequent appointment has generated anything like the level of controversy of these two nominees, but activists on both the right and left maintain substantial financial war-chests in case such a battle should erupt again.

The judicial process

How the Supreme Court decides which cases to hear

Either a lower court may send a case to the Supreme Court, by issuing a writ of certiorari, or the Court can be petitioned to hear a case involving a serious constitutional issue. It is up to the Court to decide if it will accept the case. During the course of the Supreme Court year, it usually hears about 100 cases. At the beginning of the year, in the first week of October, the Justices choose between forty and fifty cases that will occupy most of their time for the first half of the year, leaving room to accept up to fifty more before their year ends around the 4 July Independence Day holiday.

All cases are summarised by the law clerks of the Justices, and then considered. It takes four of the Justices to agree for a case to be accepted.

How the Supreme Court reaches a decision

Once the Court has accepted a case, the lawyers for each side present a brief, a written statement with their legal arguments, any relevant facts and supporting precedents.

Briefs, called **amicus curiae** or 'friends of the court', may also be submitted by other groups with an interest in the case, usually pressure groups or government departments. In a 2003 case deciding whether to allow Affirmative Action to continue, *Grutter* v. *Bollinger*, the Court freely admitted that they were heavily influenced by amicus briefs from influential groups such as major corporations and the armed forces in reaching their decision to uphold Affirmative Action.

A date will be set for oral argument, when each side will have thirty minutes to summarise their key points. The judges may interrupt at any time, to ask questions or to challenge a point, and, when time is up, the lawyer must stop speaking immediately, even if in mid-sentence.

Having read the papers and heard the arguments, the Justices meet to discuss the case and vote. All votes have equal weight, including that of the Chief Justice. It does not require a **unanimous** vote to reach a decision. An opinion then has to be written that will explain the decision to the general public and provide a guide to lower courts considering similar cases. If the Justices are split, a **majority decision** will be written, with the minority explaining their points of disagreement in a **dissenting opinion**. Judges on both sides can add points to the two main opinions by writing **concurring opinions**. In *Grutter* v. *Bollinger*, the majority decision was supported by two concurring opinions and the dissenting opinion was supported by three concurring opinions, making seven opinions issued by nine judges.

As with the selection of cases, law clerks play an important role. Often they write the first draft of the opinion to be presented by the Justice they work for, which, sometimes, is not amended. This is a huge responsibility for people who, although drawn from the most highly regarded law schools in the country, may not have had any previous legal experience. Unsurprisingly, with this start, many clerks go on to have very successful legal careers and, in some cases, have risen to become Supreme Court Justices themselves.

The power of judicial review

The 'least dangerous' branch?

Looking at the Constitution they had designed, one of the Founding Fathers declared: 'The Judiciary is beyond comparison the weakest of the three departments of power.' This attitude is reflected in the fact that, when the new capital city was being built in Washington, it did not seem to occur to anyone to provide a building for the Supreme Court. Until 1935, the Court met in a windowless committee room in Congress.

One of the Court's first decisions, however, had a powerful impact. In *Chisolm* v. *Georgia* (1793), the Court ruled that a citizen had the right to sue a state. The prospect of states being paralysed by the threat of law suits against everything they did led to the 11th Amendment, changing Article II, Section 2 of the Constitution on which the decision was based. The fact that it had been established that it took a constitutional amendment to overturn a decision of the Supreme Court was an early indication of the Court's power.

Marbury v. *Madison* (1803)

This case established that the Court had the power of **judicial review**, from which most of the Court's powers flow. Judicial review is the power of the courts to declare unconstitutional acts of the legislative and executive branches of government.

In 1789, Congress passed an act setting up lower Federal courts. In 1801, just before his term of office ended, President Adams appointed forty-two new Justices who shared his views and they were all confirmed by the Senate. Four of them had not received their letters of appointment and the new President ordered his Secretary of State, Madison, not to deliver them. One of the four, Marbury, applied to the Court to enforce his appointment. The Supreme Court's decision, to declare Section 13 of the Judiciary Act to be unconstitutional, established that they had the right to decide the precise meaning of the Constitution in relation to specific cases.

This gives Federal courts vast power to influence US society. There are two competing views on how this power should be used.

Judicial restraint

According to this view, the power of judicial review should be used as little as possible because:

- Judges are appointed, not elected.
- It is their responsibility to weigh up the legal factors that affect the cases they hear and to make a decision. It is the responsibility of the elected branches of government, Congress and the President, to make political decisions.
- If, therefore, a case comes before them that the judges see as raising political issues, their ruling should provide opportunities to resolve these issues outside the courtroom. In the words of a former Senator who believed strongly in **judicial restraint**, 'There is not a syllable in the Constitution which gives the Supreme Court any discretionary power to fashion policies.'

If a case has constitutional significance that cannot be avoided, judges should base their decisions on:

- Precedent – that is, considering the judgements of similar cases in the past.
- **Strict constructionism** – that is, considering the views expressed on the issue by the Founding Fathers in the Constitutional Convention.

Judicial activism

According to this view, it is the responsibility of judges to make use of the power of judicial review because:

- Judges are responsible for resolving current problems and addressing current needs.
- The Constitution provides a guide, but it must be interpreted to understand what it means in the modern world.
- This is not to deny the wisdom of the Founding Fathers, but their world is dead and gone and the principles of the Constitution have to be applied to contemporary reality.

This way of interpreting the Constitution is known as **loose constructionism**.

Limitations on the use of judicial review

While judicial review gives judges enormous power, it is not unlimited. There are a range of factors that restrict their powers:

- Legal process
  - Judges can only decide matters that are brought to them in the form of legal cases. While politicians can decide that there is a policy that they disagree with and try to change it, judges cannot. They can only use their power of judicial review when ruling on a case that has been submitted to them. (In practice, almost every issue on which they may have an opinion is likely to be the subject of a law suit.)
  - Judges will not offer advisory opinions, in which they explain what they are likely to do if a case is brought before them.

- Court traditions
  - Judges only consider cases where their decision will make a real difference. So, when the State of Idaho asked the Court to decide if it could withdraw its support for a constitutional amendment, the Court refused to hear the case, as the deadline for the amendment had already passed and their decision, while interesting, would have had no effect.
  - Judges will only consider cases in which a considerable number of people are affected and in which it is claimed that considerable harm has been caused. With the exception of appeals against a death sentence, the Court will not consider cases in which only an individual or a small group are affected, or cases in which people who have not been harmed to any significant degree are claiming unfair treatment.
  - The Courts are traditionally very reluctant to get involved in cases that involve American foreign policy. When, for example, the United States military imprisoned without trial people they described as 'enemy combatants' during the military operation in Afghanistan in 2001, it took two years for the Supreme Court to agree to hear a case on whether the policy was constitutional.
  - Judges do not think of themselves as politicians and are traditionally very reluctant to get involved in cases that are clearly political. If possible, they try to leave such issues to the elected representatives of the people in Congress and the White House. It is not always clear, however, which issues should be defined as 'political', and the other branches of government are sometimes unwilling to deal with very controversial issues which might cause them unpopularity.
  - Judges make the distinction between their personal views and what the law requires. As they are not elected, they have a particular obligation to use their power responsibly, which may require them to reach a decision that, personally, they would prefer not to reach.
- Lack of enforcement power
  - Under the Constitution, it is the judicial branch of government that decides what the law means, but the Executive branch of government, meaning the President at the Federal level and governors at state level, that is responsible for ensuring that

the law is upheld. Early in the Court's history, when it made a decision that the President disliked, it was reported that President Jackson said, 'John Marshall has made his decision, now let him enforce it.' There have been many examples since of the Court's decisions being ignored or actively resisted, such as the refusal by Southern states to end racial segregation in the 1950s and 60s, after a Supreme Court ruling to do so.

- Public opinion
  - Although the judicial branch is designed to be independent, so that the judges can make decisions based only on the merits of the case before them, public support for their decisions has to be considered. A series of decisions by the Supreme Court in the 1930s, which declared laws designed to reduce the suffering of people affected by the economic depression to be unconstitutional, created the impression that the judges were out of touch with ordinary people, which undermined the Court's status.
  - When weighing up a case, the Supreme Court will accept written statements in support of one or other side of the case, usually from pressure groups who have an interest in the outcome of the case. These statements, or briefs, are called amicus curiae.
- Checks and balances
  - Federal judges are nominated by the President but their appointment must be confirmed by a majority in the Senate. This ought to lead to the appointment of people who are suitable and moderate in their views.
  - Supreme Court judgements can be overturned by a constitutional amendment. This was first done in 1793, when the case of *Chisolm* v. *Georgia* was overturned by the 11th Amendment, and again in 1913, when the 16th Amendment was passed.
  - Congress can modify laws that have been declared unconstitutional so that, despite a Supreme Court ruling, a law continues to apply in an altered form.
  - Congress has the power to remove judges through a process known as impeachment (explained in Chapter 8 on Congress). In 1805, there was an attempt to impeach Justice Samuel Chase because his views clashed with the President and his party. The impeachment failed, reinforcing the independence

of the Court, and all twelve impeachments that have taken place since have been the result of personal misconduct on the part of the judge.

- Congress has the power to change the number of judges on the Supreme Court. Since 1869, there have been nine Justices on the Supreme Court. However, in 1937 President Roosevelt, frustrated that he was unable to implement his New Deal to tackle to the economic recession because the Court kept declaring his laws unconstitutional, proposed to Congress a 'Court-packing' plan. He offered to 'help' all judges over the age of seventy with their workload by appointing another judge to assist them. This would have added six new judges to the Court. The proposal was rejected by Congress but, thereafter, the Court did not reject any of the President's New Deal projects. Clearly the threat to change the number of judges made an impact and, as a judge on the Court put it, 'The President's enemies defeated the court reform bill – the President achieved court reform.'

The use of judicial power

There have been only seventeen Chief Justices in the history of the United States. Each one has, to a considerable extent, set the tone for the Court. Consequently, there have been periods when the Court has tended to adopt a philosophy of **judicial activism** or, alternatively, judicial restraint. Periods of judicial activism have created many controversial, and therefore famous, cases. There have been much longer periods, however, when the Court has chosen not to use the power available to it. Cases decided in these periods have, nevertheless, had considerable impact.

Restrained use of power

In *Plessy* v. *Ferguson* (1896), the Supreme Court upheld a Louisiana law that provided for 'equal but separate [train] accommodations for the white and colored races'. Despite the 14th Amendment, which gave former slaves the rights contained in the Bill of Rights, and the 1875 Civil Rights Act, which prohibited racial discrimination in 'inns, public conveyances and places of amusement', the Court ruled that such laws 'do not necessarily imply the inferiority of either race to the other'. By refusing to intervene in state affairs, the Court allowed them to pass laws that segregated their inhabitants by race.

A similar approach was taken during the Great Depression in the 1930s, when the Supreme Court declared unconstitutional laws which they believed undermined the system of Federalism, designed to stop the government in Washington from gaining too much power. In *Schechter Poultry Corporation* v. *United States* (1935), the Court ruled that the National Industrial Recovery Act, which provided employment through the building of bridges, schools and hospitals and introduced a forty-hour week for workers, was unconstitutional on the grounds that it regulated all companies, including those which traded only locally, which was the responsibility of the states. In *United States* v. *Butler* (1936), the Court ruled the Agricultural Adjustment Act, which provided financial help for farmers, unconstitutional on the grounds that it interfered with the responsibilities of the states. More recently, in *Texas* v. *Johnson* (1989), Justice Kennedy summed up the values of judicial restraint in a ruling that declared that the burning of the US flag during a protest was a form of freedom of expression covered by the 1st Amendment. He argued that 'the hard fact is that sometimes we must make decisions we do not like. We make them because they are right, right in the sense that the law and the Constitution, as we see them, compel the result.' Judges, in his view, should only be guided by a narrow interpretation of the Constitution and not let personal opinion influence their decisions.

Active use of power

The case of *Brown* v. *Board of Education* (1954), which ruled that seg-regation marked the separated race as inferior and was therefore unconstitutional, is widely regarded as the start of an era of judicial activism. The courts continued to play an active role during the Civil Rights campaign. Other notable rulings in this period included *Boynton* v. *Virginia* (1960), which ordered the desegregation of inter-state public transport, and *Baker* v. *Carr* (1962), when the Court ruled that the population of each electoral district must be of roughly equal size, thereby providing equal political representation.

In the 1970s, when the mass protests of the Civil Rights movement had faded away, the Federal courts continued to play a role in main-taining the drive for racial equality. In *Swann* v. *Charlotte-Mecklenburg*

(1971), the Supreme Court ruled that continued segregation in the schools of Charlotte, North Carolina, had to end and specified the means to do so – that school buses take white and black children to each other's schools. In 1974, a Federal district judge, Arthur Garrity, ordered the same remedy for the schools of Boston, Massachusetts. When the local school board refused to obey the order, the Court appointed its own administrators and ran every aspect of the Boston school system for three years, including setting the curriculum and hiring teachers, taking judicial activism to a new level that included enforcing its own decisions.

At the same time, the courts were also active in the area of criminal justice. It was clear that many suspects were not able to exercise their rights, either because they did not know them or because they could not afford to. In *Gideon* v. *Wainwright* (1963), the Court ruled that defendants in criminal cases who could not afford a lawyer were entitled to one provided by the State in order to ensure a fair trial, as required by the 6th Amendment of the Constitution. In *Miranda* v. *Arizona* (1966), the Court ruled that a suspect must be told of the right, guaranteed by the 5th Amendment, not to incriminate themselves and to remain silent during police questioning. This decision was widely criticised, as it appeared to be providing criminals with a loophole to escape justice.

The backlash against the Court gathered momentum with the landmark judgement of *Roe* v. *Wade* (1973). The Justices ruled that the 9th Amendment, which protects rights other than those mentioned in the Constitution, provided a right of privacy and that any law which made abortion illegal was an 'unjustifiable intrusion by the Government upon the privacy of the individual'.

Judicial activism is often associated with 'liberal' judges (often, but by no means always, nominated by Presidents from the Democratic Party) who extend the rights recognised under the Constitution. Judicial restraint is frequently associated with 'conservative' judges (almost always nominated by Presidents from the Republican Party). However, judicial activism applies to all rulings which re-shape society, including those which have the support of extremely conservative judges such as Antonin Scalia and Clarence Thomas (see below). Thus, if *Roe* v. *Wade* were to be overturned, that would be an example of conservative judicial activism.

'Culture Wars'

'No more Souters!'

After eleven years without a vacancy occurring on the Supreme Court, in the summer of 2005 there were two. The reaction of the President's conservative supporters was instant: 'No more Souters!'

They were referring to Justice David Souter, who had been nominated by the President's father in 1990, believing him to be a sound conservative, only to find that he joined the liberals on the Court when voting on cases. To make their point, they immediately turned their fire on the Attorney General, Alberto Gonzales, rumoured to be under consideration and far too moderate for their taste. Conservatives, in the words of one of their leaders, had 'a chance to implement a judicial revolution' and they were determined that the opportunity would not be lost. Their liberal opponents were equally determined to block any nominee who shared the conservatives' revolutionary agenda. Battle was joined. But would two new Justices make such a difference? And what were the issues that generated such intense rivalry?

The Roberts Supreme Court, 2005

The two vacancies were created by the resignation of Sandra Day O'Connor and the death, a few weeks later, of Chief Justice William Rehnquist. The first woman ever to be appointed to the Supreme Court, Sandra Day O'Connor was appointed by President Reagan (Republican) in 1981. At first she tended to support the other conservative judges appointed by President Reagan, except on issues of discrimination and abortion, but became significantly more liberal over time. William Rehnquist was first appointed by President Nixon (Republican) in 1972. Describing his appointment, he said, 'At the time I came on the Court, the boat was kind of keeling over in one direction. I felt that my job was to kind of lean the other way.' He dissented from the *Roe* v. *Wade* decision. In 1986, he was promoted to Chief Justice by President Reagan (Republican).

Although two Republicans departed, because of Justice Sandra Day O'Connor's increasingly liberal tendencies their replacement with two reliable conservatives was potentially significant, as the chart below illustrates.

Roe v. *Wade*

Few issues galvanise both conservatives and liberals as much as abortion. For liberals, the right to an abortion equals the right of a woman to control what happens to her body. For conservatives, especially evangelical Christians, abortion is murder. Neither side is prepared to yield an inch to the other.

Table 3.1 Supreme Court Justices

Justice	Voting Pattern
John Roberts (Chief Justice)	Conservative (replacing a conservative)
John Paul Stevens	Liberal
Antonin Scalia	Extremely conservative
Anthony Kennedy	Moderate conservative
David Souter	Liberal
Clarence Thomas	Extremely conservative
Ruth Bader Ginsburg	Liberal
Stephen Breyer	Liberal
Samuel Alito	Conservative (replacing a moderate conservative)

Since the ruling in 1973, conservatives have argued that the Court's decision cannot be justified by the language of the Constitution. However, they have not had enough supporters to reverse *Roe* v. *Wade*, and even with the new additions it is unlikely that the situation will change. Their interim strategy, of making abortions more difficult to obtain, may be more successful. In *Planned Parenthood* v. *Casey* (1992), a law to make women notify the baby's father before having an abortion was struck down by the Supreme Court. On its way through the appeals system the case was heard by Samuel Alito, who voted to uphold the law.

In *Stenberg* v. *Carhart* (2000), a law which banned a controversial procedure, known by its opponents as partial-birth abortion, was also struck down by the Supreme Court. Sandra Day O'Connor joined the liberals in a 5–4 vote. Her replacement is thought likely to vote the other way.

Grutter v. Bollinger

The last time the issue of Affirmative Action came before the Supreme Court, in 2003, Sandra Day O'Connor again joined the liberals in a 5–4 vote to it to continue. She also wrote the judgement expressing the view that race-conscious Affirmative Action ought not to be needed by 2028. With both John Roberts and Samuel Alito thought to be opposed to Affirmative Action, it is unlikely that it will be many years before another challenge is brought before the Court.

McCreary County v. American Civil Liberties Union

The groups that feel strongly about abortion also tend to object to the Supreme Court's interpretation of the Constitution that there can be no religious displays or ceremonies in government-funded institutions. In 2005 Sandra Day O'Connor voted with the liberals to hold that a prominent display of the Ten Commandments in a Kentucky county courthouse was an unconstitutional endorsement of religion. The new additions to the Court are thought unlikely to agree with her.

Lawrence v. Texas

Religious conservatives point out that record numbers of voters turned out to support the Republican Party in the 2004 election, motivated by votes being held to ban same-sex marriage in thirteen states. Yet they can do nothing to resist the Supreme Court's decision in 2003 to recognise gay rights. It is unlikely that the new additions to the Court will make an impact on this issues, as the vote was 6–3, with Anthony Kennedy joining the liberals.

Prospects for the Supreme Court

Unpredictable justices

Although political activists and commentators analyse in detail the judgements and decisions of Justices joining the Supreme Court, and how these compare with the retiring Justices, it is impossible to predict with any certainty how they will vote. Conservative frustration at this unpredictability is well known, but Democrats can be equally disappointed with their nominees: President Truman, in the 1950s, complained that 'whenever you put a man on the Supreme Court he ceases to be your friend'. Judges acknowledge this point. One renowned Supreme Court Justice, when asked if judges change when they put on their robes, replied, 'If he's any good he does.'

Unpredictable issues

Making predictions more difficult is the uncertainty that the most controversial issues of today will be the main issues in years to come. As recently as August 2001, it would have been difficult to foresee the current 'War on Terror', but now that poses great challenges to the Supreme Court. Traditionally, the Courts have been reluctant to second-guess the President at times of war. During the Civil War, President Lincoln expressed his view clearly, arguing that the only concern was whether the government would be 'not *too* strong for the liberties of its people [but] strong *enough* to maintain its own existence, in great emergencies', and the Supreme Court largely accepted a passive role for the duration of the war. In Second World War, the Court ruled that eight German saboteurs who had been arrested on American soil by the FBI were not entitled to a trial in the civil courts, with the protections of the Bill of Rights, such as the 5th Amendment right not to incriminate themselves. Instead, they were tried by a military tribunal, on the grounds that constitutional safeguards do not apply to offences against the law of war. Do these precedents apply to the current 'War on Terror', which may last for decades and has no conventional armies or battles? The first judgement handed down by the Court, in *Hamdi* v. *Rumsfeld* (2004), ruled that enemy combatants were entitled to constitutional rights because 'a state of war is not a blank check for the president' and because 'if this nation is to remain true to its ideals, it must not wield the tools of tyrants even to resist an assault by the forces of tyranny'. Then, decisively, in *Hamdan* v. *Rumsfeld* (2006), the Supreme Court ruled by a majority of 5–3 that all prisoners captured during anti-terrorism operations, known as illegal combatants, were entitled to the same legal protections as conventional prisoners of war. This included a rejection of the claim made by the administration of George W. Bush that illegal combatants were not covered by Common Article 3 of the Geneva Conventions, which prohibits torture and requires that detainees receive 'all the judicial guarantees which are recognised as indispensable by civilised peoples'. Justice Alito was in the minority who voted to support the President's policy and Justice Roberts did not vote because he had been involved with the case at an earlier stage (when he also supported the President) before being appointed to the Supreme Court. Within months of the Hamdan decision, Congress passed the Military Commissions Act, restoring to the President the right to identify enemies, detain them indefinitely and interrogate them without the right of appeal to the courts. This new law is certain to be challenged and other cases are sure to follow. Other cases are sure to follow, especially with early indications that the new members of the Court will follow traditional practice and respect the President's judgement in matters of military operations and foreign affairs.

At the current rate of technological development, the Courts are likely to have to rule on a range of other new issues. For example, scientists are developing a technique known as brain fingerprinting, in which it is possible to detect brain activity associated with memory. Should the police be allowed to use this technology for interrogation? Would it be a form of compulsory self-incrimination that violates the 5th Amendment? Would it be so different from blood or urine samples, which are not regarded as 5th Amendment problems?

Even some of the most controversial issues of today could be transformed by technological advances. Already genetic screening provides the means to create 'designer babies'. Women's rights activists, who fear that male embryos will be routinely selected over female embryos, are joined by anti-abortion activists in opposition to this practice. However, would those anti-abortion activists remain united if scientists were to identify a genetic predisposition to homosexuality?

Certain conflict
One thing that is certain, however, is that the USA has always been divided by what it means to be true to its constitutional ideals, and will remain so whatever the future brings. The Court's role in interpreting the Constitution will, therefore, inevitably continue to make it the focus of conflict that is likely to get more, not less, intense as society wrestles with ever more complex challenges.

Box 3.3 Comparing the US and UK judiciaries

Weighing the importance of rights v. democracy
When comparing the US and UK Constitutions (see Box 1.1), the key distinction made was between the importance of rights, defended effectively by the US Bill of Rights, and the importance of democracy, undermined by the power of the unelected US Federal judiciary. This traditional distinction is, however, being blurred by changes that are taking place in the UK judicial system.

The UK judiciary in transition
When Britain joined the European Union in 1973, the government had to submit to the rules and regulations of that organisation. Failure to do so could result in the government having to appear before the European Court of Justice in a case that could be brought by an individual or business. Then, in the 1990s, government ministers found themselves facing a growing number of challenges in court in which it was claimed that they had exceeded their powers as defined by an Act of Parliament. As the issues covered by legislation have become more complex over time, the scope to challenge exactly what the terms of an Act may mean has grown. High Court judges are presiding with increasing frequency over judicial review cases in which they evaluate ministerial decisions.

This trend was reinforced by the decision by the UK government to incorporate the European Convention on Human Rights into British law in the Human Rights Act of 1998. This meant that judges, for the first time, had the right to use judicial review to overrule an Act of Parliament if it contravened human rights law. Furthermore, the government announced in June 2003 that it would introduce a new system at the head of the judiciary to create greater separation of powers, similar to that in the USA. The position of Lord Chancellor, who was head of the judiciary while also being a Member of Parliament and the government, would be abolished. The Lord Chancellor would still be a member of the government but would no longer be head of the judiciary or sit in Parliament. In addition, the highest court of appeal, the Law Lords would also operate separately from Parliament for the first time and become a Supreme Court.

'Dictators in wigs'
The proposed reforms to create greater separation of powers have yet to be implemented and the Human Rights Act lacks the force of

the Bill of Rights in the USA. When, in 2001, the British government introduced new anti-terrorism legislation, it was able to pass a law to hold suspects indefinitely despite the Human Rights Act. However, in 2003 the High Court ruled against a government policy that made political asylum harder to claim. Then, indefinite detention was eventually over ruled by the Law Lords in 2004. This would suggest that, over time, the power of Judicial Review may lead to the UK judiciary gaining significant political power along similar lines to their US counterparts.

In one respect, the parallels are already evident. Conservative politicians and commentators have begun to complain that the Human Rights Act is a charter for minority rights, at the expense of the majority, and the members of courts have been denounced as 'dictators in wigs'.

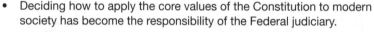

What you should have learnt from reading this chapter

- Deciding how to apply the core values of the Constitution to modern society has become the responsibility of the Federal judiciary.

- Each time the courts rule in favour of the argument that the language of the Constitution enables every generation to 'invoke its principles in their own search for greater freedom', judges effectively create policy that may affect the lives of millions of Americans. This is not a power bestowed on this unelected, unaccountable, group of people by the Founding Fathers, and the quotation from one of them, Alexander Hamilton, describing the judiciary as the 'least dangerous branch' strongly indicates that there was no expectation that the courts would make public policy.

- Failure to intervene to secure constitutional rights, as happened for fifty-eight years while Southern states practised legalised segregation with the blessing of the Supreme Court, is no less controversial.

- Whenever a case that has the potential to influence the lifestyles of Americans, such as abortion, Affirmative Action or gay rights, comes before the Courts the debate is sure to include arguments about the nature of the Constitution, how its values should be applied and whether unelected judges are the most suitable people to have the final say in the issue.

Glossary of key terms

Amicus curiae Documents or testimony from individuals or groups who are not directly involved in a case but have an interest in the outcome.

Appellate jurisdiction The constitutional authority to hear and decide cases that have been before a lower court.

Concurring opinion A written statement by a judge, supporting the conclusion reached by another judge in the same court but giving different reasons for reaching that conclusion.

Confirmation (of appointee) The process by which the Senate gives, or withholds, its support for a judge who has been put forward by the President to fill a vacancy on a Federal court.

Dissenting opinion A written statement by a judge, giving reasons for rejecting the conclusion reached by another judge in the same court.

Judicial activism Judgements that seek to apply constitutional principles to contemporary social problems and provide solutions or remedies.

Judicial restraint Judgements that seek to apply narrow legal and constitutional principles, leaving the other branches of government to resolve social problems.

Judicial review The act of declaring laws and actions of government to be constitutional or unconstitutional.

Krytocracy Rule by judges.

Loose constructionism The use, by judges, of the Constitution and precedent as guides but without being tightly restricted by them if other factors are considered more important.

Majority decision The official decision of a court, without the support of all the judges.

Nomination (of appointee) A proposal, by the President, of a person to fill a vacancy on a Federal court.

Original jurisdiction The constitutional authority to hear and decide cases that have not been before a lower court.

Strict constructionism The use, by judges, of the Constitution and precedent as guides with all other factors given far less weight.

Unanimous opinion The official decision of a court, with the support of all the judges.

Likely examination questions

Issues examiners may expect students to be able to effectively analyse include:

- Factors that enable Federal justices to be 'politicians in disguise', if they so choose
- Factors that encourage Federal justices to avoid entering the 'political thicket'
- The significance of recent appointments to the Supreme Court

- Why the judiciary has become one of the arenas for the 'culture wars' of US politics

Thus, examples of the kind of questions that could be asked include:
'The Supreme Court has too much power for an unelected body.' Discuss.
Explain judicial restraint and its political significance.

Where the question compares the US system with Britain, issues may include:

- The impact on judiciaries of codified and uncodified constitutions
- The effectiveness with which rights are protected in each country
- Whether judges inevitably play a political role
- How similar/different the two judiciaries are

Thus, an example of a question which could be asked is:
'The reality is that judges have a political role.' Discuss this view of the judiciary in the UK and USA.

 ## Helpful website

www.supremecourtus.gov and www.uscourts.gov – the two official websites of the Federal judiciary.

www.pfaw.org . and www.aclj.org – the websites of two of the organisations at the forefront of the judicial 'culture wars'. The first is a liberal group, People for the American Way, which played a major role in blocking the confirmation of President Reagan's nominee, Robert Bork, in 1987. The second is the American Center for Law and Justice, which provides speakers who regularly appears on US current affairs programmes, promoting conservative legal positions.

 ## Suggestions for further reading

A wide range of general books about the Supreme Court are available, from bookstores or Amazon, ranging from the *Oxford Companion to the Supreme Court of the United States* by Kermit L. Hall to *Supreme Court for Dummies* by Lisa Paddock.

There is also at least one biography of each member of the Supreme Court.

The judicial culture wars are also being fought out in print. On the left, this includes *Radicals in Robes: Why Extreme Right-Wing Courts are Wrong for America* by Cass Sunstein. On the right, this includes *Men in Black: How the Supreme Court is Destroying America* by Mark Levin.

**PART II: THE LIMITS OF FEDERAL POWER –
FEDERALISM AND PLURALISM**

CHAPTER 4

Federalism

Contents

Overview

On 27 October 2005, a Federal Court ruled that the State of Georgia could not enforce a law requiring citizens to use government-issued ID when voting. With car ownership much lower among the African American population than white residents and with no DMV office within nine miles of Atlanta, with its large African American population, the law would almost certainly have meant a sharp reduction of black voters at subsequent elections. 'Once again African Americans in Georgia must seek justice from the federal courts to protect us from state officials who are eager to deprive us of our fundamental right to vote,' said a local Civil Rights leader, who saw the law as part of a consistent pattern of measures, dating back to the end of the Civil War in 1865, to obstruct, suppress and intimidate black voters.

Yet Federalism was designed by the Founding Fathers as an instrument to protect the people from tyranny, one of the ways of preventing power from being concentrated in too few hands. For millions of Americans the interference of a Federal court in the affairs of Georgia is far more of a threat to civil liberties than the voter registration law.

This tension, between those who distrust state officials and those who believe that States Rights are a crucial ingredient of liberty, continues to be one of the most significant issues in US politics. This chapter examines the development of Federalism and considers the current balance between the States and the Government in Washington DC.

Key issues to be covered in this chapter

- The Founding Fathers' concern with dividing power between the central and regional governments, to cultivate diverse regional character and guard against excessive power being concentrated in the central government
- Federalism's comparative ineffectiveness in the early twentieth century, as the central government's scale and scope grew dramatically
- The efforts made in the second half of the twentieth century to re-balance the relationship between the states and the central government to one more closely resembling the original design of the Founding Fathers
- The impact on Federalism of central government policies, especially those relating to the 'War on Terror', in the twenty-first century

The states at independence from Britain

Complete dominance over the national government

When the thirteen colonies broke away from Britain in 1776, they had already been developing their own traditions and identities for up to a hundred and fifty years. Initially, these states set up a confederate system of government, in which the national government had very limited resources and was dependent on the states for money, soldiers and to enforce the law. It consisted of a legislature (Congress), with no executive (President) or courts, and nine of the states had to give their agreement before any action could be taken.

The disadvantages of a confederate system

The weaknesses of this system quickly became evident:

- Congress could not raise its own revenue and states could not be relied on to provide adequate funds.
- Congress could not regulate trade. Economic disputes broke out between a number of states and Congress could not play a role in resolving them.
- Congress found it difficult to make decisions. Often only nine or ten state delegates were present at meetings and nine votes were required for a law to be passed.
- When Congress as able to make decisions, without an executive branch or court system, they had no means of enforcing them.
- This lack of effective co-ordination meant that the country was vulnerable to invasion by powerful European imperial countries.

However, the states valued the main advantage of the system: they retained almost complete sovereignty, or control over their affairs.

Redefining the relationship between the states and the national government

A recognition of the need for a more effective national government led to the Constitutional Convention of 1787 (see Chapter 1 for more details). One of the Convention's main challenges was to ensure that the states would be able to retain as much sovereignty as possible. Consequently, they devised a system in which:

- The Constitution gave some power to the states. These were sovereign powers, which belonged to the states. Their powers had come from the Constitution, not the national government, and could not be taken away.
- The Constitution gave some power to the national government. These were sovereign powers, which belonged to the national government. Their powers had come from the Constitution, not the states, and could not be taken away.
- Neither the states nor the national government would have excessive power, meaning that the Federal system helped to protect the people from oppression and to guarantee their liberty.

Powers given to the states

Article I, Section 9 of the Constitution listed powers that could be exercised by the states but not Congress. These included, at the time, the right to trade in slaves and the right to raise an income tax. Both of these limitations were later removed but others, such as not allowing Congress to tax goods that move from one state to another, remain.

Article IV provided for 'full faith and credit', meaning that any law, government action or court decision in one state would be recognised in all of the other states. Therefore, no one would be able to evade the law in one state by escaping to another with different laws. On the other hand, it would be possible to go to another state to take advantage of their laws without punishment at home. For example, the marriage laws vary from state to state.

Article V gave the states a role in deciding whether the Constitution should be amended. No amendment is possible without the agreement of three quarters of the states (thirty-eight of the fifty states).

The 10th Amendment gave the states power over all matters which were not given specifically to the Federal government. These are known as **reserved powers**.

Powers given to the national government

Article I, Section 8 of the Constitution listed seventeen powers that only Congress could exercise. Crucially, the eighteenth clause gave Congress the right to pass any laws required to fulfil their powers.

Known as the 'elastic clause', it has been used by Congress, controversially, to intervene in matters traditionally thought of as the responsibility of the states. Section 10 listed the areas the states cannot interfere with, for example, foreign affairs.

Article II outlined the powers and duties of the President.

Article III outlined the powers and duties of the Supreme Court. At that time, the powers did not include judicial review which, like the 'elastic clause', was to become controversial.

Article VI, Section 2 was the 'Supremacy Clause', which established that when state and Federal governments were in conflict, the Federal government was supreme.

Some of the powers given to the Federal government were clearly written into the Constitution. These are known as **expressed powers** or **enumerated powers.** In order to use their powers, the Federal government also has **inherent powers**, such as the power to set up a diplomatic service to manage foreign relations. The Federal government may also have to take less obvious steps to use their powers, by making use of **implied powers**, such as the controversial 'elastic clause'.

Powers shared between the states and the national government

Both the Federal and state legislatures have always had the right to pass laws that define crimes and appropriate punishments. Since the 16th Amendment was passed in 1913, allowing the Federal government to impose income taxes, both Federal and state governments have had the right to tax individuals. These shared powers are known as concurrent powers. The consequent division of powers is shown in Table 4.1.

Federalism in the Constitution

An unsatisfactory compromise?

Before the Constitution could become law, nine of the thirteen states had to ratify it. Federalism, like so much of the Constitution, represented a compromise, and across the country there was fierce debate as to whether the right balance had been struck between the powers given to the national government and the states.

Table 4.1 Division of powers

National Government	Shared Powers	State Governments
Foreign affairs	Raise taxes	Regulate trade within the state
Defence of the nation	Borrow money	Administer elections
Resolving disputes between states	Spend money for the welfare of the population	Protect the public's health, welfare and morals
Regulating trade between the states	Pass and enforce laws	
Managing the economy		

The States' Rights position

Those who feared that the Constitution gave the national government too much power, and could become a threat to liberty, argued that:

- The original thirteen states had existed before independence and had come together to create a Constitution that placed strict limitations on the Federal government.
- Any doubts about where power belonged, perhaps caused by disagreement over an issue not directly covered by the Constitution, should therefore *always* be resolved in favour of the states.
- This approach was justified by experience, that decisions are best taken by people closest to those affected by them, and by the Constitution itself, which, in the 10th Amendment, reserved to the states any powers not specifically given to the Federal government.

The most extreme supporters of this view also developed the theories of nullification and interposition: that if the Federal government passed laws or took actions that increased its own powers, then the states should overrule them.

The Nationalist position

Those who feared that the country, and its liberties, would not survive unless the Constitution provided the national government with enough power to effectively co-ordinate affairs argued that:

- The Constitution was created to serve the people and gave both Federal and state governments the powers they needed to do so.
- Therefore, any doubts about where power belonged should be resolved according to the needs of the people, not automatically in favour of the states, and should take account of the fact that the Federal government has responsibility for all the people while each state has responsibility for only some of the people.
- Furthermore, the Constitution created a Federal government strong enough to protect the nation from external aggression and internal disputes, and had given the government the right to use 'necessary and proper' means (the 'elastic clause') to carry out its duties.

The continuing debate

When the Constitution was adopted, enough people on both sides of this dispute were able to accept the compromise, even though they still had strong reservations. Once the Constitution came into operation, however, it did not take long for these conflicting views to erupt into a dispute. In the Supreme Court case *McCulloch* v. *Maryland* (1819), it was ruled that the State of Maryland did not have the right to impose a tax on the Federal bank. The Chief Justice, John Marshall, explained that to allow states to exercise power over a Federal institution would 'render the government of the Union incompetent . . . and place all powers under the control of the State legislatures'.

Supporters of States' Rights were appalled by this decision, while their opponents felt vindicated. This decision did not finally settle the matter, however, and the debate on the correct balance between the powers of the Federal government and the States has continued ever since.

The growth of the central government

Dual Federalism

This original division of responsibilities, with the national government taking responsibility for foreign and inter-State affairs, and the state governments taking responsibility for all other matters, is known as **Dual Federalism**. It is also sometimes referred to as **layer cake** Federalism, using the image of one cake resting on top of another, completely separate, cake. This was, and remains, the model of ideal federalism: a model to be aimed for and to be changed only if absolutely necessary. However, a variety of factors made it difficult to maintain this model:

- The Supreme Court, under Chief Justice John Marshall, made a series of rulings that established that the Court was the supreme legal power in the land and could make decisions that directly affected matters that were the responsibility of the states:
  - *Fletcher* v. *Peck* (1810) This case ruled that a law passed by the Georgia state legislature had violated the United States Constitution and was therefore invalid. Before this decision, it was generally understood that the legitimacy of state laws was determined by state constitutions and state Supreme Courts.
  - *McCulloch* v. *Maryland* (1819) This case ruled that Maryland was not allowed to impose a tax on the national bank, set up by Congress, and that in a conflict between a the national government and a state the national government was supreme.
  - *Dartmouth College* v. *Woodward* (1819) This case ruled that the State of New Hampshire acted unconstitutionally when it attempted to take over a college by removing its trustees.
  - *Gibbons* v. *Ogden* (1824) This case ruled that Congress had the right to regulate inter-state commerce. Before this decision, it was generally understood that the Constitution allowed states to close their borders to trade, if they chose.
- The Constitution contained a clause, in Article I, Section 9, which prohibited the abolition of the slave trade until 1808. As soon as it was allowed to do so, however, Congress banned the slave trade, with inevitable effect on the states that depended on slavery for their prosperity.

- The Civil War (1861–65) established that no state had the right to leave the Union and that if they refused to abide by the Constitution the Federal government had the right to impose its will. Between the end of the war in 1865 and 1877, the Southern states which had tried to break away were ruled by military governors who took their orders from Washington DC.

- The 13th, 14th and 15th Amendments to the Constitution, known as the Civil Rights Amendments, were passed after the Civil War to ensure that the newly freed slaves would be given the same rights as other American citizens. For the leaders of the Southern states, who believed in white racial superiority, this was seen, like the end of the slave trade (1808) and slavery (1863), as the North deciding how their communities should be organised and imposing its values on the South.

- In the First World War, the government dramatically increased its control over the daily lives of its citizens. Conscription (compulsory military service) was introduced for the first time in 1917; a War Industries Board was set up to ensure that the weapons industry had all the resources it needed; and a Food Administration was set up to ensure that sufficient food was produced and distributed to Americans and their allies.

However, although the perfect Dual Federalism proved impossible to maintain, there were efforts to stay as close to the model as possible:

- After the death of Chief Justice John Marshall, the Supreme Court was reluctant to use its powers to overrule the states. In *Plessy* v. *Ferguson* (1896), the Court upheld a Louisiana law that provided for 'equal but separate [train] accommodations for the white and colored races'. The Court ruled that such laws 'do not necessarily imply the inferiority of either race to the other'. This ruling gave Federal permission to states to pass segregation laws (collectively referred to as Jim Crow laws), if they wished.

- In the 1875 Civil Rights Act, Congress took out a clause that specifically banned segregated schools, while the Supreme Court ruled unconstitutional a clause that prohibited racial discrimination in 'places of amusement', effectively giving the states the right to decide how racial minorities should be treated.

- Many of the steps taken by Congress and the military authorities after the Civil War to ensure that former slaves would be able to make the most of their freedom were resisted by the President, Andrew Johnson, who believed that power should be restored to the states as quickly as possible.

Thus, there has never been a neat, clear division of responsibilities between the Federal government and the states. The boundaries between the two started evolving almost as soon as the Constitution was adopted, with early signs that the national government would intrude in local affairs at times of national crisis. For those who had argued the States' Rights position, these signs vindicated their view that the constitutional safeguards against the concentration of power at the national level were inadequate.

Co-operative Federalism
The uneasy balance between the states and the Federal government in Washington DC was decisively altered by the prolonged economic depression that struck the USA after the Wall Street Crash in 1929. The proposals of the President to end the economic crisis, which meant interfering in matters that were traditionally the responsibility of the states, met with fierce resistance. Before the election of Franklin D. Roosevelt and his 'New Deal' programme, the welfare of citizens was considered to be the responsibility of the states. During the depression of the 1930s, however, state governments proved unable to rise to the challenge of mass unemployment and homelessness because:

- Conservative politicians, running some states, believed that the economy would correct itself and the problems they faced would be solved by market forces.
- Liberal politicians, running other states, were limited by the requirement of all state constitutions (except Vermont's) to balance their budget, meaning they could not borrow money to provide help in difficult times.

The Federal government faced no such restrictions, and it was Roosevelt's plan to provide financial help for the unemployed in the short term and to provide employment programmes to get people back to work in the long term. The work programmes were expected to have two benefits:

1. The income for people on the programmes would be spent on produce, which would create new jobs, which, in turn, would create demand for more produce – the 'multiplier effect'.
2. The programmes would produce new roads, bridges, hospitals and schools, which would benefit everyone in society.

For the Federal government to take responsibility for unemployment benefit, work programmes and providing local schools was a major departure from traditional Federalism, and altered the balance between the national government and the states. With both having a role in local affairs, the image of two cakes, one sitting on top of the other, was no longer accurate. The new relationship, **Co-operative Federalism**, was more like two different mixtures contributing to the same cake, or **marble cake Federalism**.

The New Deal was seen as destroying Federalism and was fiercely opposed by conservatives. However, Roosevelt's Democratic Party controlled both the White House and Congress. Conservative resistance was therefore led by the Supreme Court, where they were in the majority. Between 1933, when Roosevelt gained power, and 1937, the Supreme Court ruled key elements of the New Deal unconstitutional:

- The National Industrial Recovery Act provided employment through the building of bridges, schools and hospitals, and introduced a forty-hour week for workers. In *Schechter Poultry Corporation* v. *United States* (1935) the Court ruled the Act unconstitutional on the grounds that it regulated all companies, including those that traded only locally, which was the responsibility of the states.
- The Agricultural Adjustment Act helped farmers, at a time of falling prices for their crops, by providing them with subsidies in return for reducing production. In *United States* v. *Butler* (1936) the Court ruled the Act unconstitutional on the grounds that it interfered with the responsibilities of the states.

In response, in 1937, President Roosevelt proposed his 'Court-packing' plan. Congress has the power to change the number of judges on the Supreme Court. In 1937 President Roosevelt, frustrated that he was unable to implement his New Deal, offered to 'help' all judges over the age of seventy with their workload by appointing another judge to assist them. This would have added six new judges to the Court. The proposal was rejected by Congress but, thereafter, the Court did not reject any of the president's New Deal projects and the new balance in Federalism became firmly established.

Although the effects of the depression ended when America entered the Second World War in 1941, Co-operative Federalism continued because:

- During the war, the government needed to control much of the economy to ensure that the armed forces had the equipment they needed.
- When the Second World War was over, the government played a major role in providing support to those who had risked their lives for their country, in the form of financial and medical help for the wounded and educational opportunities for all former soldiers. This meant that the Federal government became a major provider of healthcare and education.
- As soon as the Second World War was over, the Cold War with the Soviet Union began and the government invested heavily in new weapon systems to ensure that the USA kept a technological lead over its enemy. This meant that the government became a major source of employment.
- The Cold War, at times, erupted into a hot war, although not directly with the Soviet Union: in the 1950s the Korean War broke out and in the 1960s America was drawn into the civil war in Vietnam. This meant that conscription was, for the first time in American history, used when the country was not officially at war.

For those who feared that constitutional safeguards against the concentration of power at the national level were inadequate, Co-operative Federalism was a troubling development. Of particular concern was the inability of the Supreme Court, as defenders of the Constitution, to resist the pressure from the President to redefine the relationship between the states and the Federal government. To this day, staunch States' Rights advocates argue that the New Deal permanently damaged the fabric of US society as crafted by the Founding Fathers. Referring to Co-operative Federalism, Justice Janice Rogers

Brown, who sits on the Court of Appeals for the District of Columbia Circuit (widely regarded as the second most powerful court in the country), has argued that 'Where government moves in, community retreats, civil society disintegrates, and our ability to control our own destiny atrophies. The result is: families under siege; war in the streets; unapologetic expropriation of property; the precipitous decline of the rule of law; the rapid rise of corruption; the loss of civility and the triumph of deceit. The result is a debased, debauched culture which finds moral depravity entertaining and virtue contemptible.'

Creative Federalism

The next significant change in the relationship between the national government and the states occurred not as a result of a change of circumstances, but because of the political priorities of Lyndon Johnson when he became President after the assassination of President Kennedy.

Lyndon Johnson had been chosen as John F. Kennedy's running mate in the 1960 Presidential election to 'balance the ticket'. His role had been to attract voters to whom Kennedy did not appeal. The main reasons of this arrangement can be seen in Table 4.2.

This 'balanced ticket' worked well in the election campaign, but less well once the presidency had been won. President Kennedy's closest advisors distrusted Lyndon Johnson and he played a minor role as Vice President. When he became President, however, he was determined to demonstrate that he was committed to the policies they

Table 4.2 Comparison between Kennedy and Johnson

Kennedy	Johnson
From 'liberal' Massachusetts	From 'conservative' Texas
Youthful and glamorous	Extremely experienced in both the House of Representatives
Relatively inexperienced	and the Senate
Catholic	Protestant

had campaigned for together in the election and that, with his experience, he could deliver more than his young predecessor. Four months after he became President, Johnson announced the **Great Society** programme, with the liberal (some would even say socialist) objective of eliminating poverty.

Poverty in America tends to be concentrated in specific groups. President Johnson believed that if there were an intense effort to improve the quality of life for these groups, poverty would become a thing of the past. However, he also believed that such an effort would have to come from the Federal government because:

- Only the Federal government could have the resources for a massive anti-poverty programme.
- Only the Federal government could co-ordinate such a large programme.
- Only the Federal government could be relied on to have sufficient commitment to make the programme work: poverty in some areas was as the result of neglect or active discrimination by state governments.

The groups to be targeted were:

- The elderly, many of whom could not afford healthcare and had many medical needs.
- Inner-cities, where unemployment and crime was high and the quality of housing, education, leisure facilities and public transport was low.

There were three methods used to deliver the programme:

1. Direct federal aid/support for targeted groups: This was the first time that aid of this kind had been offered when there was no national crisis – which was a change in the nature of Federalism.
2. Providing financial support for local government, by-passing the state government: Since many of the areas of concentrated poverty were in the cities, it was logical to work closely with the local authorities in those areas. However, local government is, constitutionally, accountable to the state government, and for the Federal government to intervene in this relationship amounted to a change in the nature of Federalism.

3. Providing categorical grants instead of block grants: Previously, grants from the Federal government had been in the form of **block grants**, which could be used in whichever way the state chose. **Categorical grants** were given by the Federal government for a specific purpose, and the state could not put the money to any other use, regardless of local priorities. For the Federal government to dictate how states spent money also amounted to a change in the nature of Federalism.

In relation to the healthcare needs of the elderly, in 1965 the government introduced:

- Medicare, to provide help with the cost of medical treatment and medicines.
- The Older Americans Act, to ensure that communities provided effective planning and services to the elderly, especially the most frail.

In relation to the inner-cities, the government introduced:

- The Equal Opportunity Act (1964), to address employment discrimination that meant that many inner-city residents, African-Americans and other racial minorities either could not get jobs or were denied promotion.
- The Mass Transit Act (1964), which provided funds to subsidise bus, subway and rail systems so that if inner-city residents were offered jobs, they were able to get to work.
- The Higher Education Act and Head Start Act (1965), which improved funding and new approaches to education in inner-city areas, to provide the basic skills needed to qualify for employment at a time when the number of unskilled manufacturing jobs was declining.
- The Demonstration Cities and Metropolitan Act (1966), which aimed to improve the quality of life in inner-cities by funding parks and leisure facilities.
- The Housing and Urban Development Act (1968), to clear slums and provide decent, affordable housing in inner-cities.

The effect of the Great Society programme was that the amount of money spent by the Federal government on the welfare of citizens, traditionally the responsibility of the states, rose dramatically. For the first time, the amount of money spent by the Federal government on welfare programmes was greater than spending on defence. Welfare spending increased from $10.6 billion when President Johnson came to power in 1963 to $259 billion by the time he left the White House in 1969.

During this period, the Supreme Court also played an important role in defending the interests of vulnerable groups, particularly suspected criminals, from the actions of their state governments. In *Gideon* v. *Wainwright* (1963), the Court ruled that defendants in criminal cases who could not afford a lawyer were entitled to one provided by the State in order to ensure a fair trial, as required by the 6th Amendment of the Constitution. In *Miranda* v. *Arizona* (1966), the Court ruled that a suspect must be told of the right, guaranteed by the 5th Amendment, not to incriminate themselves and to remain silent during police questioning.

Restoring powers to the states

New Federalism
For conservatives, who had opposed Co-operative Federalism but learned to live with it, the Great Society programme was a step too far. They had three main objections:

1. Many believed that the programme undermined the core principles of American society. They believed that prosperity had been built on rugged individualism, in which people had to rely on their own hard work, determination and creativity. Taking away the incentive to use these qualities was, in the view of the programme's opponents, damaging to society as a whole, and to the poor in particular, who would never learn how to compete or tap their own inner resources.
2. Many believed that the programme undermined Federalism and the states' ability to decide which issues were a priority and what where best ways to deal with them. The **New Deal**, in the 1930s, had eroded Federalism and President Johnson's 'War on Poverty' had virtually destroyed it.
3. Above all, for the Federal government to be making decisions on what happened in housing estates and parks in cities as far away

as 3,000 miles from Washington DC appeared to undermine the core principle of Federalism, which was designed to ensure that such decisions were taken as close as possible to the people affected, and to ensure that there were limits to the power that could be accumulated by the national government.

These attacks, coupled with the unpopularity of his other flagship policy, the war in Vietnam, were the principal reason that President Johnson did not run for re-election in 1968. The winner of that election, Republican Party candidate Richard Nixon, came to power having campaigned for the support of conservatives who wanted to move back towards the traditional model of Federalism.

President Nixon and New Federalism
To reverse the policies of the Great Society, which involved social policies being developed in Washington DC rather than in the states, President Nixon reduced the total amount available for anti-poverty projects. At the same time, the President introduced a policy of General Revenue Sharing, in which many categorical grants, given to cities for specific purposes, were replaced by block grants that could be spent as each state saw fit.

However, it took time for the general political climate to change, and while the President was attempting to pass power to the states, the Supreme Court continued to insist on Federal standards being applied to state laws and actions. In 1972, in *Roe* v. *Wade* (1973), the Court struck down a Texas law that severely restricted abortion, ruling that the 9th Amendment, which protects rights other than those mentioned in the Constitution, provided a right of privacy and that any state law that made abortion illegal was an 'unjustifiable intrusion by the Government upon the privacy of the individual'.

In 1974, the Court went even further, in *Garcia* v. *San Antonio Metropolitan Transit Authority*, ruling that the 10th Amendment, which restricts the Federal government from becoming all-powerful, was not a guaranteed safeguard for the states.

President Carter and New Federalism
By the time President Carter came to power in 1976, it appeared that a pattern had developed of the Democratic Party centralising control

in Washington DC, undermining Federalism and the importance of the states, and the Republican Party defending the interests of the states and loosening the grip of the Federal government. However, President Carter, although a Democrat, was formerly the Governor of Georgia and believed that governors should have as much freedom as possible to decide what was in the best interests of their states.

President Carter did not alter the system of General Revenue Sharing. Also, there was growing public concern about the size of the Federal deficit and one way in which the President reduced expenditure was to reduce financial aid to the states. This required them to depend to a greater extent on their own resources.

President Reagan and New Federalism

During his election campaign, one of the slogans of President Reagan (Republican) was 'Government is not the solution to our problem, government is the problem.' He was a firm believer in the conservative view that Federal government support undermined individual hard work, determination and creativity, and eroded Federalism. He believed that the New Federalism of Presidents Nixon and Carter had not gone far enough. Therefore, he proposed two policies to create a modern form of Dual Federalism:

- Reduce Federal aid to the states: President Reagan believed that the states had become so used to dependency on Federal financial aid, especially anti-poverty programmes, that they would never return to depending on themselves unless they were forced to. Accordingly, he reduced Federal anti-poverty programmes, cutting expenditure by $18 billion in his first two years in office. The effect on some areas was dramatic: New York was made effectively bankrupt and the number of Americans living in poverty rose from 29 million to 35 million.
- Swaps – instead of states and the Federal government each having some responsibility for the three main anti-poverty programmes, the states would take full responsibility for two of them (welfare and food stamps) and the Federal government would take full responsibility for the third (Medicaid – medical care for the very poor). This would give the states an incentive to once again take primary responsibility for the welfare of their residents, as had been the case

before the New Deal. While the states found the idea of 'swaps' attractive, it was clear that they would not be able to fund such large welfare programmes without raising taxes or cutting benefits, both politically unpopular, and they rejected the scheme.

President Reagan's programmes demonstrated the limitations of New Federalism. Despite their resentment at the steady drift of power to the national government over the previous fifty years, the leaders of the states knew that they were not capable of taking over, and funding, substantial portions of policy.

President Bush Snr and New Federalism

Although he was a Republican, and committed to States' Rights, foreign policy was the main focus of his four years in office, and issues of Federalism were largely neglected. In 1989, the Communist governments in Eastern Europe collapsed, leaving the USA as the world's only super-power, and the President concentrated on how the USA should use its military power: he intervened in Kuwait after it had been invaded by Iraq, overthrew the corrupt ruler of Panama and used troops to attempt to restore order in Somalia when civil war engulfed the country.

Ironically, in this time the needs of the states came to the fore only when there was a crisis, as in 1992, when America's worst-ever riot swept through Los Angeles and a hurricane hit Miami, leading to the Federal government providing emergency aid and, overall, the first significant increase in Federal financial support for the states since President Johnson.

However, a change in the political atmosphere was becoming evident. In 1989, the Supreme Court gave back to the states the right to impose limited restrictions on abortion, which had been taken away by the *Roe* v. *Wade* decision in 1972. In *Webster* v. *Reproductive Health Services*, the State of Missouri was allowed to impose regulations on late abortions and to restrict the use of public facilities to perform the procedure.

President Clinton and New Federalism

The change in atmosphere created by Republican President Reagan accelerated during the presidency of Bill Clinton, a Democrat, driven by a range of factors:

1. Like the previous Democratic President, Jimmy Carter, President Clinton had previously been a governor, of the state of Arkansas, and believed that governors should have the freedom to decide what was in the best interests of their states.

2. This aim was helped by the growing professionalism of state governments. In the 1960s, with most important decisions being made in Washington, the ability of people running for election at state and local level declined: the most able politicians wanted to be where the key decisions were being made. By the 1990s, this trend had been reversed and state politicians increasingly co-operated with each other to solve common problems and to lobby Washington on matters that affected them. The National Governors Association, the National Conference of State Legislatures and the US Conference of Mayors all became far more prominent and effective in demanding that the Federal government recognise their importance in this period.

3. The Supreme Court also appeared to become increasingly willing to rule in favour of the states in any conflict with the Federal government. In *New York* v. *United States* (1992), the Court ruled that Congress could not instruct a state on what to do with radioactive waste that was 'generated within their own borders', even though it was clear that any accident involving the waste could have consequences beyond their borders. In *Printz* v. *United States* (1997), the Court ruled that Congress could not instruct states to carry out background checks on people buying handguns, as this was a matter for the states to decide.

4. Two years after Bill Clinton became President, a group of conservative Republicans, committed to States' Rights, gained control of the House of Representatives. In 1994, they passed the Unfunded Mandates Act, restricting the Federal government from imposing regulations on the states, such as environmental standards, unless the Federal government was prepared to pay for the cost of enforcing them. In 1996, they passed the Welfare Reform Act, which transferred most of the responsibility for welfare to the states – as President Reagan had attempted to do fourteen years earlier.

5. Most importantly, under President Clinton, the United States enjoyed the longest economic boom in modern times, which led

to a dramatic increase in tax revenues for the states and less reliance on income from the Federal government. This was accompanied by a series of financial settlements with the tobacco industry, in which the states were provided with billions of dollars to pay for the medical costs associated with smoking-related diseases.

This combination of circumstances provided the states with the opportunity to experiment with new policies, some of which went on to be adopted by other states and even by the Federal government. For example:

- Wisconsin introduced school vouchers. Instead of paying schools for the cost of educating each student, the money went to families who could decide which school to spend it in. This would, in principle, increase choice and force schools to improve their performance or close for lack of students. This policy was adopted by George W. Bush for his presidential election campaign in 2000.
- New York City pioneered 'zero tolerance' on crime. Based on the idea that small crimes previously neglected by the police started young delinquents on the 'ladder' of crime, the New York police had their numbers significantly increased and concentrated on reducing petty crime, such as graffiti. The city became cleaner and more attractive, and crime – including serious offences such as murder – declined dramatically. The policy has since been adopted in other cities in America and around the world.
- Texas adopted a different method to New York in dealing with crime, emphasising deterrence through harsh penalties. As a result, it leads the nation in executions by a very wide margin, and one in ten of America's entire jail population is found in the state.
- California passed three propositions (opportunities for citizens to give other residents to vote on issues of importance) that particularly affected minority groups. In 1994, Proposition 187 withdrew benefits, including education, from the families of illegal immigrants, the majority of whom were from Mexico. In 1996, Proposition 209 banned Affirmative Action to ensure access to higher education for groups who had been historically discriminated against in the state's universities. (A similar initiative was passed in the state of Washington, and others were proposed in

Colorado, Florida and Ohio.) In 1998, bilingual education, usually English and Spanish, was banned in the state's schools.

Federalism in the twenty-first century

The tide turns again

By the time that President Clinton left office in January 2001, it was clear that the original model of Federalism, Dual Federalism, would never be restored. Yet it appeared that New Federalism had infused the states with an increasing self-confidence, and they were becoming increasingly self-reliant.

The new President, George W. Bush, was not only a former governor, committed to giving the states as much freedom as possible, he was also conservative Republican with the enthusiastic backing of fiscal conservatives who believed that the national government should play a less intrusive role in the lives of ordinary Americans. Bush took office committed to a fiscal conservative agenda, believing that, if taxes were cut, the national government would be forced to do less and people would increasingly rely on their personal resources and local government, which understood their needs. This approach, which its supporters call 'starving the beast', would encourage personal responsibility and further strengthen state governments. However, within months, two developments led to this policy being reversed.

Bursting the 'dot-com' bubble

Much of the boom in the 1990s was based on new, high-technology companies exploiting the opportunities offered by the Internet and the soaring prices of their shares on the stock market, even though many of them had yet to make a profit. The surge in income of many states was based on taxing these shares. When the bubble burst, so did the value of the shares and the income of the states. In 2000, state governments had built up financial surpluses of $47 billion, but by 2003 thirty-one states were cutting spending, while eighteen were increasing taxes.

As with previous crises, the states looked to the Federal government for solutions. Reluctantly, President George W. Bush gave $7.7 billion in aid to the states in 2003, with the promise of more the following year.

9/11

With business already struggling to cope with the collapse of the stock market, the attack on the financial district of New York and the destruction of the World Trade Center tipped the country into an economic recession. The states found themselves facing the effects of failing businesses, resulting in reduced taxation and a reduction in tourism revenue.

More significantly, there was a sharp shift in public opinion, which looked to the national government, in particular the President as Commander-in-Chief, to improve protection from further attacks and take the fight to the leaders of al-Qaeda and its supporters around the world. As a result, far from 'starving the beast', the national government has been fed with billions of dollars of additional funds to spend on reconstruction in New York City, military interventions in Afghanistan and Iraq and the development of new weapons to fight a different kind of conflict in which the enemy is not a conventional army.

Instead of the government becoming less intrusive, a new government department for Homeland Security has been set up, which can direct state and city governments to provide protection against potential terrorist attacks. For example, in the city of Seattle, with two sports stadiums and a busy seaport to protect, the Federal government provided $11 million in 2003 to pay for civil defence equipment and training. However, the Federal government was not prepared to pay for staff salaries of the police trained to use the equipment, which, they insisted, was the responsibility of the city.

The spending habit

The growth of spending by the national government was not restricted to national defence and supporting the states through an economic downturn. Once the administration began to loosen the purse strings, they seemed to find it hard to stop. New spending commitments made between 2002 and 2005 included:

* In May 2002, the Farm Act was signed into law, providing financial support to the agricultural sector at the cost of an estimated $83 billion over ten years.
* The Medicare Act, signed into law in December 2003, to improve medical care for the elderly, was estimated at the time to cost $400

billion over ten years. By September 2004, the cost estimate from White House had risen to $534 billion.

- Less than a month after making the immense financial commitment to Medicare, in January 2004 the President announced a plan to send astronauts to the Moon and Mars, at an initial cost of $12 billion over five years. Commentators estimated the full cost of a manned Moon programme at $15 billion, with the cost of the Mars programme at ten times that amount.

- In August 2005, the President signed into law two more expensive pieces of legislation: the Energy Act, which provides funding for projects intended to guarantee that the country has sufficient energy to meet its needs, cost $12.6 billion over four years; and the Highways Act, which funds the upkeep and improvements in the country's transport systems, cost $286 billion over five years. Among the projects included in the latter Act was the $223 million 'Bridge to Nowhere', which linked a small Alaskan town (population 8,900) with its local airport, replacing a seven-minute ferry ride.

Little in these measures had a direct impact on the powers of the states. However, as one of the purposes of Federalism was to limit the size and scope of the national government, such a dramatic growth in spending at a time when the states were cutting expenditure ran counter to a central principle of Federalism.

Education: interfering in state affairs?

Additionally, one of the most significant measures of President George W. Bush's first term was the passage of the No Child Left Behind Act, which not only increased spending by the national government but extended control over an area of policy that was traditionally the responsibility of the states. The Federal government's contribution to the cost of education in schools rose from $28 billion in 2000 (out of a total of $400 billion) to $42.5 billion by 2004. In return for this money, it required the states to introduce a federal system of accountability which meant that, unless schools met specified targets in reading, maths and science, students would be allowed to transfer to other schools which were meeting the targets.

The Act was challenged in 2005 by a teachers' trade union, in coalition with school districts in Michigan, Vermont and Bush's home state of Texas, arguing that schools should not have to meet requirements that were not fully paid for by the Federal government. Illinois, for example, faced an annual bill of $15.4 million to meet the law's requirements on curriculum and testing, but received only $13 million a year. The case was thrown out by a Federal judge, who ruled that the Federal government 'has the power to require states to set educational standards in exchange for federal money'.

Not a one-way street

Despite the apparent tide of power flowing in the direction of the national government, the states have demonstrated a willingness to assert themselves whenever the opportunity arises.

By 2005, with an economic recovery under way and finances improving, states were able to invest in their own priorities. In Delaware and Florida, this meant providing expanded pre-school programmes. In States as diverse as Hawaii, New York and Oklahoma, it meant additional funding for colleges and universities.

More significantly, with the President refusing to sign international agreements on measures to tackle climate change, eleven states have (or plan to) introduced air quality regulations that are much more strict than those of the Federal government. Unless the regulations are overruled in the courts, as a result of law suits brought by car manufacturers, greenhouse gases from cars will have to be reduced by roughly 30 per cent between 2009 and 2016. With these states, including California and New York, accounting for about one-third of auto sales, they may create a situation in which it becomes uneconomic for car companies to produce two varieties of each of their models and simply build cars with lower emissions.

How Federal is the USA in reality?

For States' Rights advocates, the Federal model designed by the Founding Fathers is hard to recognise in modern USA. The government in Washington DC has far more power than was ever envisaged and intervenes in local affairs in ways that the Founding Fathers intended to prevent. From this point of view, the watershed was the New Deal, in which the President was able effectively to bully the Supreme Court into accepting a fundamental change in the relationship between the states and the Federal government. This demonstrated the validity of the concerns long voiced by States' Rights advocates: that the constitutional safeguards against the concentration of power at the national level are inadequate.

Furthermore, developments since the introduction of New Federalism have indicated that even politicians who support States' Rights, such as Ronald Reagan, are unable to do more than slow the drift of power to the centre and, in the case of George W. Bush, a Republican former-governor, even supporters of this position are unable to resist the temptation to use a national crisis to increase the powers at their disposal.

This pessimistic view of developments is strongly contested by other commentators. In many states, for much of America's history, far from being a protection from a tyrannical national government, local rule has itself been oppressive to minority groups. In the Southern states, political leaders have turned the slogan 'States' Rights' into a doctrine of the denial of rights for anyone not like themselves. Insofar as it has taken the intervention of the government in Washington DC to ensure that the aims of the Constitution, as outlined in its preamble, to 'establish justice' and 'promote the general Welfare and secure the Blessings of Liberty to ourselves and our Posterity' are met, the evolution of Federalism is to be welcomed.

Moreover, while the relationship between the states and the Federal government may have changed, it remains the case that most decisions governing the daily lives of Americans are taken within their state, and where local authorities effectively promote the interests of all of their communities, the Federal government is highly unlikely to interfere. Indeed, when politicians at the Federal level believe they can learn from their counterparts at state level, as with the Wisconsin school vouchers policy, they have proved willing to do so, and there is the very real prospect of the larger states working together to effectively overrule the Federal government on climate-change policy.

So how Federal is the modern USA in reality? As with the debate on the role of the Supreme Court in the political system, the answer depends on the political viewpoint of the person answering the question. Since the original compromises that shaped Federalism, there have been people dissatisfied with the balance of power and who have struggled to alter it. That struggle continues.

Box 4.1 Comparing the Federal system of the USA with the Unitary system of the UK

Apparent similarities

For much of US history, the trend has been for the national government to grow in size and scope, intruding into areas of policy traditionally belonging to the states. This has been most noticeable since the development of co-operative Federalism in the 1930s, but was already evident before in times of crisis, such as wartime. Even under President George W. Bush, a Republican former-governor who was elected with a commitment to States' Rights, the role of the national government has expanded.

Meanwhile, in Britain, a unitary state with all power belonging to the national government in Westminster, recent years have seen the voluntary transfer of power to Scotland, Wales, Northern Ireland and London, as well as attempts to strengthen local government through the creation of directly-elected mayors, holding similar powers to those in US cities.

Put the two systems alongside each other and they look very similar. Appearances, however, can be misleading.

Contrasting political cultures

The US Constitution, despite not actually using the word Federalism, made clear the dividing line between the roles of the national government (mainly foreign and inter-State matters) and the states (largely responsible for affairs within their borders). Americans have a clear understanding of this line and while, for reasons of practicality, they are prepared to see the roles of the national government and the states overlap, they are not prepared to give up the constitutional protections provided for the states. Consequently, whenever the conditions allow them to do so, the states re-assert themselves. The conditions may be political, such as the determined effort by Presidents since the 1970s to move back towards the traditional model of Federalism, known as new Federalism. Alternatively the conditions may be economic, such as the prolonged economic boom that enabled states to pioneer new policies. Furthermore, even when the conditions are not ideal, states are able to implement laws that make a real impact, such as air quality regulations.

The British political tradition, in contrast, is one of all power belonging to the head of government, who shares those powers with others reluctantly. This tradition dates back to when the monarch was head of government, and some of the most famous events in political history, such as the signing of the Magna Carta and the English Civil War, were exercises in forcing the King to be more accountable when wielding power, rather than attempts to decentralise power. The unwillingness of British Prime Ministers to tolerate significant powers being exercised at regional level was illustrated in a seven-year period between 1979 and 1986. First, the Labour Prime Minister, James Callaghan, effectively blocked devolution in Scotland in 1979 by calling a referendum that required the support of 40 per cent of the electorate (including those who were eligible to vote but did not do so) in order to establish a Scottish Parliament. It received the support of a majority of the people who voted, but this was not enough to meet the threshold. Then, in 1986, the Conservative Prime Minister, Margaret Thatcher, abolished the Greater London Council because of its resistance to her polices.

Even when power was devolved in 1997, to Scotland, Wales and London, the Prime Minister has appeared reluctant to give up control. The amount of power devolved to Wales and London was extremely limited. Then, ahead of the first elections in 1999, Tony Blair made repeated efforts to ensure that loyal supporters would represent the Labour Party in each of the devolved areas. In both Scotland and London, this led to long-standing members of the party having to run as independents because the party leadership made it impossible for them to run as Labour candidates.

Consequently, most of the significant policies introduced as a result of devolution have been in Scotland. These include:

- Free long-term personal care for the elderly.
- Abolition of tuition fees for university students.
- Abolition of fox-hunting as a sport.

Even in Scotland, however, it would not be possible to introduce separate air quality regulations, and it is hard to conceive of there ever being a time when US states had as limited powers as the devolved institutions in the UK.

What you should have learnt from reading this chapter

- To restrict the power that Federal politicians could wield, the Founding Fathers relied on a system of Federalism that would place strict limits on the amount of power at the disposal of the national government.

- However, the power of the national government has grown dramatically. From the original 'Dual Federalism' model, in which the states and the national government would each have their own spheres of responsibility, the system has evolved, through 'Co-operative Federalism' and 'Creative Federalism', in ways which have served to increase the influence of Washington DC at the expense of the states. Even when there have been concerted efforts to redress the balance, through 'New Federalism', the result has been limited to slowing the drift of power to the centre.

- In terms of the values of the Constitution, this transfer of power has had its advantages. While Federalism may have been intended to ensure that fundamental rights were not infringed by the national government, it has been the states that have a record of oppressive use of power, especially in respect of minority groups. The drift of power to Washington DC has, in part, been due to interventions to secure rights that the states have failed to protect.

- Furthermore, this has been accomplished without completely stripping the states of their powers, which remain substantial.

Glossary of key terms

Block grants Financial aid from the national government to state authorities that can be used in ways that the state authorities find most appropriate to their needs.

Categorical grants Financial aid from the national government to state authorities that must be used in ways specified by the national government.

Co-operative (marble cake) Federalism Name given to the new relationship between the national government and the states resulting from the measures to cope with the economic depression of the 1930s.

Creative Federalism Name given to the new relationship between the national government and the states resulting from the measures taken in the attempt to eliminate poverty in the USA in the 1960s.

Dual (layer cake) Federalism Name given to the relationship between the national government and the states in the early decades of the history of the USA.

Enumerated (or expressed) powers Those powers belonging to the national government that are specifically mentioned in the Constitution.

Great Society Massive welfare programme, introduced by President Johnson in 1964, which aimed to eliminate poverty in the USA.

Implied (or inherent) powers Those powers belonging to the national government that are not specifically mentioned in the Constitution, but are obviously needed for the government to meet its constitutional responsibilities.

New Deal Massive welfare programme, introduced by President F. D. Roosevelt in 1933, which aimed to reduce the impact of the economic depression and stimulate the economy.

New Federalism Name given to the strategies adopted, since the 1960s, in response to concerns that the national government had acquired too much power. Each strategy was designed to empower the states and reverse the tendency of power flowing from the states to Washington DC.

Reserved powers Those powers belonging to the states because, as stated in the 10th Amendment, the Constitution did not award them to the national government.

Likely examination questions

Issues examiners may expect students to be able to effectively analyse include:

- The constitutional role of Federalism in diffusing power
- The suitability of Federalism for a country as large and diverse as the USA
- The power that local communities have over their own affairs
- The development of the relationship between the national government and the states
- The effectiveness of Federalism during the open-ended 'War on Terror'

Thus, examples of the kind of questions that could be asked include: Outline how and why federalism has changed since the 1960s. How federal is the USA in reality?

Where the question compares the US system with Britain's, issues tend to focus on the contrasting Federal/Unitary constitutions and whether, in practice, the differences between the two are as significant as may be expected.

Thus, an example of the kind of question that could be asked is: 'The US political system is Federal, whereas the UK's is unitary, but in practice the distinction is blurred.' Discuss.

Helpful websites

www.nga.org, www.ncsl.org and www.usmayors.org – the official websites of the National Governors Association, the National Conference of State Legislatures and the US Conference of Mayors, all of which have sections on state and Federal issues.

www.stateline.org – a website which has news from all fifty states.

Suggestions for further reading

For a more in-depth study of this subject, the best book is *Federalism in America: An Encyclopaedia* by Troy Smith, Joseph Marbach and Ellis Katz. Over two volumes, this work provides a comprehensive reference explaining the major concepts, institutions, court cases, epochs, personalities, and policies that have shaped, or been shaped by, American Federalism.

For an entertaining description of the diversity of the USA, read any of the books by Bill Bryson on his travels around the country. Born and raised in the USA, but having lived for extended periods in the UK, he offers an affectionate outsider's view of the American landscape and its inhabitants. *The Lost Continent*, a witty account of his travels through thirty-eight of the fifty states, is particularly recommended.

Elections

Contents

Overview

On 3 February 2005, just three months after winning re-election in a campaign that cost more than $345 million, President George W. Bush launched the campaign for the 2006 elections.

He set off on a tour of five states that had voted Republican the previous November and where there were Democratic Senators facing election in 2006. Nearly two years ahead of the next election, riding the wave of popularity that accompanies a recent victory, he was leading the attack to win additional seats for the Republicans in the Senate.

Keeping elected representatives in the public eye in this manner can be seen as a positive feature of the US political system, effectively holding them to account and preventing the abuse of power so feared by the Founding Fathers. However, given the high cost of US elections, this kind of permanent campaigning can be a cause for concern, as it creates a dependence on wealthy donors who may wield more influence than voters, contrary to the spirit of the Constitution.

This chapter examines the ways in which the electoral system contributes to the constitutional goals of holding politicians to account, and ways in which it causes politicians to rely on the wealthy, concentrating power in the hands of a tiny, privileged elite.

Key issues to be covered in this chapter

- How the electoral system works
- Efforts made to address flaws in the system
- The outcome of elections in recent years

The Founding Fathers' dilemma

The Founding Fathers' dilemma

When drawing up the Constitution in 1789, the Founding Fathers faced a version of the modern debate on elections: do they help hold potentially corrupt politicians to account, or are they a tool that can be used by politicians to manipulate the voters?

The thirteen colonies had broken away from Britain proclaiming, in the Declaration of Independence, that all men were 'created equal' with certain 'inalienable rights', and that if a government becomes oppressive 'it is the Right of the People to alter or abolish it'. This clearly suggested that the government of the new United States of America would be a democracy, with the government held accountable by the people. Furthermore, representative legislatures had been in existence in the colonies since the Virginia Assembly was set up as long ago as 1619, elected by all men aged seventeen and over.

However, the colonial legislatures did not have the final say on laws and their decisions could be overruled by the representative of the English king. Without this safeguard, the Founding Fathers were unsure whether the voters could be entrusted with electing responsible representatives. George Washington himself referred to ordinary farmers as the 'grazing multitude', Alexander Hamilton described them as the 'unthinking populace' and John Adams termed them the 'common herd of mankind'. Should such people, presumably easily led and manipulated, be entrusted with holding law-makers to account?

The debate at the Constitutional Convention

The debate between those who feared that democracy could undermine freedom and those who believed that democracy was essential to protect freedom mirrored the wider constitutional debate between the Federalists and anti-Federalists, outlined in Chapter 1 of this book. While both sides agreed that the vote would be restricted to white men, they disagreed about how much power to put into the hands of the voters.

Anti-Federalists, highly suspicious of putting power in the hands of a strong national government, wanted an electoral system that:

- Made representatives directly elected by, and therefore account-able to, all citizens.
- Gave elected representatives short terms of office before being held to account at elections.
- Placed a limit on the number of terms they could serve.
- Provided a mechanism that would enable the people to recall from office any representative who was not serving them well.

In addition, they called for a Bill of Rights that would protect individuals from oppressive laws.

Federalists, committed to an effective national government, wanted an electoral system that:

- Provided elected representatives with enough power to ensure the nation's survival in a hostile world and to ensure that there was effective co-ordination between the states.
- Ensured that this power was wielded by responsible men. This would require some form of vetting of the choices made by ill-educated voters.

As with all issues debated at the Constitutional Convention, the outcome was a compromise between the two positions, with the Federalists somewhat more satisfied with the result than the Anti-Federalists.

The electoral system

First past the post

One area of agreement at the Constitutional Convention was that elections would be decided by the candidate with the most votes being declared the winner. In the overwhelming majority of US elections, this principle continues to apply. This means no political representation for people who have not voted for the winning candidate, in contrast to systems of proportional representation in which parties are rewarded in proportion to the votes they have won.

Fixed election dates

Another area of agreement was that Federal elections would take place on specific dates, regardless of circumstances. It would not be possible for the people in power to call elections at a time when they were popular or postpone elections because of a crisis (which they could have deliberately created). Thus, in the USA, Federal elections are always held on the first Tuesday in November, every two years, even in the most extreme circumstances, such as wartime.

The House of Representatives

The concerns of the anti-Federalists were met in what was regarded as the most important of all elections. The Constitution gave the House of Representatives primary responsibility for raising taxes and deciding how Federal funds should be spent. All American males were given the right to *directly elect* one person from their district *every two years*, to represent their interests in the Capitol when these critical decisions were being made. However, despite their calls for additional measures to hold representatives to account, it was decided that the Constitution would make no provision to limit the number of terms they could serve or to have a system to recall (sack) them between elections, if their constituents were dissatisfied with their performance.

The number of districts in each state was based on the size of its population. Initially, there was to be one district for every 30,000 people, but as the population grew it was decided, in 1929, to limit the number of representatives in the House to 435. Since then, the number of seats allocated to each state has been adjusted to reflect shifts in population after each census, which takes place at the start of each decade. One consequence of this is that, as the population of the USA continues to grow rapidly, the average size of a congressional district grows proportionately. Based on the census of 2000, the average population of a Congressional district is 646,952, an increase from the average size of 572,466 based on the 1990 census.

The Senate

With the electoral arrangements for the House of Representatives clearly allowing for the possibility of 'mob politics', the concerns of the Federalists were met in the election procedures for the other house in Congress, the Senate. Senators were given six-year terms of office, enabling them to consider the long-term consequences of Congressional decisions. In addition, to ensure that the interests of their states were protected, all states were given an equal number of Senators (two) regardless of their size or population. The Senate developed rules that enabled a small minority (even just one Senator) to block measures that they strongly disagreed with. Selection to serve in this powerful body was by indirect election, with the state legislatures choosing suitable representatives.

The Constitution also set up a system whereby the terms of office of one-third of the Senators came to an end every two years. This meant that there would never be a time when everyone in the national government was replaced simultaneously. This is intended to ensure that even in the event of a tidal wave of opinion sweeping the country some of the elected representatives are insulated from it to some extent.

The 17th Amendment to the Constitution, passed in 1913, changed the method of election so that the Senate, like the House of Representatives, became directly elected. The Amendment also made arrangements for situations in which a Senate vacancy occurred (usually through death or resignation). The state governor nominates a replacement until a special election is held. In the event of a death, the governor often nominates a relative of the deceased. Thus, in 2000, when Mel Carnahan was killed in a plane crash, his widow Jean was nominated to represent Missouri in the Senate in his place. She faced a special election in 2002, which she lost by a margin of 1 per cent.

The presidency

The President and Vice President are the only people elected by voters from across the country. Although the Founding Fathers went to great lengths to limit the scope of power they could wield, this fact alone gives them the status of representative of all the people. They were given four-year terms of office and, like the Senators, they were indirectly elected, through an **electoral college** (explained below).

Although the Constitution did not provide for term limits, after the first President, George Washington, stepped down from office after two terms, it became the custom that all Presidents, however successful, limit themselves to two terms. Although both Ulysses S. Grant and Theodore Roosevelt sought third terms, this custom was not broken until Franklin D. Roosevelt was elected to a third term in 1940 and a fourth in 1944. In 1951, the 22nd Amendment to the Constitution was passed, which ensured that no one would again be elected to more than two terms.

The electoral college

The outcome of a presidential election is not determined by adding the national vote of the candidates. The Founding Fathers, concerned that the masses could be too easily tempted to support irresponsible politicians, created an electoral college to protect the nation from mob politics.

Established by Article II, Section 1 of the Constitution, the electoral college is created once every four years for the sole purpose of electing the President and Vice President. Each state is allocated a number of electors, determined by combining the number of Congressional representatives a state has (at minimum one) with its Senators (two). Thus, a state with a small population, such as Wyoming, is represented by just one person in the House of Representatives but, along with every other state, has two Senators. This means that it has three votes in the electoral college. By comparison, the state with the largest population, California, is represented by fifty-three people in the House of Representatives, which, with its two Senators, gives it fifty-five votes in the electoral college. In addition, Washington DC, which is not a part of any of the fifty states, has had three votes in the electoral college since the passage of the 23rd Amendment in 1961. (The people of Washington DC still do not have any representation in Congress.)

After each census, the number of seats allocated to each state in the House of Representatives is adjusted to reflect shifts in population; when this happens, the number of electoral college votes each state has is similarly adjusted. Thus, in the 2000 presidential elections Florida had twenty-five electoral college votes. By the 2004 election, as a result of the census that had taken place in 2000, Florida had been allocated two extra seats in the House of Representatives which was reflected in the electoral college, giving the state twenty-seven votes.

Although the distribution of votes changes every ten years, the total number of electoral college votes is fixed at 538, which means that a candidate requires a majority – 270 or more – to win.

The presidential candidate who wins a majority of votes in each state wins all of the electoral college votes for that state (with the exception of Maine and Nebraska, which allocate their electors on a proportional basis). This system means that presidential elections become fifty-one separate elections, with the candidates having to make informed decisions on which states they are almost certain to win, which ones they are likely to lose, and which are likely to be closely contested, using their resources accordingly.

Once the votes of the electorate have been counted, respected political activists, chosen by their parties, act as electors and gather in the state capital to formally cast their votes, reflecting the views of the electorate. These votes are then conveyed to the US Senate, where the final result is announced.

Since the electoral college was set up to protect the nation from an irresponsible electorate, the electors may, in principle, ignore the result of the popular vote. Occasionally this actually happens and electors who vote this way are known as faithless electors. Since the founding of the electoral college, there have been 156 faithless electors. Seventy-one of these votes were changed because the original candidate died before the day on which the electoral college cast their votes. Three of the votes were not cast at all, as three electors chose to abstain from casting their electoral vote for any candidate. The other eighty-two electoral votes were changed on the personal initiative of the elector.

Sometimes electors change their votes in large groups, such as when twenty-three Virginia electors acted together in 1836. Many times, however, these electors stood alone in their decision. No faithless elector has ever changed the outcome of an election.

In the most recent act of elector abstention, Barbara Lett-Simmons, a Democratic elector from the District of Columbia, did not cast her vote for Al Gore in the 2000 presidential election, as expected. Her abstention was meant to protest the lack of Congressional representation for Washington DC.

As the actions of faithless electors demonstrates, the electoral college is an outdated institution. Despite this, it is still seen as having advantages, as follows:

- It requires candidates to concentrate on key groups of voters (men have a different pattern of voting to women; ethnic groups vote differently; old and young, rich and poor have different concerns) and to concentrate on all regions of the nation, with their distinct issues and needs.
- It ensures that the states with the smallest populations can have a significant impact on the outcome of the election. Thus, while it is important to win large states, such as California and Texas, in a close race it is important not to neglect the small states.

However, the presidential elections of 2000 and 2004 highlighted the electoral college's disadvantages, as follows:

- Some states are solidly Democrat (often referred to as '**blue**' **states**), others solidly Republican (referred to as '**red**' **states**). Neither candidate from the two main parties mounted serious campaigns in New York (whose thirty-one electoral college votes were almost certain to go to the Democratic candidate) or Texas (whose thirty-four electoral college votes were certain to go to George W. Bush in both elections). This meant that voters in those states were largely taken for granted and had very little influence over the final result.
- Consequently, other states have a disproportionate influence over the result.
  - Disproportionate influence may arise because all states must have at least three electoral college votes, making smaller states over-represented compared to larger ones. If California had electoral votes in precise proportion to the three given to Wyoming, it would have 180 instead of the 55 it had in 2004. In 2000, a high proportion of small states were solid supporters of George W. Bush, which is why he was able to win the electoral college despite polling more than 540,000 fewer votes than Al Gore.
  - Alternatively, disproportionate influence may arise, particularly in a close election, because a state's voters are either fairly evenly split between the two main parties or has a high proportion of voters without a strong party affiliation. In 2004, there were ten of these states, known as '**swing states**' or 'battleground states', and they are expected to be decisive in the outcome of the 2008

Table 5.1 Summary of Federal elections

Institution	Number	Length of term	Directly elected?	Term limits?
House of Representatives	435 Number from each state based on the size of its population	All members face re-election every two years	Yes	No
Senate	100 Two from each state	Each Senator is elected for six years Every two years, one-third of them face re-election	Originally nominated by their state legislatures, they have been directly elected since the 17th Amendment was passed in 1913	No
Presidency	2	Four years	No	Yes The 22nd Amendment, passed in 1951, limits a President to two terms of office

election. The swing state with the most electoral college votes was Florida, but the most significant was Ohio, which President Bush won by 120,000 votes. However, had just 70,000 people switched their vote in Ohio, John Kerry would have won the presidency despite losing the popular vote in the country as a whole by 3.5 million.

- Additionally, candidates representing minor parties have little likelihood of winning electoral college votes unless they have very high levels of support in a number of states. In 1992, a Texan oil billionaire, Ross Perot, stood as an independent for the presidency and attracted 19.2 million votes, but because he failed to come first in any state this failed to translate into any electoral college votes.

State and local elections

As well as voting in Federal elections, US citizens are entitled to vote for a wide range of local officials who make decisions that can affect the quality of life in a community. The pattern varies in different parts of the country, but this may encompass the people in charge of the justice system, including the most senior police officer (the Sheriff), the senior prosecuting officer (the District Attorney) and the district judge responsible for sentencing anyone convicted. All across the USA, school boards responsible for delivering a high quality of education are elected and in many areas the commissioners of sanitation services, such as garbage collection and water supplies, are elected. In each case, the principle of accountability applies: if the quality of education at the local school is poor, or the garbage is not collected, with the associated hygiene risks, someone should be held responsible for the situation and for improving it. All this is in addition to the elected local representatives found in most countries, such as the mayor and town council.

Furthermore, in America's Federal system, there are also state representatives to be elected. As at the national level, states are run by a head of government, the governor, and a parliament which, in all but one state, has a direct equivalent to the House of Representatives and the Senate. The exception is Nebraska, which has a single-chamber assembly. Unlike the national level, however, many of the people who work under the head of government are not appointed but directly elected, such as the lieutenant governor (equivalent, at state level, to the Vice President). In addition, in many states the senior judges are also elected.

As elections for state and local representatives are often scheduled to take place at the same time as Federal elections, ballot papers can become extremely long and, at times, confusing. Adding to this is the likelihood that voters will not be asked to vote only for people but also on issues, such as amendments to the state constitution, **initiatives**, propositions or recall elections.

Amendments to state constitutions

Each of the fifty states has its own constitution, separate from the national Constitution (covered in Chapter 1). While the national Constitution is difficult to amend, state constitutions are amended frequently. In most cases, this requires the support of the electorate in that state and these decisions are added to the ballot papers at elections.

Often the issues covered are highly technical and of little interest to a majority of the voters. Thus, in Georgia in 2002, there were six proposed amendments to the state constitution, four of which were about changing the property tax regulations in order to promote the building of affordable properties and to encourage developers to clean up land contaminated with hazardous waste.

Initiatives, propositions and referenda

In twenty-three states and Washington DC, voters may be asked to vote on issues that have not been addressed by the state legislature but that groups of ordinary voters feel strongly about. These are known as initiatives or propositions. If the required number of signatures can be obtained – from 5 per cent to 15 per cent of the electorate, depending on the state – the initiative will appear on the ballot paper at the next election for the voters to approve or reject. If the initiative is approved, it becomes law.

The most-publicised initiatives in recent years have been in California. In 1994, Proposition 187 (entitled the 'Save Our State' initiative) was passed, denying all state services to anyone who cannot demonstrate citizenship or legal residency. Then, in 1997, a highly controversial campaign was started in the state to give voters the opportunity to ban Affirmative Action in state-supported programmes. Known as Proposition 209, it was passed by 54 per cent to 46 per cent.

Referenda are a similar process, but instead of proposed laws being put on the ballot by private citizens, the state legislature offers the voters an opportunity to express a view on a law they have drafted.

Recall elections

Recall elections are the process (permitted in twenty-six states) of removing officials from public office before their term has expired.

Before the vote is held, signatures of registered voters (usually equal to 25 per cent of votes cast in the previous election) have to be collected and verified; two votes are cast, one to decide whether the post-holder should be 'recalled' and another, if necessary, to choose the replacement. The winning candidate then serves the remainder of the term of office. The recall election for the post of governor of California in 2003, which led to the election of Arnold Schwarzenegger, brought this process to public attention around the world.

Recalls, like votes on amendments to state constitutions, initiatives, propositions and referenda, is a form of direct democracy. This form of democracy has a number of obvious advantages, as outlined below:

- It gives people a direct say in decisions that many of them feel strongly about and that may have a significant impact on everyone in the state.
- It strengthens popular control of government, ensuring that elected officials remain acutely aware of the views of the electorate.
- By providing a means of taking direct action on issues of great interest, it helps to maintain a high level of interest in the political system.
- Discussion of political issues, which surround direct-democracy campaigns, help educate the electorate.
- In the case of recall elections, the procedures allow voters to correct electoral errors, as long complicated ballot papers may allow incompetent officials to slip unnoticed into elected positions.

However, direct democracy also has a number of disadvantages, as outlined below:

- Many of the issues people are asked to vote on may be highly technical and of interest mainly to specific groups of people, such as the amendments to the Georgia state constitution (see above), which were of particular concern to property developers. The majority of voters may have a poor grasp of the full implications of their vote, made worse if there is a campaign in which the only voices heard are the most extreme supporters and opponents of the measure.

- Campaigns around single issues on a ballot paper will attract the support of groups that may be well-funded and able to be disproportionately influential.
- Direct democracy may undermine the effectiveness of elected representatives, as they will have to apply laws that they may find unhelpful. Additionally, elected representatives may be overly cautious when making proposals, concerned that they may trigger a recall campaign by any powerful group that opposes the proposal. Effectively, recall elections can be used as a form of political harassment.
- As direct democracy can be used by large or wealthy groups to advance their political agenda, it can work to the disadvantage of already vulnerable minority or poor groups unable to muster the number of votes or funds to defend their interests. It is notable that the two successful initiatives in California (see above) worked to the disadvantage of Mexicans and African-Americans.
- In the case of recall elections, democratic principles may be undermined rather than reinforced by the process:
  - In all states that use recall elections, there are provisions to remove corrupt officials by impeachment and officials found guilty of crimes unrelated to their office are automatically barred from public service. Therefore, recall elections are used to remove people prematurely from office for inadequate reasons.
  - Recall elections give the losing party a second opportunity to win office.
  - The incumbent has to win more than 50 per cent of the vote to stay in office; the replacement, especially in a crowded field, does not and could win with 20 per cent of the vote or less. (In the California recall, there were 135 candidates. Governor Gray Davies won 45 per cent of the first vote; Arnold Schwarzenegger won 48 per cent of the second vote.)

Primaries

Before most elections in the USA, from town council to President, voters are given an opportunity to play a part in selecting which candidate will represent the main parties.

Early in the twentieth century, concern by ordinary members that the party leaders were controlling who could stand for election, blocking anyone who did not agree with them, led to the introduction of primaries, which are elections allowing voters to express their views on who should represent the party at the next election.

After the First World War, use of primaries declined, with the main form of selection being a caucus. This is a series of meetings in which party members attempt to persuade each other to support their preferred candidate. Caucus meetings tend to be dominated by party activists who are sufficiently committed to the party's cause to take part in each stage. Supporters of the caucus system believe that it leads to the best candidate being selected. However, meetings are closed (that is, not opened up to anyone other than a party member) and historically they have been dominated by a small group of influential men selecting people with whom they were comfortable.

Primaries re-emerged after the 1968 presidential election campaign, in which leaders of the Democratic Party chose a candidate without consultation with ordinary party members, and have become the dominant method for choosing candidates.

Primaries take two forms:

- **Closed primaries**: Only voters who have declared their affiliation to a party can participate in this form of primary. In most states, people are asked to declare an affiliation when they register to vote and may, as a result, participate in any closed primary for the party they support. In some states, people are allowed to declare their affiliation at the polling station when they arrive to vote. Then they cast their vote for their preferred choice. Thirteen states use this form of primary, with another thirteen using a modified form of closed primary in which independents are allowed to vote in at least one party's primary.
- **Open primaries**: Anyone can vote in this form of primary, including people who have not declared a party affiliation. On arriving at the polling station, voters are given two ballot papers, one for each of the main parties. Voters have to decide which party's primary they wish to participate in and return the ballot paper they do not wish to use. Then they cast their vote for their preferred choice. Twenty states use this form of primary.

In addition, four states used to use blanket primaries, in which voters could participate in the primary of both main parties, but this form of primary was declared unlawful by the Supreme Court in 2000, in the case of *California Democratic Party* v. *Jones*, as it allowed non-party members to decide who would represent the party in elections.

The use of primaries has a number of advantages:

- They are more democratic than party leaders deciding on the candidates that voters can choose from at the election. It is also possible that the electorate will find neither of the candidates chosen by the leaders of the main parties appealing but such a situation is less likely when the voters have played a role in their selection.
- As a result of the influence of party leaders being diluted, candidates who would have had little chance of being selected by them may stand for election.
- The competing candidates usually offer a range of policies and election strategies, and the result of the primary will provide a strong indication of which approach has the most electoral appeal, especially if independents have been allowed to participate.
- In the case of open primaries, all voters have the opportunity to participate at this stage of the election process, which increases political participation by a wide cross-section of the adult population.

However, primaries also have a number of disadvantages:

- Experienced party leaders may make a more informed decision on suitable candidates for their party than the wider electorate.
- Some candidates may campaign on their personal qualities, rather than issues, serving to obscure rather than promote the party's message.
- The competition between candidates of the same party can become so intense, with mutual insults and accusations, that the party's public image is seriously damaged ahead of the election.
- In the case of open primaries, there is the opportunity for 'raiding' by supporters of one party who cross over and vote for a weak candidate of the opposing party.

Opportunities to participate

For much of US history, all of these mechanisms for selecting people to be political representatives and holding them to account have not been available to all. The next section will examine how voting rights have expanded.

Making the electoral system genuinely democratic

Votes for African-Americans

When the Constitution went into effect in 1789, African-Americans – both free and enslaved – made up about 10 per cent of the US population. Not only were slaves not entitled to vote, they were defined by the Constitution as less than fully human, as three-fifths of a person. Despite this, they were counted when calculating how many seats each state should have in the House of Representatives, helping to boost the representation of those who enslaved them. Even free African-Americans were only allowed to vote in a few states.

This situation was supposed to be transformed, after slavery was abolished, with the passage of the 15th Amendment, passed in 1870, which stated that no citizen could be deprived of the right to vote 'on account of race, color, or previous condition of servitude'. However, each state has always been entitled to regulate who can vote and many states, especially those that had resisted the abolition of slavery, used regulations to limit and discourage the participation of African-American voters. The three most common devices were:

- The Grandfather Clause: Incorporated into the Constitutions of most Southern states, this stipulated that only people whose grandfathers had voted before 1867 were eligible to vote. Although clearly contrary to the 15th Amendment, such clauses ruled out anyone whose forefathers had been slaves.
- Literacy test: Many states have required citizens to pass literacy tests before qualifying to vote, to ensure that they were able to read newspapers and election literature and, therefore, cast an informed vote. In those states that were determined to stop African-Americans from voting, election officers used their discretion to declare literate any white voter who could write their own name while disqualifying any African-American who failed to adequately explain the meaning of parts of the state or national

constitutions. Even African-Americans with advanced degrees in Political Science were known to fail the tests.

- Poll tax: This was a payment which had to be made before voting. As it had to be paid for all previous unpaid years, as well as the current year, it made the cost of voting unmanageable for the poorest people. This affected people of all races but, because of slavery and subsequent forms of racial discrimination that impoverished black citizens, African-Americans were disproportionately affected by this device. The 24th Amendment, passed in 1964, outlawed this practice.

In practice, the vote only became available to most African-Americans after the passage of the Voting Rights Act (1965). This gave Federal government officials the power to take over the registration process in any district where less than 50 per cent of African-Americans were on the electoral register, or where it appeared that local officials were discriminating against African-Americans. It also required states to get clearance from the Federal government before they introduced any new electoral regulations, to make sure that new devices did not replace the old ones.

While these measures led to a significant increase in the number of African-American voters, they did not at first lead to a significant increase in the number of African-American representatives in the corridors of power. Then, in 1976, the Supreme Court ruled in *Beer* v. *United States* that any plan to redraw district boundaries should not leave ethnic minorities worse off in terms of political representation. In the spirit of increasing political representation for minorities, some states created race-conscious districts in which voters of the same race were grouped together. Since 2004, there have been forty African-Americans in the House of Representatives, up from ten in 1970, but only one Senator.

Clearly, a lot of progress had been made but there continue to be concerns about the ability of African-Americans to exercise their right to vote. Despite the Voting Rights Act, suspicion remains that in some Southern states there are political leaders who are always looking for ways of disenfranchising African-Americans, such as the ID registration law in Georgia, covered in the introduction to Chapter 4.

Votes for women

Women had to fight for the vote for over seventy years, from the mid-1800s, before the 19th Amendment was passed in 1920, stating that the vote 'shall not be denied or abridged by the United states or by any state on account of sex'.

The campaign had been fought in each individual state, as well as in Washington DC. By 1914, women had won the right to vote in eleven states, all of them west of the Mississippi River. Before the successful passage of the 19th Amendment, however, it had to be introduced in Congress 118 times.

Votes for Native Americans

Despite their presence on the continent for centuries before the arrival of European settlers, Native Americans were not recognised as US citizens until the Snyder Act of 1924. Even then, they were not entitled to vote in all states, as there were provisions in many state constitutions restricting the voting rights of Native Americans. In 1948, the Arizona Supreme Court struck down a provision of its state constitution that kept Indians from voting. Other states eventually followed suit, concluding with New Mexico in 1962, the last state to enfranchise Native Americans. Even with the lawful right to vote in every state, Native Americans suffered from the same mechanisms and strategies – such as poll taxes, literacy tests, fraud and intimidation – that kept African-Americans from exercising their voting rights, and they were beneficiaries of the Voting Rights Act (1965).

Votes for 18-year-olds

Until the 1960s, the minimum voting age in most states was twenty-one. During the Vietnam War, however, the average age of the soldiers fighting in South East Asia was nineteen, and it was argued that if they were old enough to die for their country then they were old enough to vote in elections for/against the people who sent them to fight and funded the war.

The 26th Amendment, ratified in record time, was passed in 1971 and stated that the right of people 'who are eighteen years or older to vote shall not be denied or abridged by the United states or by any state on account of age'. The amendment expanded the electorate by more than 10 million people.

Concerns about the system: campaign finance

Concerns about the system

With almost every US citizen able to vote, and so many opportunities to choose their political representatives and hold them to account, it would be reasonable to expect that the US electoral system would be highly valued at home and a model to be copied abroad. Instead, it is the subject of considerable debate and legislation, with the USA widely criticised in other countries, mainly for two reasons: the cost of elections and the relatively low turn-out by voters.

The cost of elections

The first stage of a US election campaign is the primary. With candidates competing with members of their own party, they have to use their own funds or campaign donations to promote their agenda. In the case of campaigns for the House of Representatives, this means addressing an electorate of more than 600,000 people; for the Senate, this may mean an electorate of several million people (more than 26 million in California) over a vast territory (equivalent to the size of Britain and France combined in Texas); for the presidency, this means an electorate of well over 200 million, who have to be appealed to, state by state, across a geographically and culturally diverse continent.

Even after the primaries, when the political party they represent starts making financial contributions to the campaign, candidates continue to need substantial donations. Having gained the support of people affiliated to their party during the primaries, they have to reach out to the wider electorate through distributing leaflets, putting up posters, organising campaign rallies and co-ordinating volunteers who canvass voters in person or by phone. In a race for a Congressional district, this requires setting up a campaign office with full-time paid staff, and in a Senate race a number of offices will be required in the main towns/cities in the state. To judge the success of the campaign, and for guidance on any improvements that need to be made, the candidate will need to hire opinion pollsters and public-relations specialists. Above all, because neither the candidate nor the support team can expect to encounter a majority of the voters, the main method of conveying the campaign theme is TV and radio advertisements, which are expensive both to make and to broadcast. The pressure to raise so much money has two effects:

1. People will only run for office in districts they have a reasonable chance of winning. There is little point in challenging a well-funded, popular incumbent. Consequently, there are a significant number of Congressional districts in which the incumbent may face no challenger for several elections. For example, in Georgia's 5th District, which covers the predominantly African-American city of Atlanta, Congressman John Lewis – who was a Civil Rights leader alongside Martin Luther King Jnr – has not faced a challenge in either a primary or in an election since 2002. In 1998, the Republican Party – in an act of desperation – nominated a candidate also named John Lewis, in the hope that the people of Atlanta might vote out their Congressman by mistake.

2. Where an effective challenge is mounted, the cost of an election is likely to be substantial. In 2004, there were 433 candidates for the House of Representatives who raised, collectively, $525,513,868. The 98 candidates for the Senate raised $251,623,440. In the presidential race, the winner, George W. Bush, raised $367,728,811, while the loser raised $326,236,288. These figures do not include the campaign funds raised during the Democratic primary, which had nine contestants. Of these, Howard Dean alone raised $52,968,040. Additionally, during the presidential contest a number of groups ran their own separate campaigns against the candidate they most disliked. Six of these groups raised more than $25 million each, with the largest, America Coming Together, raising $79,795,487. When the funds raised for local campaigns, such as governor and state legislatures and so on are added to these totals, the campaign funds amassed in 2004 exceeded $3 billion.

The concerns that have emerged from such expensive contests are that:

- They make it impossible for people who do not have personal wealth, or connections to prosperous individuals or organisations, to run for office.

- Elected representatives, highly reliant on the individuals and organisations that fund their campaigns, may be more responsive to the needs/wishes of their donors than their voters.
- Donors, in turn, prefer to support candidates who have a proven record of electoral success and who have a record of supporting their interests. This means that incumbents usually have a significant advantage in fund-raising, reducing the likelihood of an effective electoral challenge.

The widespread suspicion that, once elected, representatives can remain in office for as long as they have the support of wealthy donors has raised questions of whether the electoral system fulfils its primary goals of holding representatives to account and limiting the amount of power they wield.

Watergate: political corruption and campaign finance regulation

Such suspicions were shown to be well-founded during the Senate investigations into the Watergate scandal in the early 1970s. After the discovery that senior advisers to President Richard Nixon had paid people, out of campaign donations, to break in to the headquarters of the Democratic Party, to find out their election campaign strategy, further probing revealed a number of questionable relationships between the President and his donors. International Telephone and Telegraph contributed $400,000 at the same time as the Justice Department settled a law suit against the company, and milk producers saw an increase in Federal subsidies after donating $600,000 to the President's re-election campaign.

The hearings demonstrated a clear need for campaign finance to be strictly monitored, and Congress passed a series of laws in the following years regulating how much could be donated and how the money could be used.

The Federal Elections Campaign Acts (FECA)

The first of the Acts was passed before the Watergate scandal broke. All the legislation passed since 1908 to address political corruption was replaced by the Federal Elections Campaign Act (1972). This law aimed to reduce the influence of wealthy donors on elections.

These measures were greatly strengthened by the Federal Elections Campaign Act (1974). Passed in response to the Watergate revelations. It required all candidates to publicly declare the sources of their income, placed precise limits on campaign donations and set up a system of public financing of presidential elections to reduce the need for candidates to rely on wealthy private donors. It also set up the Federal Elections Commission (FEC) to enforce the rules.

Together, these Acts put in place a three-pronged strategy for managing the money in politics:

- Disclosure: All campaign contributions must be declared and published so that anyone can see who has given money and judgements may be made as to whether the elected representative's actions appear to have been influenced by his/her donors.
- Restrictions on the size of donations: To limit the dependence of candidates on a small number of extremely wealthy donors, the 1974 law placed strict limits on the donations they could accept. This would, it was expected, lead to such a wide range of donors for each campaign that it would be unrealistic for them all to expect some form of reward for their contributions. The terms of the law were:
  - Individuals were limited to contributions of $1,000 per candidate in a primary or election.
  - Individual could donate up to $20,000 to a political party each year.
  - Organisations were limited to contributing $5,000 per election through a Political Action Committee (PAC). Again, to discourage too close a relationship between a candidate and a donor, the law stated that PACs had to receive contributions from a minimum of fifty donors and make contributions to a minimum of five candidates, thereby acting as a form of financial filter.
  - Finally, to ensure that donors did not get around the regulations by making donations through many PACs, each citizen was restricted to making a maximum donation of $25,000 each year, including a donation to a political party.
- Reducing election costs and reliance on private donations: The 1974 law dangled a carrot in front of all candidates

running for the presidency. If they undertook to limit the total amount of funds raised through private donations, the Federal government would provide matching funds, boosting their campaign budget without the need to invest further time and resources in fund-raising. The limit has increased over the years, linked to inflation, and in the 2004 presidential election it was about $45 million. To qualify for the funds, candidates have to demonstrate that they have widespread voter appeal across the country by raising a minimum of $10,000 in small contributions of no more $250 each. Additionally, they must demonstrate that the contributions came from at least twenty states, with small contributions of at least $5,000 from each of those states. In this way, it will be clear that the candidate is not reliant on wealthy contributors and has the active support of people beyond his/her home region.

It was apparent from the outset, however, that candidates would be reluctant to accept restrictions on their ability to raise private campaign funds when Congress decided not to apply the matching funds arrangements to campaigns for the House of Representatives or the Senate. In the thirty years since its inception, a variety of devices have been used to limit the effectiveness of FECA.

Buckley v. Valeo
In 1976, the Supreme Court upheld a challenge to the Federal Elections Campaign Act of 1974, which argued that it was unconstitutional to restrict how much a person could spend, of their own money, on an election campaign. This meant that personal wealth would be exempted from campaign finance regulations.

Soft money
Then, in 1979, a number of technical amendments were announced by the FEC to campaign finance rules. These removed all restrictions on:

- Fund-raising to promote awareness of elections and voting procedures.
- Fund-raising to raise awareness of the issues being debated during the election campaign.

- Fund-raising to support activities to help voters, especially the elderly and people with disabilities, get to the polling stations and make sense of complex ballot papers.

This kind of fund-raising became known as **soft money**.

Money donated directly to the election campaign, according to the FECA regulations, was known as **hard money**. These funds could be used to persuade voters to 'vote for', 'elect' or 'defeat' a candidate.

In the 1988 presidential election campaign, in order to bridge the funding gap with his opponent, the Democratic campaign began using soft money to 'explain' the issues in ways that clearly encouraged people to vote for their candidate. However, by carefully avoiding the use of the words falling under the FECA regulations, the campaign was able to use soft money for purposes for which it was not intended. Once this device had been used successfully, all subsequent campaigns used it, undermining the effectiveness of FECA.

The 'Failure to Enforce Commission'

For critics of these developments, the ineffectiveness of the Federal Elections Commission has also been a cause of concern. The commission is composed of six members, three Republicans and three Democrats, who are often deadlocked when deciding whether election laws have been broken. The result is that no action is taken. Critics, who have called the FEC the 'Failure to Enforce Commission', would like to see it replaced by an organisation with independent members and strong powers to severely punish anyone who breaks the rules.

The McCain campaign

With the money being raised for campaigning continuing to grow, by the 2000 presidential election there was a strong sense that FECA had been ineffective and needed to be replaced.

Running for the Republican nomination, Senator John McCain made campaign finance reform a centrepiece of his campaign and took pride in his reliance on many small donors, rather than wealthy contributors. Although he lost the nomination to George W. Bush (who went on spend $187 million), his stand on this issue gave momentum to the drive for reform.

The Bi-partisan Campaign Reform Act (BCRA)

In 2002, Congress passed a new Campaign Reform Act, sponsored by John McCain and Russell Feingold in the Senate and by Christopher Shays and Martin Meehan in the House of Representatives. The terms of the new law were:

- The maximum hard-money contribution an individual could give to a candidate was doubled to $2,000 per year. If a candidate faced a wealthy opponent, self-financing a campaign, the hard-money ceiling would be raised, depending on how much money the opponent was spending.
- Contributions from PACs remained limited to $5,000 per campaign.
- Total contributions that an individual could make to individual campaigns, PACs and political parties was raised to $95,000 every two years.
- Soft-money donations to candidates and political parties were banned.
- Pressure groups were banned from airing TV or radio electioneering advertisements one month before a primary election and two months before a general election.

The intention of the law was to reduce the total amount of money being spent in Federal elections and to make candidates more dependent on a large number of donors making hard-money contributions, rather than on a small number of donors making immense soft-money contributions. Like FECA, however, it was immediately encountered efforts to evade its regulations.

527s

Having specified that candidates and political parties were banned from raising soft money, political activists were quick to spot that the rule did not apply to non-party organisations. Ahead of the 2004 presidential election, a group of trade union leaders set up organisations, under Section 527 of the tax code, for the specific purpose of raising soft money to spend on anti-Bush advertisements and to mobilise voters likely to vote against him.

In the election, 527s spent around $400 million. Of this, $146 million was donated by just twenty-five people. How influential they were, however, is questionable. As they were not allowed to co-ordinate with the political parties, it may be that they duplicated their work rather than complemented it (see below).

'Money, like water, will always find an outlet'

On 10 December 2003, the provisions of the BCRA were challenged by a range of groups, both left- and right-wing, who believed that it limited their ability to express their political views, contrary to the 1st Amendment of the Constitution. In *McConnell* v. *FEC*, the Supreme Court upheld the BCRA but expressed doubt as to whether it would be able to achieve its goals of limiting the role of money in US politics. 'Money, like water, will always find an outlet,' they wrote.

Campaign finance reformers face the challenge of trying to reduce the supply of money while demand rises. Factors that drive up the cost of elections include:

- The length of elections: As the introduction to this chapter indicated, election campaigns begin almost as soon as the previous one has ended. In early 2004, badges were on sale promoting Hillary Clinton for the presidency in 2008, months before the 2004 election had taken place.
- Campaigning has become more professional: Highly-paid campaign managers are often credited with doing more than the candidate to win elections, such as George W. Bush's strategist, Karl Rove.
- Campaign techniques have become more sophisticated: As well as television and radio advertisements designed to appeal to a range of specific groups of voters, candidates use opinion polls, focus groups and, in recent years, the Internet to identify potential supporters, recruit volunteers and raise funds.

However, reformers have one major asset. It is clear that public confidence in the electoral system, and the politicians it produces, is being eroded by the perception that political decisions are unduly influenced by wealthy donors. Campaigns to 'strengthen public participation and faith in our institutions' and 'ensure that government and political processes serve the general interest, rather than special interests' strike a chord with many voters.

Concerns about the system: redistricting

Gerrymandering

After each census, at the start of each decade, the number of Congressional districts in each state may change to reflect population shifts, and the boundaries of each district may also be altered to reflect population changes within the state. This process is known as redistricting; but when it is done in such a way as to benefit one party over another, it is often referred to as gerrymandering.

Gerrymandering – to create districts that virtually guarantee victory for one of the main parties – can undermine confidence in the electoral system by causing voters to feel that there is little they can do to effectively hold representatives to account.

Redistricting commissions

Only one state, Iowa, puts the redistricting process in the hands of neutral civil servants. Five others set up commissions made up of members from both the Republican and Democratic parties. In every other state, the party that has a majority in the state legislature controls the redistricting process. The result is often blatant gerrymandering. In Florida, for example, where George W. Bush beat Al Gore by just 537 votes in the 2000 presidential election, the Republican-controlled legislature produced a map with eighteen Republican-leaning districts and seven Democratic ones. In Michigan, a Republican Congressman won the 8th District by just 160 votes in 2000, but after redistricting his seat became so safe that in 2002 he did not even have a challenger.

Furthermore, commissions are aided in recognising the pattern of political support in each community by sophisticated software and powerful computers, making it easier than it used to be to draw reliable electoral maps.

Mid-decade redistricting

Redistricting took place in Texas after the 2000 census. However, in 2003, after the Republican Party had won control of the state legislature, they embarked on a second round of redistricting that gave their party six extra seats in the House of Representatives. The Texas redistricting plan was challenged in the Supreme Court but upheld in June 2006.

Following the success of this initiative, other states have drawn up plans to redraw district boundaries before the next census, raising the possibility that redistricting could take place each time a state Legislature changes hands or data becomes available that can be used to its advantage by the majority party. As a consequence of these developments, the leading electoral commentator in the USA, Charlie Cook, has warned that there may be fewer than 30 truly competitive districts in the whole country, compared with more than 120 in the early 1990s.

Concern about the system: participation

Low turn-out

As the amount of money in US politics has grown, and the number of competitive Congressional races has fallen, the percentage of Americans voting in elections has declined. In the 1960s, participation hovered around 62 per cent of the adult population in presidential elections, with about 45 per cent turning out in mid-term elections. By the late 1990s, these figures had fallen to 48 per cent and 38 per cent respectively. Such low, and declining, figures have been a source of concern in the USA that people have sought to understand and address.

Voting-age population

It is some comfort in a country often held up as a beacon of democracy that voter turn-out is comparable with other Western industrialised countries. In the USA, turn-out is measured as a percentage of all people old enough to vote – the voting-age population – regardless of whether they have registered to vote. In most other countries, turn-out is measured as a percentage of registered voters. If the USA used this second method, turnout in presidential elections would be around 85 per cent, well ahead of Britain, which used to average around 77 per cent before a slump to around 60 per cent since the turn of the century.

Nonetheless, there has been concern in US political circles that participation is not higher, and explanations have been sought for non-participation so that more people can be encouraged to vote.

Voter mobility

Almost one-fifth of American voters move to a new location every five years. At any given election, many voters will not have met their new district's registration requirements or may simply not have got around to registering in their new districts.

The 'Motor Voter' Act of 1993 was introduced to allow voters to register when they renew or change their address on their driving licence. Since its introduction, an estimated 9 million additional people have registered to vote, but there is some evidence that many of these people have not used their vote in elections.

Poverty

The motor voter law was aimed at people who were not sufficiently motivated to make an effort to register to vote, usually the poorest in society. This lack of motivation may stem from a lack of belief that politicians are able, or willing, to effectively address many of the issues that are of greatest concern to the poor and vulnerable, such as racial tension and spiralling healthcare costs.

Campaign finance and safe seats

Scepticism about the willingness of politicians to address the needs of poorer voters is linked to the factors outlined above, the cost of elections and the lack of competitive districts. The poor tend to be the least organised in society and unlikely to be able to field a candidate able to compete with the well-financed candidates from the main parties.

Voter fatigue

Some factors affecting voter participation relate to all voters. With the opportunity to participate in so many elections at local, state and Federal levels, with primaries for many of the posts (see above), voters may find the range of choices confusing or simply become jaded with the frequency of elections and choose not to participate.

State restrictions

All states have their own conditions for electoral registration. Some states limit the participation of adults who have served a prison sentence or suffered mental illness. In thirteen states, a felony conviction results in disenfranchisement for life. In the 2000 presidential election, this meant that more than 200,000 people in Florida alone were excluded from the electoral process despite having 'paid their debt to society'.

Alternative forms of political participation

Some citizens may feel that they make more of an impact through direct participation in groups that campaign for issues that are important to them than by voting. It is argued by some political commentators that low participation in elections could be directly related to high participation in pressure groups.

Rising participation

From the low point of 48 per cent turn-out in the 1996 presidential election, turn-out has been rising. The explanation for this appears to be simple: competitive presidential elections focusing on a politician, George W. Bush, who inspires devotion and hatred in equal measure, as outlined below.

Elections in the twenty-first century

Two types of presidential election

Presidents are not allowed to run again after serving two terms. When this happens, as in the 2000 and 2008 elections, a number of candidates from both parties run for office. To some extent, candidates from the party that already controls the White House will be judged by the performance of the out-going President, but there will be opportunities for all candidates to establish their own identities as the campaign unfolds.

When the President is running for re-election after one term, as in 2004, the election campaign becomes effectively a referendum on his performance. It is conventional political wisdom that an effective, or popular, President is highly unlikely to be defeated, even if facing a strong opponent, and therefore does not usually face a strong challenge – the most effective opposition politicians will wait for a more promising time to stand for the nation's highest office.

The start of the process: testing the waters

Indications that politicians are seriously considering running for the presidency include:

- Visits to the states where the first primaries and caucuses will be held (New Hampshire, Iowa and South Carolina).
- Appearances on TV talk shows.
- In some cases, the publication of a book outlining the politician's ideas/compelling life story.

The response of political commentators and colleagues to these activities may determine whether these potential candidates have the credibility for a full campaign. Other potential candidates who are considered promising may find themselves having to declare their intention even if they are not testing the waters. By early 2005, Republicans Condoleezza Rice and Jeb Bush had been forced to firmly rule themselves out of the 2008 campaign.

The invisible primary
Once a candidate formally announces that he/she will run for office, that individual must file with the FEC a statement of Candidacy and becomes bound by campaign finance rules. After a number of candidates have declared, the 'invisible primary' begins. This is the term given to the period, before the official primaries, when the candidates have to become sufficiently well-known and to have raised sufficient funds to be able to present themselves as a credible presidential candidate.

The Democratic challenge 2004
In 2004, to the surprise of many commentators, a long list of Democratic candidates put themselves forward to challenge George W. Bush. He appeared to have a formidable range of advantages, including:

- A successful set of mid-term elections in 2002 (when all members of the House of Representatives and one-third of the Senate face re-election), in which the Republican Party had gained seats in both the House of Representatives and the Senate, something that had not happened in mid-term elections since 1934. Active campaigning by President Bush for Republican candidates was seen as the principal reason for these gains.
- A united party behind him, with no challenger in the primaries and little criticism of his performance by other Republicans.

- A target of $200 million to be raised to fund the campaign, which no one doubted would be met.
- High levels of public confidence in his role as a war leader in the wake of 9/11 and concerns about further attacks.

Yet no fewer than ten Democrats put themselves forward to challenge him. They were attracted to the race because, despite the President's high standing in the opinion polls, they believed that his success since the events of 11 September 2001 concealed an ineffective leader whose limitations could be exposed during a long, gruelling election campaign. The reasons why they believed that he could be defeated included:

- The 'stolen' election of 2000 – the Democratic candidate, Al Gore, had won the popular vote but had lost Florida's critical electoral college backing by just 535 votes. Despite evidence that there had been counting irregularities, the Supreme Court (with a majority of Justices appointed by Republicans) ruled against a recount, handing the Presidency to George W. Bush. Democrats believed that they could tap a reservoir of anti-Bush feeling left over from those events.
- The 2002 mid-terms election campaign – President Bush used his status as the leader of the 'War on Terror' to suggest that the Democrats could not be entirely relied upon to do everything necessary to defend the nation. This included giving his active support to the Republican challenger to Max Cleland, a US Senator from Georgia, who had lost both legs and one arm during the Vietnam War. During the campaign, the Republicans ran TV ads against Cleland which included pictures of Osama Bin Laden and the Iraqi dictator Saddam Hussein. Democrats believed that these tactics would add to the reservoir of anti-Bush feeling.
- The divisive President – George W. Bush had only won the presidency by wafer-thin margin but he proceeded to govern as if he had a strong mandate from the people. He appointed extremely right-wing people to key positions, notably John Ashcroft, who was appointed Attorney General. Bush's main policy was to press Congress for massive tax cuts, which benefited the (mainly Republican) wealthy at the expense of welfare programmes that benefited the (mainly Democrat) poor.

- The war in Iraq – although presented by the President as part of the 'War on Terror', the absence of evidence of links between Osama Bin Laden and Saddam Hussein, and the flimsy evidence regarding weapons of mass destruction, meant that the level of support the President's policies enjoyed at home and abroad diminished rapidly in 2003.
- High levels of unity within the Democratic Party – George W. Bush had become so hated by Democrats that, by the time the campaign started, the candidates were determined to avoid giving the President political ammunition by attacking each other.
- The emergence of '527' groups, such as America Coming Together, exploiting a loophole in the campaign finance regulations to raise money from traditional Democratic supporters, not to campaign *for* the Democratic nominee but to campaign *against* the President, erasing his financial advantage.

The first televised debate between the candidates (ignored by most of the country) took place in South Carolina in May 2003. The favourite, at that time, was John Kerry. He had been a national figure since denouncing the Vietnam War in the early 1970s, had fought for his country – which equipped him to be Commander-in-Chief – and had more than twenty years experience in the Senate. It was Howard Dean, however, who most effectively tapped the reservoir of Democratic anger towards the President and through the autumn of 2003 he raised far more money from party supporters than did his opponents. Indeed, John Kerry's campaign was doing so badly that, in November 2003, he fired his campaign staff and appointed a new team. Before the first primary, Howard Dean had raised over $40 million, with John Kerry trailing with a mere $22 million. (George W. Bush had already raised over $100 million.)

The presidential race 2008
Ahead of the 2008 campaign, with George W. Bush term-limited, a lengthy list of candidates from both the Republican and Democrat parties of emerged. Early Republican candidates, in order of probable victory, were:

- John McCain, Senator for Arizona and author of *Faith of my Fathers*, which chronicles his experiences as a POW in Vietnam.

Not always loyal to his party, he was very popular with independents and had made a strong showing in the 2000 presidential primaries.

- Rudy Giuliani, former Mayor of New York City and one of the few politicians to win *Time*'s 'Man of the Year' for his role in managing the aftermath of the destruction of the twin towers on 9/11. Like Senator McCain, he was a moderate who had demonstrated an ability to reach out to voters outside his party.
- Sam Brownback, Senator from Kansas, also campaigned as a social conservative.
- Mitt Romney, Governor of Massachusetts; Chuck Hegel, Senator from Nebraska; and George Pataki, former Governor of New York State, were considered outsiders.

Early Democratic candidates, in order of probable victory:

- Hillary Clinton, former First Lady and Senator from New York state, was the overwhelming early favourite to win the Democrat nomination, having made speeches to appeal to moderate Republicans and independents since early 2005.
- Barack Obama, the only African-American Senator, whose profile was raised by the publication of a book, *The Audacity of Hope*, that outlined his political philosophy.
- John Kerry, losing candidate in the 2004 presidential race and Senator from Massachusetts, who had kept his list of supporters and maintained a high profile in the Senate.
- John Edwards, losing vice-presidential candidate in 2004. Although youthful and charismatic, he had the disadvantage of not being in frontline politics since stepping down as Senator for North Carolina in 2004.
- Joseph Biden, Senator from Delaware, who had served in Washington for thirty years.
- Rod Blagojevich, Governor of Illinois, and Tom Vilsack, Governor of Iowa, were considered as vice-presidential candidates in 2004.

The primary campaign 2004
The process of deciding which of the ten Democratic candidates would be chosen to challenge the President began, officially, on 20

January 2004, with the Iowa caucus, followed a week later by the first primary in New Hampshire.

Despite the formidable lead established by Howard Dean in the invisible primary, it was John Kerry who won these early contests, with John Edwards coming a strong second. It appeared that Democratic supporters had concluded that Howard Dean's appeal was too narrow, too partisan, and that John Kerry was more likely to defeat the President. John Edwards' success was put down to his positive campaign, concentrating on his agenda and not criticising his opponents. In the primaries that followed, at a rapid pace, John Kerry continued to win while Howard Dean's support slumped, and by mid-February it was already clear that the race was effectively over.

This swift conclusion was, in large part, due to the front-loading of primaries. In 1988, in order to strengthen their influence on the issues dominating the election debate, sixteen Southern states scheduled their primaries on the same day in early March. This became known as 'Super Tuesday'. In the following election, in 1992, other states responded by holding their primaries a week before Super Tuesday, to have a similar impact. This process, which as continued, resulted in 72 per cent of convention delegates being selected by the seventh week of the campaign, compared to just 19 per cent forty years before.

Front-loading has been subject to criticism for sevaral reasons, including:

- The importance of the 'invisible primaries' has grown. Candidates need to have raised substantial funds, established name-recognition and gained endorsement from prominent party members to make an impact in the first, crucial, weeks of the primaries. Anyone who has failed to do this may find themselves effectively written-off as a credible candidate before the primaries even begin.
- The importance of the first primary, in New Hampshire, and the first caucus, in Iowa, is also magnified, as carrying early momentum into Super Tuesday is essential.
- Candidates who perform unexpectedly well in the first primaries, such as John Edwards did in 2004, have little time to build on their success through fund-raising, building their campaign teams and buying additional campaign advertising.

- The primary season can develop the feel of a cross-country tour bus, with the candidates stopping just long enough in each state to wave and then move on to another contest.
- This, in turn, may mean that the public do not get to know the candidates well.
- Voters in states that do not hold their primaries early in the season are effectively disenfranchised in the selection process.
- The process, overall, creates a sense that election campaigns start very early and last too long.

There are also advantages to front-loading, including:

- With the race virtually over by the end of March, any battles that erupt between members of the same party will be short, reducing the damage to the party ahead of the general election campaign and preserving resources for that phase.
- Backing from the most prominent leaders of the party is highly beneficial to candidates in a compressed primary calendar, giving the leaders an opportunity to influence the choice of candidate to represent them in the election.

In March 2004, as soon as it was evident that John Kerry would be the Democratic nominee, the Bush/Cheney campaign unleashed an advertising blitz in the battleground states to present their view of their challenger. With more than $200 million at their disposal, they emphasised every contradiction in John Kerry's voting record during his twenty-two years in the Senate to suggest that he was indecisive and lacking the kind of clear sense of direction needed at a time of international crisis. This presentation of Senator Kerry as someone who 'flip-flops' had some initial success and his opinion poll ratings began to decline.

The spring of 2004, however, was a time of terrible news coming out of Iraq, all of which damaged the President's standing. Security in the country seemed to be collapsing, Spain pulled its troops out of the American-led coalition, the number of American soldiers being killed continued to rise and it was becoming increasingly clear that there were no weapons of mass destruction. In addition, to everyone's surprise, John Kerry raised more campaign funds in the spring than did the President.

The national conventions

By the time of the Democratic National Convention, in July 2004, the two candidates were virtually even in the polls. Usually, after a week of dominating the news, a National Convention leads to a boost, or 'bounce', in the opinion polls, but there were doubts as to whether John Kerry could produce one.

The President's political difficulties over the previous months had all been caused by events in Iraq, not by John Kerry, and questions were being asked about his campaigning style, which was seen as long-winded and dull. His only notable contribution to the campaign was the announcement of Senator John Edwards as his candidate for Vice President. This was a choice that was widely applauded as helping to 'balance the ticket', as Edwards was from the South and had a youthful appeal. Kerry's speech to the convention also helped further to allay doubts about his style, although it did not completely erase them. There was no post-convention 'bounce', however, because attention shifted to a national security alert, with warnings issued by the government of a possible attack on prominent buildings in New York City. It later turned out that these warnings were based on three-year-old intelligence.

Over the rest of the summer, the campaign was dominated by what Democrats saw as dirty tricks by their opponents. A '527' linked to the Republicans, Swift Boat Veterans for Truth, ran TV ads in key states questioning whether John Kerry's account of his participation in the Vietnam War was true and questioning his suitability to be Commander-in-Chief. The 'evidence' provided by the group was proved to be fabricated but sowing the seeds of doubt proved extremely effective and Senator Kerry's poll ratings fell. Republicans also provided funding and volunteers for the campaign of Ralph Nader. In the 2000 campaign, Nader represented the Green Party and, had he not stood, most of his support would have gone to the Democrats. Although he won only 2.7 per cent of the vote nation-wide, he won more than 97,000 votes in Florida, a state George W. Bush won by just 537 votes.

The Republican National Convention took place in New York in September, later than usual and one week before the third anniversary of the destruction of the World Trade Center. Most of the prominent speakers were moderate Republicans with a record of attracting support from independents and Democrats, such as Arnold Schwarzenegger and Rudy Giuliani. All of them emphasised the President's steadfast leadership at a time of crisis and presented Senator Kerry as a 'flip-flopper'.

A week after the convention, the Bush/Cheney campaign had established a ten-point lead in the opinion polls and leading Democrats were publicly complaining that the Kerry/Edwards campaign was ineffective at responding to political attacks. The picture was not quite as bleak as it appeared, though, as the Bush/Cheney campaign established only slim leads in the swing states. However, the earlier doubts about Senator Kerry's campaigning style had resurfaced and there seemed to be signs of panic in the team, with key workers being replaced by people who had worked on President Clinton's successful election campaigns.

The election debates
By the time of the four presidential election debates, which began in early October, it looked as if it would require Senator Kerry to deliver a knockout blow to stop the momentum of the President and to salvage his campaign.

In the first debate, in the swing state of Florida, it seemed that he almost succeeded. There was general agreement that he won the debate and a week later the two candidates were again neck and neck in the polls. The second debate, in the swing state of Ohio, was the only one to feature the vice-presidential candidates and was generally seen as a draw. The third debate, in the swing state of Missouri, was also seen as a draw, but in the days which followed the Democrats drew attention to a strange, box-shaped bulge under President Bush's suit, suggesting that the President needed help to perform well. The final debate was also seen to be a draw, with little between the candidates on election day.

The election result
Overall, turn-out increased dramatically. In 2000, 105 million Americans voted; in 2004, 122 million people voted. As a percentage, turn-out rose from 51 per cent of the voting-age population in 2000 to 61 per cent in 2004.

George W. Bush won 50.7 per cent of the electoral vote, a total of

62,040,606 votes. This resulted in 286 electoral college votes. John Kerry won 48.3 per cent of the vote, a total of 59,028,109 votes. This resulted in 252 electoral votes.

In the Senate, the Republicans made a net gain of four seats, giving them a margin of 55–44, with one Independent.

In the House of Representatives, the Republicans increased their representation by six, mainly as a result of redistricting in Texas (see above), Republicans holding a majority of 232–203.

Overall, with the opinion polls indicating a close outcome, how was such a decisive victory achieved?

Why George W. Bush won

The traditional approach to winning an election is to secure the vote of the party's traditional supporters and attempt to win the support of independents. In 2004, both Democrats and Republicans went into the campaign aiming to win by registering as many supporters as possible, and getting them to the polling stations, rather than persuading uncommitted voters.

Both parties succeeded in increasing their vote. If the Democrats had performed as well in 2000, they would have won the presidency by a wide margin. However, the Republicans were more successful because of the strategy they adopted. Their chief strategist, Karl Rove, believed that the percentage of genuinely independent voters had declined from 15 per cent in the late 1980s to no more than 7 per cent at the turn of the century. After the 2000 election, the Bush campaign built up a bank of 6 million e-mails of potential supporters. They also built up a network of 1.4 million active volunteers, organised into teams with targets for registering voters and ensuring that they were committed to actually voting. In addition, they commissioned market research on 'anger points' of Republican-leaning groups, such as motor-racing fans, and produced tailored messages to be conveyed by e-mail or via their teams. A particular 'anger point' was gay rights. After the Massachusetts Supreme Court ruled that gay marriage was permitted by the state constitution, initiatives were placed on the election-day ballot in eleven states to ban gay marriage.

The Republican strategy was recognised by their opponents, but its effectiveness was not. On 17 June 2004, the Democrat-leaning *New York Times* ran an article on the Bush campaign's courtship of Baptist churches. Another, the following month, questioned whether church leaders were straying into politics beyond the scope of their tax-exempt status. A third, in August, covered the role of committed Evangelical Christians in the Bush campaign. None of them appeared to be ringing alarm bells about the effectiveness of the get-out-the-vote strategy of the President. On the contrary, another *New York Times* article in September reported that 'a sweeping voter register campaign in heavily Democratic areas has added tens of thousands of new voters to the rolls in the swing states of Ohio and Florida, a surge that has far exceeded the efforts of Republicans in both states'.

The Kerry campaign, the Democratic National Committee and anti-Bush 527s spent some $344 million on political advertising, compared to £289 million by their opponents. On the ground, however, the rules that banned 527s from co-ordinating with the Kerry campaign led to some voters being canvassed as many as a dozen times while others were not canvassed at all. They also relied too heavily on volunteers and paid workers from reliably safe Democratic states. For example, in Miami, Florida, two weeks before the election, a group of America Coming Together campaigners were led by a paid worker from New York and a volunteer from California, who got lost and spent most of the day leafleting an affluent community that was certain to vote for the President.

Finally, the Bush campaign appeared to gauge more effectively where to invest their resources. In the final two weeks of the campaign, Kerry spent much of his time in Florida, which Bush won by more than 200,000 votes. The President put more of his time into Ohio, including an unprecedented rally on election day itself, and won the state by 120,000 votes.

The 2006 mid-term elections

Following the 2004 elections, political analysts in the USA pointed to the fact that, in the electoral college, George W. Bush won 31 States which, if replicated in elections to the Senate, would give the Republicans 62 Senators. He also won a majority in 255 congressional districts, indicating considerable potential for the Republicans to extend their majority in the House of Representatives. It appeared, therefore, that the prospects for the Democratic Party were unpromising. However, in the 2006 mid-term elections, when all of the members of the House of Representatives and one-third of the Senators face re-election, the Democrats gained control of both houses of Congress. In the House, they overturned a twenty-nine seat deficit to hold a 233–202 advantage. In the Senate, they overturned a ten seat deficit to hold a 51–49 advantage (including the support of two independents).

The key factors which shaped this outcome were:

- The war in Iraq, which had led to the death of nearly 3,000 American servicemen by November 2006, was particularly unpopular with no sign of a positive outcome in the foreseeable future.
- Accusations of sleaze in relation to the Republican Party, with the indictments of the lobbyist Jack Abramoff, the resignation of 'Duke' Cunningham, Tom DeLay standing down as leader of the party in the House of Representatives and, above all, the revelation that a Republican Congressman, Mark Foley, had made sexual advances towards young men working in Congress and that the Republican Party leadership had taken no action against him despite knowing of the allegations for several years.
- The handling of the Hurricane Katrina catastrophe in 2005 had damaged the President's reputation for effective crisis management.
- A growing sense that the President, who should be the leader of all Americans, was too partisan, with Democrats in Congress excluded from all policy-making.
- A collapse of support for Republicans, even moderates, outside the party's heartland (particularly New England) where the President was particularly unpopular.
- The recruitment of Democratic candidates with conservative views to compete in Republican strongholds such as Montana and Virginia.

Did this outcome demonstrate that the analysis of commentators after the 2004 election was misplaced? Three factors suggest that, despite the result, the Republicans remain a potent electoral force:

- As in the previous two elections, the Republican Party was the main focus of attention, with polls consistently demonstrating that voters were not particularly inspired by the Democrats' message.

- The reliance on conservative candidates in Republican strong-holds suggests that social issues which have helped Republicans win previous elections, such as abortion and gay rights, remain politically significant.
- Despite the unpopularity of the Republicans, eighteen of the seats they lost in the House of Representatives were decided by the wafer-thin margin of less than 5,000 votes, suggesting that the chamber could easily be recaptured in 2008.

Furthermore, President George W. Bush took immediate steps to address the issue that was primarily responsible for the unpopularity of Republicans: the Iraq war. He indicated that a change of strategy was needed and accepted the resignations of Secretary of Defense, Donald Rumsfeld, and John Bolton, US ambassador to the United Nations, both leading supporters of the war. He also indicated a will-ingness to co-operate with the Democratic leaders in Congress. Ahead of the 2008 elections, the political focus was on whether this more moderate stance, together with the Democrats being subject to more intense scrutiny as a result of their control of Congress, would lead to a revival in Republican fortunes.

How accountable are politicians in reality?

At a time when democracy was seen as potentially dangerous, putting power into the hands of a poorly educated population, the Founding Fathers took the risk of using elections to hold politicians to account. Their concerns about giving this authority to 'the mob' were out-weighed by their concerns that even people of the highest integrity could be corrupted by power unless they were held to account. As democracy became more widely accepted, this principle was applied to almost everyone with the power to take decisions that could affect the quality of life of Americans, often with representatives serving a limited number of short terms of office. Under these circumstances, the question of accountability should hardly be worth debating.

Yet, over time, concerns that politicians would become unhealth-ily attached to power have been justified by events. They have found ways of insulating themselves from realistic challenges at elections, whether it be through the drawing of district boundaries or through raising massive campaign funds that intimidate and overwhelm rivals. This, in turn, has led to the suspicion, reinforced by periodic instances of corruption, that politicians may pay more attentions to the wishes and needs of their financial donors than they do to the voters.

The electorate, however, is keenly aware of these weaknesses in the electoral system, with public interest groups such as Common Cause actively publicising any flaws that undermine the impact of ordinary voters, as well as campaigning for improvements to enhance account-ability. The result is a system that is constantly being refined to ensure that it effectively fulfils its role of making sure that the powerful are closely monitored by the people who are affected by their decisions.

Box 5.1 Comparing elections in the USA and UK

The voting systems

The electoral system used in both countries for national elections is first-past-the-post. The impact of this system raises questions in both countries about the lack of representation for people who do not back the winning candidate.

Responses to these questions, however, have been contrasting in both countries. In the USA, the response has been to increase the opportunities to 'throw the rascals out' in both frequent elections and primaries. In the UK, the response has been to try out forms of pro-portional representation at lower tiers of government, notably in the devolved assemblies and in elections to the European Parliament. With this has come a higher profile for smaller parties, such as the UK Independence Party, and coalition government that has given the third party, the Liberal Democrats, an opportunity to share meaning-ful power in government in Scotland. It is worth considering which system provides more effective representation.

The nature of the campaigns

Another significant contrast between the two countries is the way in which election campaigns are conducted. US elections, especially presidential campaigns, are so long, with so many strategies used to deliver the candidates' messages, that there is really no excuse for not knowing who the candidates are and what they stand for. In the UK, party election broadcasts are fairly easily avoided, especially by those who do not watch the news on a regular basis, and election posters and literature are in limited supply in safe seats. On the other hand, US voters can legitimately complain of voter fatigue, while this is a poor excuse for British voters. It is worth considering which system provides for a higher calibre of candidate.

The nature of political representatives
Finally, in Britain it is difficult for people to be elected to office unless they represent one of the major parties. In recent years, a number of independents have proved successful, but the pattern remains. For some, the dominance of candidates hand-picked by the party leadership, often having worked as political advisers before selection, produces characterless clones with little to offer the political system. In the USA, the use of primaries to select candidates means that 'insurgents' win nomination, and even election, primarily on their personal qualities and/or wealth. It is worth considering whether this kind of 'personality politics' is more or less desirable than the leadership-controlled selection procedures used in British parties.

What you should have learnt from reading this chapter

- The Founding Fathers, despite reservations about ordinary people being entrusted to hold politicians to account, relied on elections to remove from office any elected officials who failed to implement policies effectively or, more importantly, abused their powers.

- Despite the many opportunities for voters to choose political representatives and hold them to account, the electoral system has been widely criticised because of the cost of elections and the relatively low turn-out by the voters, suggesting that the wealthy disproportionately influence the outcome of elections and many voters doubt that they can affect the outcome.

- However, elections are subject to almost constant scrutiny and action is taken to address concerns about their effectiveness, whether it be the 'Motor Voter' law (passed in 1993) to increase electoral registration, the Help America Vote Act (passed in 2002), in response to the flaws exposed by the 2000 presidential election, or the Bipartisan Campaign Reform Act (also passed in 2002) which sought to limit the influence of wealthy donors. This, coupled with the campaigning of public-interest groups such as Common Cause, who are dedicated to making democracy work to the benefit of all Americans, means that politicians take their electorate for granted at their peril.

Glossary of key terms

'Blue' states Those states consistently won by the Democratic candidate at presidential elections.

Electoral college The mechanism used to elect the President, in which each state is allotted a number of votes, based on its population, which are then awarded to the candidate who wins the most votes in each state. Candidates need to win 270 electoral college votes to win the election.

Hard money Campaign donations made directly to candidates.

Initiatives (also known as propositions) A vote providing the public with an opportunity to support or oppose a proposal put forward by their fellow citizens (only used by some states, never the Federal government).

Primaries (open and closed) The mechanism used to select candidates to represent the main parties at elections, in which the general public can vote for the person they think would make the most suitable candidate (open primary) or registered supporters of the party vote for the person they think would make the most suitable candidate (closed primary).

Recall election A procedure enabling voters to remove an elected official from office before his/her time has expired.

'Red' states Those states consistently won by the Republican candidate at presidential elections.

Referenda A vote providing the public with an opportunity to support or oppose a proposal put forward by the government (only used by some states, never the Federal government).

Soft money Donations given for the purpose of expanding political party activities, political education or promoting political participation.

'Swing' states Those states not consistently won by either party at presidential elections.

Likely examination questions

Issues examiners may expect students to be able to effectively analyse include:

- How the electoral system works
- Whether the system makes it possible for minor parties to emerge and whether this is a good or bad thing
- Whether the electoral system is effective in holding elected representatives to account
- Ways in which the electoral system is deficient in holding elected representatives to account
- The outcome of recent elections and the factors that have shaped the outcome

Thus, examples of the kind of questions that could be asked include:
Why has it proved so difficult to reform campaign finance?
Analyse the factors that influenced the outcome of the most recent presidential election.

Where the question compares the US system with Britain's, issues may include:

- The selection system in the two countries
- The effectiveness of the two systems in providing effective representation
- The development of the two electoral systems
- The opportunities for minor-party representation offered by the two systems

Thus, an example of the kind of question that could be asked is:
Account for the level of electoral participation in the UK and USA.

 ## Helpful websites

www.pcl.stanford.edu/campaigns – contains past political advertising, including almost all of those broadcast by Bush and Kerry in 2004.

www.opensecrets.org – provides detailed information on campaign contributions and spending, with sections on 'who gives' and 'who gets'.

www.commoncause.org – 'a nonpartisan nonprofit advocacy organization founded in 1970 as a vehicle for citizens to make their voices heard in the political process and to hold their elected leaders accountable to the public interest'.

 ## Suggestions for further reading

For an in-depth account of elections at all levels, consult *US Elections Today* by Philip John Davies, in the Politics Today series published by Manchester University Press.

Alternatively, the *Almanac of American Politics* by Michael Barone includes profiles of every member of Congress and every governor, alongside in-depth and up-to-date narrative profiles of all 50 states and 435 House districts, covering everything from economics to history to, of course, politics. Available on Amazon.com and the website of its publisher, the *National Journal*, it is quite expensive at around $70, but is the 'ultimate guide for political junkies'.

Political Parties

Contents

Overview

On 24 May 2001, Senator James Jeffords of Vermont announced that he was leaving the Republican Party. Although he would remain in the Senate as an independent, he felt he could no longer represent the Republican Party as it had become far too right-wing, leaving no room for moderates.

Three years later, in April 2004, another moderate Republican Senator, Arlen Spectre of Pennsylvania, was challenged in the primary by a committed conservative, Pat Toomey. 'The problem we've got,' argued Mr Toomey, 'is a handful of Republican senators who never really bought into the idea of the Republican Party in the first place.' One of his principal backers, Stephen Moore, re-emphasised the point that the campaign was not about getting one man elected to the Senate, but complete conservative dominance of the party. 'If we beat Spectre, we won't have any trouble with wayward Republicans any more,' he said. 'It serves notice to others who have been problem children that they will be next.'

Yet, in 1973, just thirty years earlier, David Broder won the most prestigious literary prize in the USA for his book *The Party's Over*, in which he argued that political parties in America had become such broad coalitions, with party leaders having such little control over their supporters, that they had little ideological identity and were becoming almost irrelevant in US politics.

This chapter surveys the development of political parties, through periods of decline and resurgence, and considers whether, in the twenty-first Century, increasingly ideological parties undermine the constitutional goals of limiting the amount of power in the hands of any group of people.

Key issues to be covered in this chapter

- The changing nature of US political parties
- The main contemporary strands of opinion in the two largest parties
- Which groups support the two largest parties, and why
- The extent to which minor parties are able to make a significant political impact

The emergence of two 'umbrella' parties

Federalists v. anti-Federalists

The Founding Fathers were extremely suspicious of political parties, with their writings consistently expressing the view that they would be divisive and used to promote the interests of their members at the expense of the wider community. Even as the Constitution was being written, however, the Founding Fathers themselves divided into two camps on the central issue of how much power an effective national government could have without the risk of it becoming oppressive.

A passionate debate erupted (outlined in greater detail in Chapter 1) between the Federalists and anti-Federalists. The former, led by Alexander Hamilton, believed that a strong national government was needed to protect the country from foreign threats and deliver the freedoms promised by the Constitution. The latter, led by Thomas Jefferson, believed that a strong central government would itself become a threat to freedom and would undermine the Constitution.

By the time the first President, George Washington, left office in 1797, two parties had clearly emerged, each believing that they were fighting to protect the values embodied in the Constitution. The antagonism between them was so deep that it contributed to an amendment to the Constitution. Originally, the winner of the presidential election became president and the runner-up (invariably from another party) became Vice President. After the 12th Amendment was passed in 1804, the two positions were elected jointly.

The emergence of the Republicans and Democrats

The issues dividing Americans changed over the following decades, as did the names of the parties, but the issue that produced the parties that now dominate US politics, the Republicans and Democrats, was slavery.

The Republican Party was founded in 1854, primarily as an anti-slavery party, and rapidly attracted support in the Northern states, where slavery no longer existed. However, after the Civil War (1861–65), as the party of the North, it became associated with the interests of the rich industrialists who dominated the region. Thus, the party that enabled slaves to become citizens developed as the party of business and the middle class.

The Democratic Party, which had a much longer history, enjoyed support among poorer people in Northern cities and in the South. These two branches of the party split when the Civil War broke out, but gradually came together again after it was over. The two groups appeared to have virtually nothing in common. In the South, the party represented the interests of racist, Anglo-Saxon Protestants in mainly rural areas. In the North, it represented ethnic groups from parts of Europe often looked down on by Anglo-Saxons, such as Ireland, Italy and Poland. These immigrants were overwhelmingly Catholic and worked in the most heavily industrialised parts of the country. However, compared to the people represented by the Republican Party, both groups felt like outsiders.

Two 'umbrella' parties
By the twentieth century, therefore, each party represented such a diverse range of people that it was difficult to describe either as standing for something distinctively different to the other.

The Republicans, as the party of business, were conservative, resistant to change and to government intervention in the economy. With a history of abolishing slavery, however, the party attracted some **liberals** who believed that government had a moral duty to look after the interests of those genuinely unable to help themselves.

At the same time, the Democrats in the South were even more right-wing than most Republicans. Determined to assert white racial superiority over the freed African-Americans who had previously been their slaves, they used every method available to them, including violence, to enforce the 'Jim Crow' laws that segregated the races (outlined in more detail in Chapter 2). Like the Republicans, however, the Democrats had their liberal wing, mainly in Northern cities, which used the resources of local government to provide jobs and homes for poor, newly-arrived immigrants.

Further, unlike in other parts of the world, no significant socialist party emerged, committed to capturing political control to redistribute resources from the rich to the poor to ensure not just equality of opportunity but equal outcomes. Periodically, parties representing groups disenchanted with the Democrats and Republicans emerged to threaten their dominance, such as the Populists, who represented small farmers suffering great hardship in the 1890s, and the Progressives, who represented people determined to eradicate political corruption before the First World War. Each time, however, either or both of the main parties adopted many of the policies of the minor party, eliminating the threat and leading to an even wider range of people and policies in each party.

With both parties covering most of the political spectrum, from the extreme right to the moderate left, and no major party offering a clearly left-wing alternative, both parties became known as '**umbrella**' **parties**, covering most people. The main reasons that voters chose one party over the other was often linked to their community's historical ties. Catholic immigrants were grateful to the Democrats for providing for their needs when they first arrived in the country. White Southerners were taught from a young age that it was considered treason to vote for Abraham Lincoln's Republican Party, which had invaded their region and imposed its values upon them. Even a century after the Civil War, the Democrats' slogan in the South was 'Vote as you shot'.

The 'New Deal Coalition'

In the 1930s, the Democrat umbrella was extended to cover another group – African-Americans. Over the previous decade, African-Americans had adopted a range of strategies in response to legalised segregation in the South. One of these was simply to leave the region and move to the Northern states, which, at the time, were going through an economic boom and recruiting workers. When, after the Wall Street Crash of 1929, the USA went into a period of prolonged recession, African-Americans were particularly hard hit, as employers adopted an attitude of 'last hired, first fired' towards their black workers.

African-Americans were, therefore, among those with most reason to be grateful to the Democrat President, Franklin D. Roosevelt, when he introduced his 'New Deal' programme, providing benefits for people without work, generating jobs and improving the employment rights for people in work. Before the introduction of this programme, the few African-Americans with the right to vote usually gave their support to the Republican Party because of its role in ending slavery. With the wave of migration to the North, the number of African-Americans able to vote increased dramatically, and after benefiting from the policies of FDR, their support swung over-whelmingly to the Democrats.

'The party's over': the decline of political parties

The party's over

By the 1950s, the tensions within the Democratic Party in particular were evident on television screens around the world. African-Americans prepared to risk their lives in the Civil Rights movement were loyal supporters of the same party as committed segregationists prepared to kill as they resisted the advance of black Civil Rights. Furthermore, in the 1960s the party saw an influx of anti-Vietnam War protesters, many of them very left-wing, who questioned the role that the USA was playing in the world.

By the early 1970s, it was being argued by political commentators, most notably David Broder in his book *The Party's Over*, that the party system in the USA was failing to fulfil the role it should play in a healthy democracy.

Policy formulation

Political parties *should* play the role of providing the electorate with choices of how the country should be run, and visions of its future. The umbrella parties that had developed by the 1960s were seen by commentators as offering no distinct alternatives.

Recruitment and nomination

In addition, parties *should* be responsible for providing suitable candidates and the resources for them to stand at election, with a view to winning office and implementing their vision. The increasing use of primaries, since the 1960s, to nominate candidates for elections (see Chapter 5) meant that party leaders played a diminishing role in choosing who represented their party. In addition, during primaries competition between candidates of the same party can become so intense, with mutual insults and accusations, that the party's public image is seriously damaged. Moreover, they encourage candidate-centred campaigns that emphasise personal qualities rather than the party's agenda, and provide an opportunity for 'raiding' by supporters of one party who cross over and vote for a weak candidate of the opposing party.

Fund-raising and campaigning

Once a candidate has been selected, parties *should* provide them with funds and teams of volunteers to fight the general election against the other party. However, to pay for elections, candidates often rely more on their own fund-raising resources than financial support from their parties.

Candidates may also assemble their own campaign teams. In part, this has been due to the decline in the number of people joining political parties or expressing a strong commitment to either of the main parties. Between the Second World War and 1976, the number of voters defining themselves as independents doubled, peaking at 26 per cent.

In roughly the same period, the proportion of voters who engaged in split-ticket voting, supporting candidates from different parties at the same election (for example, voting for the Republican candidate for President at the same time as voting for the Democratic candidate for Congress) rose from just 12 per cent after the Second World War to a peak of 30 per cent by 1972.

Governing

If a party wins an election, it *should* work in a co-ordinated fashion to implement its policies. However, the decline of parties as vehicles for formulating policies; the lack of dependence on parties by many of their members at elections; the growing dependence on independent groups for election funding and campaigning; and the system of separation of powers between the legislature and executive – all combined to create a situation whereby political parties struggled to implement a programme that commanded the clear support of most of their active supporters.

In 1968, President Lyndon Johnson decided not to seek re-election, partly because he was exhausted after five years of having to bully his fellow Democrats in Congress to pass his legislative proposals and partly because the most severe criticisms of his two main programmes (the Vietnam War and the Great Society policy) were coming from activists within his own party who wanted the war to end and much more money invested in the Great Society programme.

Two empty bottles

The overlap in policies between the parties, and the difficulties they faced in implementing their programmes, led to the charge that they were 'like two bottles, with different labels, both empty'. However, as commentators in the early 1970s were explaining why political parties were in steep decline and at risk of becoming almost irrelevant, trends were developing that would transform the party-political landscape.

Two ideological parties: the resurgence of political parties

Party realignment

In 1964, after signing the Civil Rights Act, President Johnson commented to a young aide, 'I think we delivered the South to the Republican Party for your lifetime and mine.' Events were to prove him right, as the African-Americans who had previously supported the Republicans switched their support to the Democrats, and whites in the South began to contemplate the possibility of voting for the party of Abraham Lincoln.

Conservatives of the heart

The white voters of the South who had fought the abolition of slavery replaced it with legalised racial segregation and then violently resisted the Civil Rights movement, were outraged that the Democratic Party they had loyally supported for generations passed the laws that gave meaningful political rights to African-Americans. They were still more outraged when the Democratic Party gave its support to Affirmative Action programmes designed to ensure that African-Americans had the means to take advantage of their newly-won rights. Yet, the tradition of 'Vote as you shot' was so deeply ingrained that many of them could not bring themselves to vote for the Republican Party, and in 1968 they were able to turn to an independent, segregationist Democrat George Wallace, who won almost 10 million votes and 46 electoral college votes. No similar candidate appeared thereafter and by 1980 the white South was prepared to give a Republican who shared their values a chance.

Other traditional supporters of the Democratic Party began to desert it at the same time. In the North, some of the Catholic ethnic groups that had migrated from Europe in the nineteenth century, and had always voted for the party that had supported their communities when they first arrived in the USA, began drifting towards the Republican Party. In part, this was because many of them had become wealthier and moved to suburban areas in which the Republican Party was seen as the most effective defender of their interests. In part, it was also because they resented Affirmative Action programmes that were seen as giving one community opportunities that others, as outsiders also facing discrimination, had had had to fight for. Furthermore, at a time when many Americans perceived Communism to be a growing threat to the USA's interests and values, the Democrats were widely seen as weak on defence issues. A significant group left the party in the 1980s, in response to the Carter presidency, which was perceived as appeasing America's enemies.

These 'conservatives of the heart' came together to join traditional supporters of the Republican Party to elect Ronald Reagan in 1980. After winning the party nomination, he launched his presidential campaign in Philadelphia, Mississippi, where the local community had refused to co-operate with investigations into the murder of three Civil Rights workers in 1964 (featured in the film *Mississippi Burning*). Like the Catholic voters he attracted, Reagan was of humble origins and had used his talents and determination to reach the top. Those who felt strongly that the USA needed to strengthen its defences and be more confrontational towards its enemies found, in Ronald Reagan, a man who shared their views with equal passion.

The core of the modern Republican Party had been established. People with conservative views who had previously voted Democrat, because of historical community ties to the party, had switched sides. Once President Reagan had to leave office in 1988, however, having served two terms, there was no strong conservative leadership to keep these groups together. His successor, President George Bush Snr, was more moderate and, with Communist regimes around the world collapsing, focused on the USA's role as the world's only super-power.

In 1994, the rise of another forceful conservative Republican, Newt Gingrich, helped reunite conservatives of the heart, and towards the end of the decade the torch was passed to George Bush Jnr, who has led this group into the twenty-first century.

Liberal Democrats

As conservatives who used to vote Democrat have left the party, the remainder of the old 'New Deal coalition' are, on the whole, relatively liberal.

The industrial white working class, which looks to government to provide high-quality education for their children, protection from unfair employment practices and support through periods of economic or medical misfortune, remains overwhelmingly loyal to the Democratic Party. African-Americans have proved even more loyal since the 1970s, with 90 per cent, or more consistently voting for the party because of its support during the Civil Rights movement and its commitment to Affirmative Action since.

Other groups who believe that government has an important role to play in protecting the vulnerable are less reliable supporters of the party, including sections of the various Hispanic communities and some of the super-rich, especially those in the entertainment industry who believe that the more fortunate should share their wealth with the less fortunate.

The modern Republican Party

Although it is increasingly accurate to describe the Republican Party as conservative and the Democratic Party as liberal, both parties have distinct strands running through them.

The Republican Party is dominated by two strands, both conservative. People who fall outside these strands can still be found in the party, even in important positions, but they are a declining minority.

- Social conservatives: It is a core conservative belief that human beings are essentially selfish. Some conservatives reach this conclusion by observation of the world around them; others refer to religious texts, such as the Bible, which they say teaches that all people are sinful. In order to live and work together, they enough, everyone needs clear moral guidance, strong effective leadership and disincentives to giving in to selfish desires.

  Clear moral guidance, for social conservatives, requires a shared understanding, throughout society, of what is right and wrong. Without this, society can crumble under the strain of managing reckless, irresponsible and dangerous behaviour. People learn their values in strong family units in which parents provide both a moral framework and strong role models. Moreover, this moral framework needs to be reinforced outside the home by policy-makers ranging from education, through business to politicians. This kind of positive leadership, for those who overcome their instincts, needs to be balanced by punishment for those who do not, and these penalties must be severe enough to act as a deterrent to wrongdoing.

As an organised political force, social conservatives began to emerge in the 1970s in response to what they saw as the country's downward moral spiral. The previous decade had seen the breaking down of many social taboos. For social conservatives, free sexual expression, rising divorce rates, more single-parent families and increasing crime were all evidence of moral and social decay. Then, in the Supreme Court decision *Roe* v. *Wade*, women were given the constitutional right to abort a pregnancy, violating what social conservatives saw as one of the most fundamental moral principles – the right of the vulnerable and innocent to live. New political groups sprang up to channel what many Americans saw as their civic, and in many cases religious, duty to turn the tide and rescue their nation from moral decay.

Unsophisticated and amateurish at first, these groups have developed into a highly organised, well-resourced network with a clear set of linked goals:

- Protecting the unborn child – sanctity of life is the most fundamental moral principle in a society operating on Judeo-Christian values and, consequently, one of the highest priorities of social conservatives is to have *Roe* v. *Wade* overturned. This means working to ensure that one of their allies is in the White House when a Supreme Court vacancy occurs and that there are enough of their supporters in the Senate when a suitable nominee is being confirmed. In the absence of *Roe* v. *Wade*, restrictions on abortion would be made by elected officials at state level, who would be subject to pressure from anti-abortion groups.
- Protecting the home from immoral influences – as children are being raised in homes promoting traditional, religion-based values, they are subject to a range of influences that undermine

those values, including: a casual attitude towards relationships and marriage by celebrities; provocative sexual imagery in adverts and music videos; violent computer games; pornography on the Internet or at the corner shop. Social conservatives have been pushing to reduce access to inappropriate material, especially that imported into the home via the television. Since 2000, by law, every television sold in the USA must be equipped with a V chip that blocks any programme a householder finds inappropriate. So, when inappropriate material finds its way into mainstream family viewing, such as Janet Jackson baring a breast during the half-time show of the 2004 Superbowl (the programme with largest audience in the country), it generates a storm of protest. Conversely, social conservatives actively support material that promotes religious, especially Christian, values. When *The Passion of Christ*, which tells the story of the crucifixion of Jesus Christ, was released in 2004 it was actively promoted by social conservatives in order to demonstrate that films with a strong moral theme can be commercially successful.

- Protecting moral values at school – social conservatives believe that schools have a responsibility to reinforce society's moral values, based in large measure on biblical principles, and have invested heavily in recent years in campaigns to increase religious influences in schools. With notable exceptions, these campaigns have not been successful, but the battle continues to be fought. Social conservatives would like to see the *Engel* v. *Vitale* (1962) Supreme Court decision ruling that school prayers were unconstitutional in publicly-funded institutions overhead because the 1st Amendment keeps government out of religious matters. This has been challenged, but upheld, on six occasions, most recently in *Santa Fe Independent School District* v. *Doe* (2000), which ruled that prayers could not be delivered over the public address system before school football games. Social conservatives also tend to be suspicious of sex education in schools, fearing that it has the effect of encouraging teenagers to become sexually active and promiscuous. They have promoted, as an alternative, 'abstinence only' sex education, which encourages teenagers to understand the risks associated with becoming sexually active. These programmes have benefited from millions of dollars of Federal funds since the passage of the Adolescent Family Life Act, passed by Congress in 1981, and have survived a legal challenge, *Bowen* v. *Kendrick* (1988). (These principles have also influenced foreign policy: when, in 2003, President George W. Bush announced $15 billion to fight AIDS in Africa, a third of it was for abstinence education and none of it was distributed through organisations that provided abortions.) Above all, social conservatives have been at the centre of a battle over the teaching of evolution in science lessons, which, as they see it, undermines the biblical account of creation. This, it is argued, subtly erodes the moral foundations of a society based on biblical principles. They favour putting scientific theories (note that they are called theories, not facts) of how the world was created, and of its development, on the same academic basis as bliblical accounts. This approach, known as creationism, was ruled unconstitutional by the Supreme Court in *Edwards* v. *Aguillard* (1987) on the grounds that it was a way of promoting a religious viewpoint. The controversy continued, however, with the development of an alternative to creationism, called Intelligent Design, which argues that there is scientific evidence that 'certain features of the Universe and living things are best explained by an intelligent cause, not as part of an undirected process, such as natural selection'. In December 2005, in the case of *Kitzmiller* v. *Dover*, a Federal judge also ruled this Intelligent Design as unconstitutional, as it advances a version of Christianity. Despite these setbacks, two avenues have emerged that can be used by families who feel they cannot get a school education that respects their values. One is a school voucher scheme, offered in a number of states, starting in Milwaukee, Wisconsin, in 1990. This provides families with a voucher equivalent in value to the cost of educating a child in a community school, but which can be used in any school, including private schools. As a significant percentage of private schools are religious, this scheme was seen by critics as another device to introduce the values of social conservatives into the school system. However, this use of taxpayers' money was upheld by the Supreme Court in 2002 in *Zelman* v.

Simmons-Harris. The other avenue is via the development of the homeschool network. Some two million students are taught at home by a parent, free from restrictions on religion. These families are able to offer each other mutual support through the Home School Legal Defense Association, which, in 2000, set up its own university, Patrick Henry College.

- Protecting the moral values of the community – social conservatives believe that, even if people come through childhood with their moral values intact, the world is full of pressures that can lead adults astray. This is less likely to happen, however, if positive influences are promoted and negative forces confronted. Among the negative forces to be eliminated from the community are drug use and crime (often linked), and the most effective means of confronting them are well-resourced law enforcement agencies and punishments that will serve as deterrents. The most positive influence is traditional marriage and protecting this institution has become, since 2003, the highest priority on the social conservative political agenda. In the case of *Lawrence* v. *Texas* (2003), the Supreme Court ruled that laws banning homosexual sex were unconstitutional and then went further, proclaiming that 'the state cannot demean their existence or control their destiny by making their private sexual conduct a crime'. This apparent assertion of gay rights, invalidating laws that can be interpreted as 'demeaning' gay people, was seen by many as opening the door to gay marriage. Further, when the Supreme Court in Massachusetts ruled, four months later, that gay marriage was constitutional in that state, the judges mentioned the Lawrence case. The campaign to resist this rising tide of gay rights led to ballot initiatives banning same-sex marriage in thirteen states in 2004. These contributed to some 4 million additional social conservative voters coming to the polls, the majority of whom voted for George W. Bush, who went on to win the presidential election by 3.5 million votes. Thus, these 'values voters' have firmly established themselves as a dominant force within the Republican Party.

- Fiscal conservatives: Just as social conservatives are driven by the concern that the selfish nature of human beings can lead to the collapse of order in society unless people are bound by a strong moral code, so the other main branch of American conservatism is driven by the belief that selfishness can be harnessed to produce a dynamic, productive society.

For fiscal conservatives, people can be trusted to make sensible, appropriate decisions in their own best interests and, through the free market, those choices will lead to progress and general benefit. In common with social conservatives, they believe that society needs well-resourced law enforcement agencies and punishments that will serve as deterrents for individuals whose self-ishness exceeds the bounds of social norms. However, fiscal conservatives are less concerned that people are likely to make choices that will lead to a breakdown of social order. Rather, they believe that market forces will, almost invariably, guide people to make the most profitable use of the resources available to them, leading to economic growth and a shared sense of well-being. Consequently, they are highly suspicious of any form of government intervention beyond maintaining law and order and defence of the nation.

Fiscal conservatism emerged as a force in the 1970s at the same time as social conservatism was coming to public prominence, and together they were referred to as the 'new right'. However, fiscal conservatives were motivated by a different set of concerns and developed a different set of policy priorities. During the 1970s, the US economy was barely growing, while inflation was a serious problem. Led by two economists at the University of Chicago, Friedrich Hayek and Milton Friedman, the theory argued that this was due to years of government intervention, which had distorted market forces, created a culture of dependency though welfare programmes and undermined incentives for the wealthy to invest through high taxes. Their solution – to cut back the role of government and allow creativity and resourcefulness to flourish – stuck a chord with many Americans, especially in the West, who associated such qualities with the expansion and development of their nation.

Small government – meaning lower taxes and fewer rules and regulations – had obvious attractions for businesses, but the idea also attracted other groups. Advocates of gun rights also resent government interference in what they see as their constitutional right to 'keep and bear arms' of their choice. Advocates of property rights resent restrictions on the use and development of their land, often as a result of environmental regulations. Even recreational fishermen and off-road vehicle enthusiasts, both subject to government regulation, are attracted by this political creed.

In order to reduce the scope of government, fiscal conservatives have a range of policy objectives:

- Promoting tax cuts – when Ronald Reagan became President in 1981, he proclaimed that 'Government is not the solution to our problem; government is the problem.' Fiscal conservatives wholeheartedly agree and see tax cuts as the solution. As long as government has the resources to fund an ever-increasing range of programmes, interfering in the daily lives of Americans and distorting the free market, it will do so. Tax cuts are a way of 'starving the beast', leading to a reduction in the size and scope of government. Additionally, allowing citizens to maximise the benefits of their labour and/or investment encourages an atmosphere of self-reliance, reversing the dependency culture that fiscal conservatives view as the source of irresponsible behaviour in society. There would be fewer single-parent families, for example, if mothers could not depend on welfare to support them. Conversely, if they knew that they could keep most of their earnings, then they would be encouraged to work, provide for their families and be positive role models to their children. Finally, they argue, tax cuts stimulate the economy, providing more disposable income, which leads to demand for products, which leads to competition to meet the demand, which in turn leads to innovation, increased production and more jobs. Since George W. Bush became President, this wing of the party has been delighted to see two massive tax cuts, in 2001 and 2003, with smaller packages in 2002 and 2006. They have been distressed, however, to see that these measures have done nothing to 'starve the beast'. Rather, Federal spending has dramatically increased during the presidency of George W. Bush. In part, this has been due to the expenditures associated with the aftermath of the 9/11 attacks, on both military action and improving homeland security.

This, fiscal conservatives can accept. Yet much of the additional spending has gone on expensive commitments such as expanding Medicare (healthcare for the elderly), increasing Federal financial support for education and paying for the reconstruction of New Orleans after Hurricane Katrina and so on, which fiscal conservatives find much harder to accept, especially as the combination of tax cuts and increased spending has resulted in a record deficit of nearly £9 trillion.

– Eliminating earmarks and line-item veto – to complement tax cuts, fiscal conservatives want to see wasteful spending curtailed. Congressmen attach projects for their districts, known as earmarks, to bills as they pass through the legislature (as outlined in Chapter 8), which accounts for a significant proportion of Federal spending. The influence of pressure groups tends to inflate this kind of expenditure. Fiscal conservatives would like to see this kind of spending drastically curtailed or even eliminated. As a fallback position, they would like the President to have the power of a line-item veto that would enable him to strike out wasteful spending from bills before signing them. A line-item veto was passed by Congress in 1996 but was struck down as unconstitutional by the Supreme Court in *Clinton v. City of New York* in 1998, on the grounds that if the President modified laws he breached the constitutional requirement that only Congress legislates. Fiscal conservatives would like to pass a modified version of the 1996 law that takes account of the Supreme Court's objections.

– Social security reform – all working Americans pay a proportion of their wages, matched by their employers, into a fund to cover pensions and disability benefits. This money is used by the Federal government to fund general spending, as well as pensions. Current projections are that there will be insufficient funds in the budget to cover the benefits paid to retired people by 2041, and it is generally agreed that action needs to be taken now to address the projected deficit. In January 2005, immediately after his re-election, President Bush announced a plan to reform social security so that some of the contributions by employees would go into a personal account that they would then control. This approach, long advocated by fiscal conservatives, would remove from Congressional control some of the funds they currently have available; it would make people (not the government) responsible for their own future; it would encourage more people to learn about investing money; and it would (if the stock market remained buoyant) result in higher pension benefits. The progress of this initiative in many ways reflected the relationship between the President and his fiscal conservative supporters: they were elated by his decision to adopt one of their ideas as his flagship policy for his second term, but deeply disappointed by his lack of determination to fight for it in the face of determined opposition from those who believed that the plan would create uncertainty over benefits for retirees.

- Promoting a balanced budget amendment – ultimately, fiscal conservatives would like to see these measures become unnecessary because they would like to see the Constitution amended so that the Federal government would not be able to spend more than it raised. If a balanced budget amendment were passed, any tax cuts would inevitably 'starve the beast'; but the most recent attempt, in 1997, failed to gain the necessary two-thirds support in the Senate by just one vote.

- Promoting welfare reform – as well as financial responsibility by the government, fiscal conservatives want to see financial responsibility on the part of citizens. One of their highest priorities was achieved under a Democrat President, Bill Clinton. The welfare programme, Aid to Families with Dependent Children, was seen as a subsidy to unemployed single mothers, discouraging them from seriously looking for work. By the time it was replaced, it covered 14 million people in 5 million families. The replacement law, Temporary Assistance for Needy Families, required welfare recipients to be in some kind of work-related activity for at least thirty hours a week and, with some exceptions, families could not receive benefits for longer than five years. Since the programme was introduced, the number of welfare recipients has halved, in part because of an expanding economy providing more jobs, and in part because some have exceeded the time they are allowed to remain in the programme.

- Promoting school vouchers – fiscal conservatives favour providing families with a voucher equivalent in value to the cost of educating a child in a community school, but to be used in any school, including private schools. This policy is also supported by social conservatives, albeit for different reasons. For fiscal conservatives, vouchers are about giving people control over important areas of their lives by giving them a viable range of options and introducing market forces into education, forcing poor schools to raise their standards in order to retain their students. For social conservatives, vouchers are primarily about providing a religious-based education for those who want one. However, only about 32,000 students across the country participate in such programmes.
- Opposing Affirmative Action – of the range of arguments against Affirmative Action, fiscal conservatives are most likely to adopt the view that it is a form of discrimination that distorts the labour market. While acknowledging that it is a measure to compensate for decades of discrimination against minority groups, especially African-Americans, fiscal conservatives argue that all discrimination causes fear and anxiety, and that while African-Americans continue to experience the fear of discrimination, Affirmative Action has extended that fear to white Americans, making the overall situation worse rather than better. The most recent challenge to Affirmative Action, the Supreme Court case *Grutter* v. *Bollinger* (2003), left the constitutional position unchanged, to the disappointment of fiscal conservatives.
- Promoting tort reform – small-government advocates have, arguably, been more successful under the presidency of George W. Bush in non-budgetary matters. In February 2005, the President signed into law the Class-Action Fairness Act, which authorised federal courts to hear law suits involving damages greater than $5 million, and involving persons or companies from different states. Business has long complained that they operate in constant fear of lawyers who can shop around for the state court where they expect to win the most money for clients who may not even have a valid claim, making it cheaper to settle the law suits, rather than risk a massive jury award. That threat has been reduced by the Act.

- Protecting gun manufacturers from law suits – in October 2005, the President signed into law a bill that protects the gun industry from law suits by victims of crimes in which their weapons have been used. Without this law, manufacturers and dealers would have had to be much more careful about who they sold guns to, a kind of gun-control through the courts.
- Reductions in environmental regulation – of all the small-government groups, opponents of environmental regulation appear to have had the most to smile about since the election of George W. Bush. Very publicly, when he came to office in 2001, he withdrew the USA from the Kyoto Protocol on Global Warming because of the costs it would impose on American businesses. Less publicly, in his first term his administration eased controls on coal-fired power plants, expanded logging and oil developments on Federal lands, and encouraged the military to get exemptions from the endangered species act. One of the President's top second-term priorities has been to open up the Arctic National Wildlife Reserve to oil drilling.

Conservatives have also developed a distinctive approach to foreign policy. Led by a group known as neo-conservatives, their response to the end of the Cold War and the emergence of the USA as the sole super-power was to develop a set of guiding principles for foreign policy. These are:

- To increase defence spending significantly.
- To strengthen the ties between the USA and its democratic allies, while challenging regimes hostile to its interests and values.
- To promote the cause of political and economic freedom abroad.

These principles have played a major role in guiding policy, especially since the attacks of 9/11, and explain the decision to attack Iraq despite the absence of evidence of involvement in those events.

Other groups also play a role in the Republican Party but are far less influential. Moderates with a less conservative agenda (especially on abortion) are organised in a faction called the Republican Main Street Partnership. This wing of the party, ironically, is supported by some of the best-known politicians in the nation, including the former

Mayor of New York, Rudy Giuliani, his successor, Michael Bloomberg, Governor Arnold Schwarzenegger of Calfornia and Senator John McCain. However, the group has been steadily losing influence. In the 2006 mid-term elections, two of its Senators were defeated, reducing its membership in the Senate to just six, and ten of the most liberal Republican members of the House of Representatives were also defeated.

At the opposite extreme, the Republican Party has always had a 'nativist' faction that opposes large-scale immigration. In the nineteenth century, this group was extremely influential in the party and was a significant factor in ethnic groups giving their support to the Democrat Party. For much of the past century this faction has been small, but noisy, with periodic upsurges of support. In 1994, the Republican Party rode a wave of anti-immigrant feeling in California by campaigning for Proposition 187, which denied social services, healthcare and education to anyone who could not prove that they were legal immigrants. This measure, aimed primarily at Mexicans, passed but gave the party such a reputation for extremism that it ruined its election prospects in the state until Arnold Schwarzenegger's victory in 2003. Another upsurge began in the states bordering Mexico in 2005. Armed anti-immigrant activists, calling themselves 'minutemen' (after eighteenth-century elite militiamen who defended their communities from foreign invasion), began patrolling the border to illustrate their claim that the authorities were failing to stem a tide of illegal immigration. Condemned as vigilantes by the President, they were hailed as 'heroes' by the leader of the nativist tendency in Congress, Tom Tancredo, who chairs the Congressional Immigration Reform Caucus.

Splits such as these occur within all parties. The effectiveness of a party depends on how well its leaders reconcile different strands. This can be particularly difficult when one of the main strands favours strong leadership, providing moral guidance, while the other favours minimal government intervention. Despite these tensions, throughout the 1990s and the first few years of the twenty-first century, the party has maintained a high degree of unity. This has been due to two main factors:

1. Willingness to compromise – the two main wings of the party have proved willing to focus on what they have in common rather than

what divides them. Sometimes this is straightforward, such as on school vouchers, which both strands support although for different reasons. At other times they have found creative ways of harmonising their policies. When fiscal conservatives have proposed packages of tax cuts, for example, they have made families the main beneficiaries, providing a financial incentive for marriage, which appeals to social conservatives. Co-operation is also helped by regular contact between the leaders of the two wings of the party. In Washington DC there is a regular programme of conservative breakfast meetings, lunches, seminars and dinners attended by supporters of both wings of the party. This kind of overlap is also evident in their grassroots supporters, with high levels of gun-ownership among Evangelical Christians and nearly half of small-business owners defining themselves as born-again Christians. Above all, conservatives are agreed that they need, at all costs, to keep out of power a Democrat Party that they see as regulatory and secular.

2. Forceful leadership – since the current generation of conservatives gained control of the House of Representatives in 1994, their leaders have organised party affairs in Congress in such a way as to ensure that they deliver as much of their electoral agenda as possible. Under Newt Gingrich, then under Dennis Hastert and Tom DeLay, the House leadership have selected influential committee chairmen on the basis of loyalty to the conservative agenda rather than the traditional basis of seniority; designated 'leadership issues' that require committee leaders to consult with the House leadership before making decisions; placed all of the staff working for Republicans under the direct authority of the Speaker; and completely bypassed committees when drafting legislation, if they have felt it necessary. In this way, they were able to make life extremely difficult for the Democrat President, Bill Clinton, while his Republican successor, George W. Bush, vetoed only one bill in his first six year in office (see Chapter 8 for more details).

The extent to which the Republican Party has become a conservative party was demonstrated by the outcome of the 2004 presidential election. Guided by the political strategist Karl Rove, Republicans made little effort to reach out to moderates but concentrated instead on galvanising voters who supported an undiluted conservative agenda (see

Chapter 5, for more details). Dubbed the Three Gs campaign by some commentators (Guns, God and Gays) or the Three Fs by others (Faith, Flag and Family), George W. Bush used this approach to succeed in boosting his support from 50 million voters in 2000 (when he ran a more moderate campaign based on 'Compassionate Conservatism') to 62 million in 2004.

The modern Democratic Party

It is less easy to define what the Democratic Party stands for than the Republicans. As long ago as 1989, a leading pollster wrote, 'Democrats have been struggling to assert an identity, constrained by their narrowing base, bedeviled by Republican mischief, and muted by the party's own caution about Democratic principles.' That analysis remains, largely, valid.

Republicans, on the whole, measure the health of their political system by the extent to which it interferes in people's lives or promotes moral values, and their policies appeal to people who are dissatisfied with aspects of modern America and want to see traditional values restored. Democrats, on the whole, measure the health of the political system by the extent to which it protects constitutional rights and their policies appeal to people who welcome many of the extension of rights in the twentieth century to previously excluded groups such as African-Americans, women and people with disabilities. This, however, makes the Republicans the party of change (which generates enthusiasm among supporters) while the Democrats have become the party of protecting the status quo (which is far less inspiring), or of extending the rights of minority groups who are often unpopular among the wider population, such as gays and lesbians. The modern Democratic Party, as a result, is divided between a range of strands of opinion on how to develop a rival agenda for change that will inspire supporters in the way that the Republican Party has done so successfully in recent years, and how best to stem the tide of Republican electoral success.

- Blue Dog Democrats: This faction argues that Americans have become increasingly conservative and that Democrats have to respond to this trend by presenting an agenda that protects the interests of the vulnerable while respecting traditional Christian values and keeping taxes low. This agenda enables them to work with Republican moderates and they are the least likely to vote on party lines of any identifiable group in Congress. Criticised by other members of their own party as 'Republican lite', this group boosted its influence by increasing its Congressional membership from 37 to 44 in the 2006 mid-term elections, making inroads into Republican strongholds.

- Democratic Leadership Council: This faction, founded in 1985, also seeks to establish a political agenda for the Democratic Party that appeals to the conservative heartland of the USA. The group is often identified with Bill Clinton, who became its leader in 1990 and, of course, went on to become President two years later. He argued that the Democrats had not been trusted by middle-class voters to 'defend our national interests abroad, to put their values into social policies at home, or to take their taxes and spend it with discipline'. According to the DLC, therefore, party policy has to combine 'progressive ideals, mainstream values, and innovative, non bureaucratic, market-based solutions . . . promoting opportunity for all; demanding responsibility from everyone; and fostering a new sense of community'.

- The Internet left: This is not an organised faction, but a grassroots movement that emerged during the 2004 presidential election campaign. Responding to the confrontational campaign of Howard Dean, during his run for the Democratic nomination, the website MoveOn.org helped raise £40 million to promote the message that there can be no compromise with conservatives and that the way for the Democratic Party to win back power is by fighting every conservative policy that threatens hard-won rights such as abortion, civil rights for racial minorities, gay rights and so on. This kind of 'rainbow coalition' politics, galvanising a range of minority groups who do not tend to vote in large numbers, has a long history on the fringes of the Democratic Party but has now established itself as a major force, providing both £120 million in campaign funds and thousands of volunteers to remove President George W. Bush from office in 2004. They may have been unsuccessful in their goal but they contributed towards raising the Democrat vote from 50 million in 2000 to 59 million in 2004. The argument of MoveOn.org and the other prominent leftwing internet campaign, The Daily Kos, is that this base is motivated by determined resistance when the party's core values are being attacked by the right, and that future election victory is more likely if the Democrats get their committed voters to the polling booths (as the Republicans did in 2004) than if they moderate their message in an attempt to attract moderate conservatives. Liberals in Congress, who share the political priorities of the internet left, saw their influence enhanced after their party's victory in the 2006 mid-term elections. Many of the chairmanships of the powerful Congressional committees went to liberals who had spent years in the political wilderness while Republicans and moderate Democrats controlled Washington DC.

With both the right and left wings of the Democratic Party having been strengthened in 2006, the observation that the party is 'struggling to assert an identity' continues to be valid.

Strengthening party leadership

At the same time that the two main parties were becoming more ideologically cohesive, steps were taken to enhance the leadership role of the most senior members of each party.

Historically, the national headquarters of each party only had a significant role to play once every four years, during presidential elections. During the 1980s and 1990s, both parties established permanent headquarters in Washington DC, which played an increasingly important role in fund-raising, keeping databases on supporters and identifying vulnerable districts that would benefit from help in the form of money or volunteers.

Additionally, the Democratic Party, in the mid-1980s, introduced super-delegates to the national convention, which selects their presidential nominee. This gives elected office-holders, such as members of Congress and governors, voting rights equivalent to 20 per cent of the total when choosing the nominee. In a tight contest between two candidates, one of whom enjoyed the confidence of the senior members of the party, the influence of the super-delegates could prove decisive. As yet, no such situation has arisen.

Has party renewal been a positive or negative development?

Considering the suspicions of the Founding Fathers, that political parties would contribute to the concentration of power in the hands of one faction, the emergence of two ideological parties could be seen as a negative development. In particular, in the case of conservatives, tight links have been forged between a network of like-minded groups including think-tanks, TV and radio stations, magazines, newspapers, campaign groups and policy strategists who all work together to advance their political agenda. The Republican Party can be seen as the political wing of this movement. Arguably, this level of political control and influence is precisely what the Founding Fathers sought to avoid when they crafted a constitutional framework that fragmented power and set up a system of checks on its misuse.

Certainly, commentators have long argued that when US political parties were broad-based coalitions they were more reflective of the country's very diverse society, its Federal nature, and that they operated in a way that was consistent with the intentions of the Founding Fathers. However, this analysis has been challenged. As long ago as 1949, the social commentator V. O. Key argued that 'over the long run, the have-nots lose in a disorganised politics'. When policy is made through deals struck between competing groups, the poor and marginalised who have little to bargain with are poorly placed to secure their interests, while the already wealthy and powerful are well placed to reinforce their dominance. Consequently, as parties, especially the Democrats, encompassed an ever wider range of people and policies in the 1960s, political participation declined, especially among the poor. By the early 1990s, before party renewal became evident, 86 per cent of the wealthiest Americans were regularly voting compared with barely half of the poorest. Early in the twenty-first century, by contrast, the two polarised parties have galvanised voters of all races and income-brackets in record numbers.

Thus, while it is easy to conclude that party renewal has been a negative development, especially in respect of the aims of the Founding Fathers, careful analysis of broad-based parties indicates that they may have been even more effective vehicles for establishing political and economic dominance than the 'factions' the Founding Fathers so mistrusted.

Party supporters

Identifying the party faithful

With the Republican Party now clearly identified as having a conservative agenda, and the Democrats in large part motivated by resistance to that agenda, it is crucial to each party to identify who their supporters are and persuade them to vote.

In the 2004 presidential election, the Republican electoral strategist kept a card in his pocket showing that the percentage of independent voters had fallen from 15 per cent in 1988 to 7 per cent in 2002. Hence his strategy to almost ignore undecided voters and concentrate on maximising turn-out among committed Republicans. The Democrats adopted a similar, if less successful, approach. So who are the committed Republicans and Democrats?

Race and ethnic identity

One of the clearest indicators of party support in the USA is race or ethnic identity.

African-Americans have tended to vote Democrat since the New Deal in the 1930s, and have overwhelmingly given their support to the party since the Civil Rights movement in the 1960s. In the 2000 presidential election, the Democratic Party won 90 per cent of the African-American vote, and in 2004, on a higher turn-out, this percentage fell by just 3 per cent.

Jews have also been reliable supporters of the Democratic Party over the same period because of the party's association with Civil Rights and moving forward the standard of living for minority groups. In the 2000 election, 81 per cent of Jews voted Democrat. In 2004, this fell to 75 per cent, in part because of the unwavering support that the Bush administration gave to Israel during its first term.

European Catholics, primarily those who came to the USA in the nineteenth century from Italy, Ireland and Poland, have also been traditional supporters of the Democratic Party. This support has been steadily eroding, however, since the 1960s. In part, this is due to income: as an increasing percentage of these ethnic groups have become wealthier they have migrated to the suburbs, away from the communities that have historically voted as a bloc. In part, this is due to the Civil Rights movement, which opened up new competition for jobs in sectors traditionally dominated by white Catholics, especially in services such as the police force and firefighting. They tend to be particularly hostile to Affirmative Action, which they see as giving minority groups an advantage in competition for these jobs. Moreover, in recent years social issues have significantly influenced Catholic voters, adding to defections to the Republican Party. In the 2004 presidential election, the church took a public stand on abortion, effectively encouraging Catholics to vote for President Bush, who took 52 per cent of the white Catholic vote (against a Catholic candidate, John Kerry), up by 5 per cent on the 2000 result.

The other large Catholic group of voters in the USA, the Hispanics from Central and South America, is difficult to categorise, as it is made up of many nationalities. Based on past experience, recent immigrants with low incomes can be relied on to vote Democrat. This has generally proved to be the case with Mexicans and Puerto Ricans. Other factors, however, seem to play a significant role in Hispanic voting patterns. The periodic upsurges of the 'nativist' faction within the Republican Party, typified by proposition 187 in California, which appeared hostile to Hispanic groups, drives them into the arms of the Democrats. When the 'nativist' faction is quiet, Hispanic voting patterns are more fluid. Politicians who reach out to them, such as the former Governor of Florida, Jeb Bush, who speaks good Spanish, are rewarded with high levels of support. The Republican Party has demonstrated an ability to attract wealthier members of these communities and some of the party's social policies, such as opposition to abortion, accord with Catholic teachings. Additionally, fiercely anti-Castro Cubans are unswervingly loyal to the Republican Party, which they see as taking a tougher line with their arch-enemy. Overall, though, the Democrats hold a distinct, but insecure, lead among this diverse group. The 2004 and 2006 elections illustrate the fluid nature of Hispanic support. In the 2004 presidential election, President Bush secured 44 per cent of their votes but in 2006, after a forceful campaign against illegal immigrants led by the nativist faction, the Republican Party won just 30 per cent of the Hispanic vote.

Gender

There is a longstanding pattern of women being more likely than men to vote Democrat. Surveys consistently demonstrate that health-care is the highest priority amongst women, followed by equal pay and job security. Third is education, providing the best opportunities for their children. The Democrats are seen as the more committed to taking action on each of these issues.

Research indicates that the gender gap grows as education increases. A survey of more than 40,000 women in 2003 indicated that among those with a high school diploma or less, women were 10 per cent more likely than men to vote Democrat. For those who had gone on to university, but failed to complete their degree, the gender gap grew to 15 percentage points. Among those with a degree, it rose to 20 per cent. And for voters who had taken postgraduate courses, it reached 28 percentage points, almost triple the gender difference among the least-educated voters. On the other hand, when women get married their voting patterns change and the gender divide almost disappears.

The result, overall, is a fairly consistent pattern of 54 per cent of women voting Democrat and 53 per cent of men voting Republican.

Geography

The political parties, as well as examining how and why specific sections of the electorate vote, also pay close attention to regional patterns of support, which is particularly important when making electoral college calculations.

When evaluating the outcome of recent elections, and their implications for the future, Michael Barone, author of the *Almanac of American Politics*, has divided the country into three parts, each with roughly equal population. One is the east and west coasts, around New York state and California, which has consistently cast around 55 per cent of its votes for the Democratic party over the mid-1990s. Another is the 'heartland' of the Midwest and Rocky Mountain states, which has cast around 53 per cent of its votes for the Republican Party over the same period. The third is the South, made up mainly of the Confederate states that fought against the Union in the Civil War, which has cast around 55 per cent of its votes for the Republicans.

Adding to this depressing picture for the Democrats, in the 2004 presidential election, Mr Barone pointed out that John Kerry was most successful in those districts with slow population growth, or even population loss, while George W. Bush won a majority of the districts undergoing the fastest growth in population, suggesting that geographical voting trends favour future Republican success.

Religion

Before 1972, there was no difference in the voting patterns of those who regularly attended a place of worship and those who did not. Then, in the 1972 election, a 10 per cent gap emerged as Richard Nixon appealed to the 'silent majority' who favoured a return to traditional values after the social upheavals of the 1960s. This gap widened during the presidency of Bill Clinton amidst rumours, then admissions, of marital infidelity.

By the beginning of the twenty-first century, religion had become one of the clearest indicators of voting behaviour among white Americans. (The votes of African-Americans, Jews, Hispanic Catholics and other non-Christians, including Muslims, do not appear to be affected by how regularly they attend religious services.) The more frequently white Americans go to church, the more likely they are to vote Republican, as follows:

- Of the Protestants who attend church at least once a week, 70 per cent voted for George W. Bush in 2004, while 56 per cent of observing Catholics also voted for him.
- Of Protestants who attend church less frequently, 56 per cent voted for George W. Bush, while 49 per cent of Catholics who were not frequent attenders voted for him.
- Of the white electorate who never attend religious services, 36 per cent voted for George W. Bush.

In short, white Americans no longer 'Vote as you shot'. Instead, they vote as they pray – or do not pray.

Lifestyle

Added to the array of indicators that parties can use to identify who is likely to vote for them, experts in voting behaviour can now provide indicators from people's lifestyles to help more precisely target their messages. For example, of the two most popular evening talk shows, Republicans are more likely to watch the one starring Jay Leno, while Democrats are more likely to watch the one starring David Letterman. The overwhelming majority of men who watch NASCAR, stockcar racing, vote Republican. Almost everyone who drives a Volvo votes Democrat.

Minor parties

Obstacles to success for minor parties

Every President since the Civil War (1861–65) has been either a Democrat or a Republican. Only Vermont and Connecticut have returned an independent Congressman and an independent Senator to Washington DC in recent years. At the local level, third parties have had some electoral success, such as the Liberal Party in New York, and Jesse 'The Body' Ventura (a former professional wrestler) was elected Governor of Minnesota in 1996. So why is it so difficult for members of minor parties to gain high office?

The most important factor is the lack of ideological 'space'. For most of American history, the political arena has been filled with two 'umbrella' parties large and broad enough to organise and draw support across an extremely large, extremely diverse country. With no room on the political spectrum for more than two umbrella parties, minor parties have tended to be focused on specific issues and highly ideological in character. Consequently, they have had difficulty attracting wide support unless they have promoted an issue the main parties had ignored and which resonated with many of the voters. Even when this has happened, the main parties have woken up to the issue, absorbing it into their programmes.

Furthermore, the evolution of the main parties, in recent years, has not created any vacant political territory space for the minor parties. Both Democrats and Republicans appeal to approximately 50 per cent of the nation and offer two clear ideological choices, encouraging voters to support one of the two main parties in order to keep out of power the party they most dislike, even when what they themselves are offering is not very attractive, rather than casting a 'wasted' vote for a minor party.

Third parties also suffer a number of disadvantages arising directly from electoral rules and practices, including:

- The first-past-the-post electoral system, which has a tendency to produce two dominant parties wherever it is used. This is particularly true of US presidential elections, where candidates have to win a majority of the votes cast in each state in order to win electoral college votes. It is so unlikely in most elections that minor parties will achieve this goal that they generally lack credibility.
- Many states have restrictive regulations that make it difficult for candidates to be included on the ballot unless they have already demonstrated (by raising signatures) that they have significant levels of support. This often causes expensive distractions from campaigning by the candidates who may have the fewest resources.
- Many states allow 'straight ticket' voting, which encourages voters to cast their votes for one of the main parties in all posts being contested. This penalises minor parties that may have not have candidates for all posts. Minor candidates receive, on average, twice as many votes in districts that do not allow straight-ticket voting.
- Limited Federal funding is only available to parties that gained more than 5 per cent of the vote in the previous presidential election and full funding is only available to parties that gained more than 25 per cent.
- Campaigns are getting steadily more sophisticated and expensive, and minor parties often have limited funds and expertise at their disposal.

Limited success for minor parties
Despite these obstacles, third-party candidates have also had some impact in recent years:

- In the 1992 presidential campaign, multi-billionaire Ross Perot managed to get his name onto the ballot in all fifty states. He spent more than $65 million on his campaign, much of it on thirty-minute 'infomercials' that outlined his strategies to reduce the budget deficit and criticised the lack of policies on the issue from the two main parties. His support in nationwide opinion polls enabled him to participate in the presidential debates, and in the election he won 18.9 per cent of the vote. However, he won no electoral college votes.

The success of his campaign can be measured by the votes drawn away from the Republican Party and the effect it had on the policy platforms of both main parties. Had Perot not been in the race, election analysts estimate that a majority of the 19 million votes cast for him could have gone to President Bush, who would have been re-elected as a result, instead of Bill Clinton. Also, deficit-reduction measures were a prominent feature of the 'Contract with America', the manifesto that enabled the Republican Party to win control of the House of Representatives in 1994. The bill they passed was then signed into law by President Clinton, who was as keen as his political opponents to claim credit for a policy that had proved so popular, and by the end of the decade the Federal budget was in surplus.

Perot's less successful campaign in the 1996 presidential election illustrates how difficult it can be for minor parties to maintain momentum. His main policy had, by that time, been adopted by both of the dominant parties and he won just 8 per cent of the vote.

- In the 2000 election campaign, Ralph Nader, a veteran consumer-rights activist represented the Green Party, forcing the issue of the environment to be debated. He won just 2.7 per cent of the vote, but this included more than 97,000 votes in Florida, almost all of which would have gone to the Democratic candidate, Al Gore. George W. Bush won Florida by just 537 votes, which gave him the 25 electoral college votes that determined which of the two men became President.

Even in the 2004 presidential election, when Ralph Nader won only 0.38 per cent of the vote, the possibility of his participation leading to a repeat of the 2000 election result meant that both of the main parties diverted time and funds: the Democrats fought to keep him off the ballot in many states and the Republicans provided assistance to help him.

Box 6.1 Comparing political parties in the USA and UK

A reversal of roles?

While US political parties have traditionally been characterised as large umbrellas covering a wide range of views and people, with little ideological cohesion, British political parties have traditionally been thought of as ideologically distinct and highly disciplined. This chapter has illustrated the extent to which the traditional character-isation of US political parties is no longer accurate. What of UK parties?

As recently as the 1980s there was an ideological gulf between the Conservative and Labour parties. When Margaret Thatcher became Prime Minister, she was determined to shake up a workforce that, in her view, had become used to relying on government support and had lost its competitive edge. Adopting a much more right-wing set of policies than her predecessors, she was prepared to see a sharp rise in unemployment. The Labour Party, in response, undertook to defend all vulnerable groups from what they saw as an attack on their welfare. Moving sharply to the left, they promoted the interests of not only the working class but of other minorities, such as ethnic groups and gays and lesbians.

The electorate, presented with such a sharp ideological divide, rejected Labour's platform. They were kept out of office until they abandoned most of their socialist policies and transformed themselves into New Labour. When Labour won the 1997 general election, they undertook to abide by the spending plans of the gov-ernment they were replacing and refused appeals from traditional socialists to repeal Margaret Thatcher's reforms.

The extent to which New Labour has invaded traditional conserv-ative ideological territory was illustrated when, in 2004, Michael Howard, leader of the Conservative Party, complained that every Conservative policy was being stolen by New Labour within days of being unveiled.

A swift survey of New Labour policies appears to validate the charge. Having a choice of public-service providers and private com-panies providing some services on behalf of the public sector were originally Conservative Party policies, as were heavy prison sen-tences as the main means of curbing crime and to use military force to defend the country's interests. All of these policies are now New Labour policies. New Labour privatised the Air Traffic Control Service. Private companies perform operations, such as hip replace-ments, on behalf of the National Health Service. City academies, run by private organisations, are being rapidly expanded to provide education for the children of Britain's most deprived communities. Under New Labour, there are a record number of prisoners and the government has sent the British armed services to fight in Sierra Leone, Kosovo and Iraq. Even the support patterns for New Labour have changed, appealing as much to middle-class Conservatives as their traditional working-class base. With both the Labour and Conservative parties vying to be seen as the more competent administrators of a free-market economy, Margaret Thatcher's transformation of the political landscape appears to be complete. With the Labour Party keeping the Conservatives out of office by offering the electorate a kinder, gentler version of Thatcherism, the new leader David Cameron has set a new tone, which, to many, echoes his opponents. The old criticism of US political parties, that they are like two identical bottles, now appears to be more applicable to the UK.

Two-party politics?
Minor parties in the USA are a periodic irritant to the two major parties, occasionally delivering substantial blows. What of the UK?

The main reason that the minor parties in the USA find it hard to make a sustained impact is the lack of ideological space available to them. That is not a problem in the UK. Traditional socialists who oppose the right-wing policies of New Labour appear to have been almost completely marginalised within the party. Yet there are still left-wing alternatives available to voters, in the form of minor parties.

In the 2005 general election, the Liberal Democrats stood on a platform of opposition to the war in Iraq and questioned whether a choice of providers in the public sector was the best way to improve services. These policies represented the main left-wing alternative in England and won the Liberal Democrats their greatest number of seats in Parliament since the 1920s. Yet it did not lead to the inroads that might have been expected at a time that the government was unpopular and the main opposition was even more unpopular. The Liberal Democrats are reviewing their policies and the signs are that they will not be offering such a clear left-wing alternative at the next general election.

In Scotland and Wales, other left-wing alternatives are available. In most countries, nationalism is associated with right-wing politics, but both the Scottish National Party (SNP) and Plaid Cymru are well to the left of the Labour Party. Although neither party has enjoyed recent electoral success, they remain the largest opposition parties in the Scottish Parliament and Assembly for Wales respectively and, as a result, tend to drag the Labour Party to the left. By refusing to introduce foundation hospitals, or variable fees for university education and by providing free nursing care for the elderly, the Labour Party in Scotland has crafted a clear distinction between itself and its sibling in England. Similarly, despite having far fewer powers, the Labour Party in Wales has abolished league tables for schools just as the Labour Party at Westminster has developed and refined league tables for English schools.

In addition, recent years have seen the emergence of pockets of support for other minor parties who represent an alternative to the policies of New Labour and the Conservatives. When, in 2001, it was proposed to close down Kidderminster Hospital, the voters of Wyre Forest did not turn to the Conservative candidate but replaced their Labour MP with an independent, Dr Richard Taylor, who had worked as a consultant at the hospital for twenty years. Similarly, in 2005, the voters of Bethnal Green replaced New Labour loyalist, Oona King, with the leader of the Respect Party, George Galloway, in protest against the invasion of Iraq. Scotland has seen a surge of support for the more left-wing Greens, Scottish Socialist Party and Solidarity Group, which now have seven, four and two seats, respectively, in the Scottish Parliament.

Similarly, on the right, disaffected Conservatives can vote for the UK Independence Party (UKIP). Offering a range of policies often associated with Margaret Thatcher, including hostility to the European Union, increasing penalties for criminals and promising 'zero net immigration', UKIP established its credibility as an electoral force in the 2004 European Elections, when it attracted 2.6 million votes, winning twelve seats, which was more than the Liberal Democrats received and more than half the numbers that voted Labour or Conservative. UKIP followed this up later the same year by coming third in a Parliamentary by-election, relegating the Tories to fourth place.

Thus, while more contrasts than similarities have long been made between the two-party systems in the USA and UK, the nature of those differences have altered radically over the past three decades.

What you should have learnt from reading this chapter

- The Founding Fathers were extremely suspicious of political parties, fearing that they would be divisive and promote the interests of their supporters at the expense of the wider community.

- The emergence of two 'umbrella' parties, each representing a diverse range of people, appeared to ensure that this would not happen.

- However, this led to policy being made through deals struck between competing groups who tended to marginalise the poor (who had little with which to bargain), and benefited the wealthy and powerful.

- Thus, the rise of 'factions', since the early 1990s, in the form of political parties promoting a narrow partisan interest, has not necessarily proved to be the cause for concern that the Founding Fathers anticipated. Along with the growing ideological cohesion of US politics, there has been a notable rise in political participation, especially in elections, with people demonstrating an intense determination to remove from office those who use their power in ways with which they disagree.

Glossary of key terms

Fiscal conservative A belief, found mainly in the Republican Party, that government interference in the daily lives of citizens, especially the levying of taxes, should be kept to a minimum.
Liberal A belief, found mainly in the Democratic Party, that government has a responsibility to actively intervene to protect the interests of vulnerable groups in society.
Party realignment A change in the patterns of support among the voters for the Democratic and Republican parties.
Social conservative A belief, found mainly in the Republican Party, that government has a responsibility to actively intervene to create a moral framework for society that promotes a shared set of values that bind a diverse population.
Umbrella parties Political parties with no clear ideological focus, seeking to win support from a wide range of groups with dissimilar interests.

Likely examination questions

Issues examiners may expect students to be able to effectively analyse include:

- The ideology of the two main parties; what they believe in, and why
- Who supports the two main parties; the evolution of the patterns of support and the significance of these for the ability of each party to win power
- The significance of minor parties
- The factors underpinning the current two-party system

Thus, examples of the kind of questions that could be asked include:

What is meant by party renewal, and in what sense has it happened? Are minor parties doomed to failure?

Where the question compares the US system with Britain's, issues may include:

* The extent of the ideological differences between the two main parties in the two countries
* The role of minor parties in the two countries

Thus, an example of the kind of question that could be asked is: 'The two-party system has grown stronger in the USA while it has grown weaker in the UK'. Discuss.

Helpful websites

www.rnc.org – official website of the Republican party.

www.renewamerica.us – website of the Arlington Group, which reflects the views of the social conservative wing of the party.

www.house.gov/pence/rsc/ – website of the Republican Study Committee, which reflects the views of fiscal conservatives.

www.newamericancentury.org – website of the Project for the New American Century (no longer being updated), which reflects the views of neo-conservatives.

www.republicanmainstreet.org – website of Republican Main Street Partnership, which reflects the views of Republican moderates.

www.dnc.org – official website of the Democratic Party.

www.bluedogdems.com – website of the Blue Dog Democrats, which reflects the views of the conservative wing of the party.

www.dlc.org – website of the Democratic Leadership Council, which reflects the views of the Democrat moderates.

www.moveon.org or www.dailykos.com – reflecting the views of the 'Internet left', promoting an aggressive, anti-conservative agenda.

www.Politics1.com – has a comprehensive list of US political parties, including minor parties in alphabetical order.

Suggestions for further reading

For an authoritative analysis on the unfolding patterns of political support for the two main parties, the introduction to the *Almanac of American Politics* by Michael Barone is hard to surpass. Available on Amazon.com and the website of its publisher, *National Journal*, it is quite expensive at around $70, but can also be used for its profiles of every member of Congress and every governor.

For a taste of the how passionately US conservatives dislike their liberal opponents, read *Liberalism is a Mental Disorder: Savage Solutions* by Michael Savage, available from Amazon.com.

For a taste of how deeply this dislike is returned by liberals, read *Lies and the Lying Liars Who Tell Them: A Fair and Balanced Look at the Right* by Al Franken, also available from Amazon.com.

Pressure Groups

Contents

Overview

On 2 March 2004, Senators were seen reading an e-mail message on their BlackBerry pagers from the executive vice president of the National Rifle Association (NRA), Wayne LaPierre. Objecting to an amendment that had been added at the last moment, he was urging them to reject a bill that had been expected to pass by a wide margin. When the votes were counted, the bill was defeated by 90–8. 'They had the power to turn around at least sixty votes,' said Senator Dianne Feinstein, of California, who had proposed the amendment, 'that's amazing to me.'

However, not all Americans would share the Senators' dismay at the NRA's influence. The group was only able to persuade politicians to listen to its views because of its ability to mobilise more than 3 million members. Generating this level of political participation can be seen as a positive contribution to an active, inclusive, democracy that helps ensure that the Founding Fathers' goal of avoiding concentration of political power is realised in modern America.

This chapter examines the methods used by pressure groups to achieve their objectives, exploiting the opportunities presented to them by the US political system, and weighs up the arguments that they enhance or undermine democracy.

Key issues to be covered in this chapter

- How and why the US political system creates a climate favourable to pressure groups
- The range of opportunities available for pressure groups to influence policy, and the methods by which they take advantage of them
- The impact, both positive and negative, of pressure groups on US democracy

Pressure groups and the Constitution

Creating a favourable climate for pressure groups

When drawing up the Constitution, the Founding Fathers relied on three mechanisms to avoid concentrations of power and, thereby, protect liberty: strict separation of powers in the Federal government; sharing power between the states and Federal government, and making elected officials accountable to the people. When, in the Bill of Rights, they guaranteed rights of freedom of expression and the right to 'petition the Government for a redress of grievances' in the 1st Amendment, the Founding Fathers also provided a constitutional avenue to influence political bodies at Federal and state level.

From the outset, therefore, the political landscape of the USA was favourable to pressure groups. The Founding Fathers themselves recognised that this presented a potential problem. In the public debate that accompanied the ratification process, James Madison, one of the principal authors of the Constitution, expressed concern that 'factions [would be] adverse to the rights of other citizens, or to the permanent and aggregate interests of the community'. If this happened, how would the most powerful 'factions' be held accountable? On balance, however, he reached the conclusion that safeguarding the freedoms that the Constitution was designed to protect was the higher priority.

Exploiting a favourable climate

Almost as soon as the Constitution came into effect, Americans took full advantage of the opportunities it provided to influence the political process. As early as 1835, the French commentator Alexis de Tocqueville wrote, 'In no country in the world has the principle of association been more successfully used, or applied to a greater multitude of objects, than America.'

This pattern continues to the present day, with groups using some, or all, of the political **access points** available to shape their society. The following sections outline why specific access points are targeted, the strategies used and the effectiveness of pressure groups.

Influencing individuals and the local community

Shaping individual behaviour

Although it may not appear to be a political strategy, the most effective way for a group to achieve its goals would be to persuade each member of society to behave in a manner consistent with its aims and objectives. Shared values and similar behaviour arguably benefit society as much as the groups that promote them. Historically, groups such as the scouts, Little League baseball and the League of Women Voters were credited with bringing together people of different classes and races in shared community-building activities that provided social bonds for a diverse society. They can also be a practical forum for applying democratic principles. Community groups require people to run meetings, handle membership dues and keep records. Leaders of local groups also had to be responsive to the views of their members. In the 1950s, it was calculated that the twenty largest national associations had 5 per cent of the adult population taking a leadership role in their local communities.

Such face-to-face group activity has diminished substantially since the 1950s. However, encouragement to participate in groups may have risen with increasingly sophisticated marketing by pressure groups, using direct mail and e-mail to target people who may be sympathetic to their views or goals. Following a high-profile campaign in 2005 to save the life of Terri Schiavo, a woman in a prolonged coma whose life-support system was turned off despite the objections of her parents, the list of donors who supported the campaign was sold to 'right to life' groups opposing abortion. Other groups, such as the National Rifle Association, provide services to their members, such as banking facilities, a travel service and a mobile phone service, while encouraging them to meet at events, such as gun shows, and to participate in campaigns to resist gun control.

For some groups, the specific targeting of individual behaviour is part of their wider political strategy. Anti-abortion groups are constantly devising methods to put pressure on women seeking an abortion to change their minds. In 2002, taking advantage of advances in digital photo technology, anti-abortion groups began posting pictures of women attending abortion clinics on their websites, to deter visits, until ordered to remove them by the courts. Then, pregnancy centres operated by anti-abortion groups began installing ultrasound equipment, which shows women the babies they are carrying. Reportedly, 90 per cent of women considering having an abortion change their minds if they attend one of these clinics (which often do not make it clear that they are part of an anti-abortion campaign).

Shaping communities

A political culture of accountability means that in most US communities any service that has a direct impact on people's lives may be run by elected people who can be held accountable if the service is not of an acceptable standard. This may include sanitation (garbage disposal), education and law and order. Consequently, there are many opportunities for groups to help shape their communities.

Education has been a particularly controversial area. As explained in Chapter 6, social conservatives have sought to gain control of school curriculums to ensure that moral values are a part of children's education, which has brought them into conflict with the courts. It is estimated that more than a quarter of the 15,000 school districts in the USA are dominated by groups with a social conservative agenda.

Law and order policies in the USA are also heavily influenced by local elections. In many areas, the Sheriff (who determines police priorities), the District Attorney (who decides on prosecutions) and the judges (who manage court cases and decide on sentencing) are all elected. This gives organisations such as Mothers Against Drunk Driving (MADD) an opportunity to promote their views that the police should put more resources into monitoring driving offences, the DA should push for heavier penalties for drunk drivers and judges should imprison those found guilty as a deterrent to others.

In addition, local councillors and the mayor are all elected, which provides opportunities to shape developments on a large scale. The mayor of New York City, for example, is sometimes described as the second most powerful executive in the nation. Mayor Giuliani's zero-tolerance policing policy, which has proved influential around the world, drew heavily on the 'broken windows' strategy. This was devised by two sociologists working for the Manhattan Institute, a right-wing think-tank, who argued that petty criminals developed over time into serious criminals and that this process could be stemmed by focusing on minor crimes, leading, in due course, to a reduction in major crime.

Political developments in communities can also be shaped through local democracy. In many states, voters are provided with opportunities to influence affairs through amendments to the state constitution, Initiatives, propositions or recall elections. How this is done, and the impact this can have, is outlined in Chapter 5.

Influencing state governments

Shaping policy at local level

States have enormous powers, including: levying taxes; spending money on the welfare of the population; passing and enforcing laws; regulating trade within the state; administering elections; and protecting the public's health and morals.

All of this has an effect at local level. The money available for education, road-building and so on is largely determined in the state capital by the state congress and the governor. So too are important policies such as whether or not to adopt the death penalty for certain crimes. In the 1990s, pressure groups were able to change the law in California through propositions (opportunities for citizens to vote on issues of importance) that particularly affected minority groups. In 1994, Proposition 187 withdrew benefits, including education, from the families of illegal immigrants, the majority of whom were from Mexico. In 1996, Proposition 209 banned Affirmative Action to ensure access to higher education for groups who had been historically discriminated against in the state's universities. In 1998, bilingual education, usually English and Spanish, was banned in the state's schools.

Shaping policy at national level

Policies pioneered at state level can also substantially affect national politics. In the 1990s, Wisconsin introduced school vouchers. Instead of paying schools for the cost of educating each student, the money went to families, who could decide which school to spend it in. This would, in principle, increase choice and force schools to improve their performance or close for lack of students. The policy was driven by a right-wing think-tank, the Bradley Foundation, which was close to the Republican Party, and some Democrat African-American activists who believed that existing policies were failing their community's children. It was adopted by George W. Bush for his presidential election campaign in 2000.

Since George W. Bush became President, he has refused to sign international agreements on measures to tackle climate change. Actively lobbied by environmentalist groups, eleven states have (or plan to) introduced air quality regulations that are much more strict than those of the Federal government. Unless the regulations are overruled in the courts, as a result of law suits brought by car manufacturers, greenhouse gasses from cars will have to be reduced by roughly 30 per cent between 2009 and 2016. With these states, including California and New York, accounting for about one-third of auto sales, they may create a situation in which it becomes uneconomic for car companies to produce two varieties of each of their models and simply build cars with lower emissions.

Influencing elections

Getting sympathisers into power and monitoring how they use it

With significant power being wielded at so many levels (including the Federal level, below) by so many people, it is clearly beneficial for pressure groups to:

• Help sympathetic people to win elections.
• Make sure that they use their power to advance the agenda of the group(s) that helped them win.

There are a variety of strategies used by groups to accomplish these two goals.

Creating voters

Pressure groups can, literally, create voters. Significant sections of society have, historically, been denied the right to vote, including African-Americans, Native Americans and women. Each required robust, lengthy campaigns before the franchise was extended to them. Two notable groups are the focus of continuing campaigns to extend their limited voting rights: residents of Washington DC, who cannot vote in Congressional or Senate elections (because the district is not in any of the fifty states), and released convicts who, in thirteen states, lose the right to vote for the rest of their lives.

Pressure groups also play a significant role in helping people to register to vote. At any given time, in a highly mobile society, many voters may not have met the registration requirements to be able to vote in their new districts, or may have not yet registered to vote by the next election. Others, relatively recent immigrants to the country, may be unsure of the registration procedures. Pressure groups often play a prominent part in supporting and advising people in these situations. The leading African-American Civil Rights group, the National Association for the Advancement of Colored People (NAACP), led the campaign for the 'Motor Voter' Act of 1993, which was introduced to allow voters to register when they renew or change their address on their driving licences. Since its introduction, an estimated 9 million additional people have registered to vote.

Choosing the right candidate

Registering sympathetic voters is the first step. Persuading the main political parties to adopt candidates who support the group's objectives is the second.

Before most elections in the USA, from town council to President, voters are given an opportunity to play a part in selecting which candidate will represent the main parties. Pressure groups donate funds to candidates they support; provide information to their members on why they should vote for the group's preferred candidates in the primaries; encourage their members to volunteer to work on the campaigns of favoured candidates; provide assistance to anyone who wishes to vote in the primaries but may have difficulty getting to a polling station; and may even produce their own election material explaining to the wider electorate why they support particular candidates.

Electing the right candidate

After the primary, if the pressure group's preferred candidate has won, the next task is to get the voters out to ensure that the candidate wins the election against the opposing party. This is done by assisting the candidate's campaign: distributing leaflets, displaying signs in front of homes, telephoning voters to remind them of the election and providing transport to get voters to the polling stations.

Pressure groups that are particularly effective may have helped sympathisers to win the primary of both parties, meaning that the group wins whatever the outcome of the election. For example, in the race to represent the 3rd District of Colorado in the 2004 election, the National Rifle Association (NRA) fully endorsed both candidates.

Understandably, there has long been concern that pressure groups play too significant a role in elections, potentially making politicians more responsive to their agenda than to the concerns of the voters. Attempts to limit this influence, and the response of pressure groups, is outlined in Chapter 5.

Ensuring that politicians are aware of a pressure group's agenda

While pressure groups would deny that they wield excessive influence over politicians, they do want elected officials to be fully aware of their policy priorities. Commonly, this is done by providing all elected officials with a list of their legislative priorities. This list is also distributed to members and put on the group's website. Politicians are aware that the level of support, or opposition, they can expect from pressure groups depends on the extent to which they promote the groups' agendas.

Monitoring politicians' responsiveness to a pressure group's agenda

Ahead of the next election, pressure groups will issue 'report cards' on how much support their agendas have received from politicians seeking re-election. As with school reports, politicians are graded on a scale of A–F. Those with highest grades can expect considerable support in their campaign, in terms of both funds and volunteers. Those with a grade F can expect to face active opposition throughout their campaigns.

In 2006, Republican Senator Mike DeWine of Ohio, who was facing re-election that year, was given a Grade F by the NRA for opposing the group's top legislative priority the previous year, a bill that prohibited law suits against gun manufactures for unlawful use of their firearms. The bill passed but the group vowed to punish him in the 2006 election for his decision, and contributed to his defeat.

Influencing the House of Representatives

Frequent elections

At the Federal level, the strategy of influencing politicians through electoral support is most effective in the House of Representatives because all of its members have to stand for re-election every two years. A significant proportion of the seats are so safe that the Congressmen are not seriously threatened at elections and therefore do not need to mount expensive campaigns. In competitive seats, however, members are acutely aware of the need to raise a substantial war chest, as much as $10,000 per week between elections.

However, both Congressmen and pressure groups are conscious of the suspicion aroused in the media and among voters of relationships that appear to be based exclusively on money. Both are keen to develop relationships that are seen to be constructive, bringing mutual benefit to the Congressman's constituents as well as to the pressure group.

Developing a relationship

Relationships between Congressmen and pressure groups are often based on ideology. Republicans are likely to be approached by conservative groups to promote their proposals. For example, when President George W. Bush proposed reforming social security in 2005, the Free Enterprise Fund, which had advocated such reform for years, approached Congressman Paul Ryan (Wisconsin, 1st District) to introduce a bill that reflected their views. At the same time, the Cato Institute, another conservative think-tank, which supported reform, approached Congressman Sam Johnson (Texas, 3rd District) to introduce a rival bill reflecting their proposals for reorganising the system. A similar ideological relationship is commonplace between Democratic Congressmen and liberal pressure groups.

Pressure groups will also attempt to forge relationships with Congressmen, including their opponents, because of their committee assignments. For example, John Lewis (Georgia, 5th District), a liberal African-American Congressman, consistently opposes the interests of the pharmaceutical industry, and because he sits on the Ways and Means Health Subcommittee this opposition has a direct impact on the industry. Over the years, large pharmaceutical firms have provided medical scholarships to African-Americans in his district to increase the proportion of black doctors, provided study weekends for his staff in exotic locations, and put on events to commemorate Congressman Lewis's contributions to the Civil Rights campaigns in the 1960s. None of these contributions have persuaded the Congressman to vote in their interests but they may have helped reduce the volume of his criticisms.

Relationships between Congressmen and pressure groups may be based on local priorities. For example, the largest employer in Congressman Lewis's district is Coca-Cola. Representatives from the firm are always welcome in his office and his staff are always receptive to their requests.

Relationships may also be built on the personal commitments of the Congressman. For years, Congressman Lewis campaigned for a National Museum of African-American History and Culture to be added to the Smithsonian complex of museums in Washington DC, and welcomed any support offered. Having submitted a bill to Congress to authorise and fund the project on fifteen occasions, the proposal was signed into law in 2003 and a prestigious location on the Mall allocated in 2006.

Professional lobbyists
Pressure groups employ people, on a full-time basis, to build relationships on their behalf. Professional lobbying has been a growth business since the 1930s, when, under the New Deal, the scale of government began to grow rapidly and, with it, the scale of government contracts and regulations that could benefit or harm organisations. Between 2000 and 2005, Federal spending increased from $1.79 trillion to $2.29 trillion, and at the same time the number of registered **lobbyists** in Washington DC rose from 16,342 to 34,789.

The people best placed to foster relationships with Congressmen, and their staff, are those who already know them, and the legislative procedures that they wish to influence, well. Thus, many lobbyists are former Congressional staff members or former Congressmen. For those with the best contacts in Congress, and the greatest experience of the legislative system, becoming a lobbyist can be extremely lucrative. For example, after twenty-five years representing the 3rd District of Louisiana, Billy Tauzin stepped down to take up the post of president of the Pharmaceutical and Research Manufacturers of America for an estimated $2 million per year. This is known as the **revolving door syndrome**, with people leaving Congressional employment only to reappear almost immediately as lobbyists. It should be noted, however, that periodically the revolving door takes people from lobbying into elected positions, often with a significant drop in pay. The most notable recent example would be Haley Barbour, current Governor of Mississippi, who left the lobbying firm that he had established and built up to be one of the largest, wealthiest firms in Washington DC in order to run for office.

The close relationships that exist between professional lobbyists and members of Congress has given rise to concern that meaningful power has become concentrated in a small elite who are the only ones who fully grasp the vast array of complex regulations. To address this concern, the Federal Regulation of Lobbying Act was passed in 1946. Limited to setting up a system of registration and financial disclosure of those attempting to influence legislation in Congress, the law did not attempt to regulate the conduct of lobbying. Then, in 1954, the scope of the Act was narrowed by a Supreme Court ruling in *United States* v. *Harriss* that it only applied to the paid efforts of people who spent more than half of their time directly contacting Congressmen (not their staff) on legislative matters. It took a scandal in the 1980s to push Congress into tightening up the law, when it came to light that a large corporation had hired numerous lobbyists to help win government contracts without reporting their work. In 1995, the Lobbying Disclosure Act was passed, which extended disclosure of information to all forms of lobbying, not just legislative, and included disclosing lobbying of Congressional staff. It also addressed concerns about the revolving door syndrome by requiring people who have worked in Congress to wait for a year before lobbying their former colleagues.

For critics of the system, such as Common Cause, Democracy 21 and Public Citizen, the Lobbying Disclosure Act does not go far enough. While there are restrictions on providing gifts and meals for Congressmen and their staff, these can be easily evaded. If a large corporation, for example, provides tickets to its box at a sports stadium, it will value the cost at a rate below the threshold value for gifts from lobbyists. In any event, the authorities in the House of

Representatives and the Senate do not invest significant resources into investigating violations of the law.

In 2006, there was a surge of support for further tightening lobbying regulations as a result of a series of media revelations of lobbying sliding into unethical conduct. In September 2004, an executive for the Boeing Aircaft Corporation, who had formerly worked for the Department of Defense, was convicted of conspiracy over a contract she had negotiated, worth $20 billion, knowing that she would be joining the firm. In November 2005, the Congressman for California's 50th District was forced to resign when it was revealed that he had accepted gifts to the value of $2.6 million from a defence contractor while he was on the Appropriations Defense Subcommittee. Then, in January 2006, top lobbyist Jack Abramoff was convicted of defrauding some of his clients. The investigations revealed that he had strengthened his relationship with politicians through expensive meals and golfing trips to Scotland.

Among the proposals to strengthen lobbying regulations are:

- A ban on members of Congress, or their staff, accepting gifts or meals from lobbyists.
- Disclosure of who paid for travel.
- A ban on becoming a lobbyist for two years (instead of one).
- Not allowing former members of Congress to use private areas within the building, such as the gym, which present opportunities for discreet lobbying.
- More detailed disclosure of lobbyist activities, especially expenditure.
- Heavier penalties for breaking the rules.

However, for all the concerns expressed about professional lobbyists, it is generally agreed that they can play a useful role in Congress. The legislative process can be, at times, quite chaotic, with a wide range of diverse interests holding up bills or adding amendments largely unrelated to their purpose (see Chapter 8). Professional lobbyists can be particularly helpful in:

- Negotiating deals between members of Congress to move legislation forward without losing its focus.

- Helping members of Congress to generate support for proposals through their links with important people, contributing articles to inluential newspapers and by mobilising the grassroots members of their organisations.
- Helping Congressional staff who may need guidance on the full implications of legislative proposals so that they can provide appropriate advice for their busy Congressmen. Lobbyists are usually experts in their field, making their advice particularly valuable.
- Helping members of Congress to promote causes that have not captured the public imagination, such as the campaign for a National Museum of African-American History and Culture outlined above.

In any meeting between congressional staff and a professional lobbyist, each side will ask the other what help they can offer. A healthy relationship can be of mutual benefit and help the process of government. An unhealthy relationship can lead to corruption. The challenge for political leaders, which they have yet to fully meet, is to find a way to inhibit unhealthy political relationships without damaging constructive relationships.

Influencing the Senate

Exclusive powers
Pressure groups that seek to influence the House of Representatives also seek to influence the Senate, for much the same reasons and using the similar methods. However, the Senate has some procedures and powers that are not shared by the House, which makes it particularly attractive to some pressure groups because:

- Groups opposed to the dominant party in Congress can still make an impact in the Senate because of filibusters, which enable a small group of Senators, or even a single Senator, to hold up the work of the entire chamber.
- Groups that take a particular interest in foreign-policy issues will be attracted by the Senate's exclusive power to ratify treaties.
- Groups that take a particular interest in the Federal courts will be attracted by the Senate's exclusive power to confirm presidential appointments.

The power of minority voices

Each state, regardless of size, has two members in the Senate, giving the smaller states disproportionate influence. This bias is reflected in the chamber's procedures, which make it possible for minorities to hold up its work. Between 2002 and 2005, urged on by liberal pressure groups such as People for the American Way, Democratic Senators blocked the appointment of ten of the President's Federal court nominees who they considered to be so conservative that they were 'outside the mainstream' of US politics (see Chapter 8 for more details).

Influencing presidential appointments

As Presidential appointments can be so significant, especially those to the Federal judiciary, where judges may interpret the Constitution 'during good behaviour' for a quarter of a century or more, pressure groups take a particular interest in the confirmation process. In 1986, a coalition of liberal pressure groups spent more than $15 million on a campaign, ultimately successful, to oppose the nomination of Robert Bork to the Supreme Court. On the other side of the political spectrum, in 2005 the nomination of Harriet Miers to the Supreme Court was withdrawn by President Bush in response to attacks from right-leaning activists challenging the depth of her conservative credentials.

Influencing foreign policy

Five categories of pressure groups take a particular interest in foreign policy:

- Business groups, who want an international trading climate that is to their advantage.
- Defence specialists.
- Sympathisers of countries seeking to improve or reinforce their diplomatic relationships with the USA.
- Campaign groups seeking US support for poorer nations.
- Environmentalists.

Business groups have, in recent years, been particularly concerned with the relationship between the USA and China. As China has grown as a world economic power, the USA has been torn between taking an aggressive stance towards China's export of cheap products (against which the USA cannot compete) and building a relationship with China that could turn the country's 1.3 billion people into customers for American businesses. Business groups have also been concerned with the potential costs of joining international efforts to reduce emissions of greenhouse gasses and played a significant role in lobbying the Senate to pass the Byrd-Hagel Resolution in 1988, which made clear that the Senate did not believe that such a treaty would be in the best interests of the USA. The treaty was, consequently, never sent to the Senate for ratification.

Defence specialists have also been concerned with China in recent years, which has dramatically increased its spending on weapons. They have also been at the heart of the debate on the most effective way to conduct the 'War on Terror', since the 9/11 attacks. Prominent in this debate has been a conservative think-tank, the Project for a New American Century, which argues that US security is best protected by promoting political and economic freedom abroad. These principles have played a major role in guiding policy, especially since the attacks of 9/11, and explain the decision to attack Iraq.

Prominent among groups concerned with the interests of other countries is the American Israel Public Affairs Committee, which campaigns for the USA to provide Israel with the support it needs to guarantee its security.

Under Republican leadership, anti-poverty groups and environmentalists have had a hard time being heard.

Influencing the White House

Funding the winner

Presidential elections are expensive: in 2004, George W. Bush's re-election campaign raised more than $367 million. Groups that made substantial contributions to this, coupled with successful campaigns to get their supporters to vote, have been well placed to gain access to the White House. This would include the National Federation of Independent Business, the National Rifle Association, the American Medical Association and the US Chamber of Commerce.

Supporting the President's agenda

The President and his senior advisors need a great deal of help if they are to implement their political goals. Many of their objectives depend on Congressional legislation for funding and authorisation. Sympathetic pressure groups can play an important role in persuading Congress to implement the President's agenda. Equally important, pressure groups can provide the White House with feedback on policies. With high levels of security, it is very difficult for the President, or high-profile members of his administration, to mingle with ordinary citizens, getting a feel for their views. Pressure groups can play a valuable role for the President in providing this kind of input. Groups with large grassroot memberships that play this role for President Bush include Focus on the Family, the Southern Baptist Convention, American Values and the Family Research Council.

The benefits of being an insider group

Groups that establish close ties with the White House may play a substantial role in formulating policy. They may be consulted on:

- Key appointments.
- Preparation of the state of the Union Address, in which the President outlines his political agenda for the coming year.
- Strategies for implementing policies.

Influencing the Federal bureaucracy

Building 'iron triangles'

For groups that may not have access to the White House, there is still an opportunity to influence the executive branch of government. Not all of the 3 million people employed in the Federal bureaucracy will be in sympathy with the priorities of the President and, frequently, different government departments are at odds with each other. The Defense Department, which looks towards military solutions to international disputes, has had rifts with the State Department, responsible for US diplomacy, under virtually every President. Similarly the Commerce Department, which favours minimal restrictions on business, has priorities which may clash with those of the Interior Department, which often places restrictions on businesses in order to protect America's forests, wildlife and waterways. Similarly, Congressional committees may be committed to programmes they have funded for years but which are at odds with presidential policy.

Where pressure groups can forge strong ties with departments, or senior civil servants, and with Congressional committees that fund government programmes, in combination they may create a wall of resistance to change that the White House may not be able to breach. When the three groups operate in this way it is known as an '**iron triangle**'.

Influencing the judiciary

Influencing how the Constitution in interpreted

In practice, the Constitution of the USA means whatever the Supreme Court says it means. Consequently, if a pressure group successfully influences the Court to adopt its views, it can effectively shape the framework within which all public policy operates. Such an outcome is desirable for all pressure groups, but is particularly important to minority groups who do not have sufficient representation in the elected branches of government to effect far-reaching change. There are a variety of strategies a pressure group can adopt to achieve this goal.

Influencing appointments to the Federal judiciary

Interest groups will adopt a range of strategies in support of nominees who share their political outlook, or opposition to nominees who may rule against their interests, including:

- Compiling detailed dossiers on the judgements (and private lives) of the nominee.
- Ensuring that their members know the group's views on the nominee and encouraging them to write to their representatives in Congress.
- Mounting demonstrations during the confirmation hearings.
- Funding newspaper and TV advertisements explaining why the nominee should/should not be confirmed.
- For opponents, briefing their allies in the Senate on the most damaging questions to ask the nominee.

- For supporters, coaching the nominee on how to answer difficult questions.

In the case of high-profile appointments, especially to the Supreme Court, analysis of how much impact the rival campaigns are having will dominate news programmes between the announcement of the nomination and the completion of the confirmation process, often several months.

Bringing test cases to court

Some pressure groups specialise in providing the highest standard of legal assistance in court cases that have the potential to alter the existing interpretation of the Constitution. One example of this is the NAACP Legal Defense Fund, which, in 1954, won the case of *Brown v. Board of Education, Topeka, Kansas*. This case, which outlawed racial segregation, may have had a greater impact on US society than any other pressure-group initiative in the twentieth century. The organisation has continued to fund Civil Rights cases, including those that uphold the constitutional right to implement Affirmative Action programmes.

Meanwhile, fighting to have Affirmative Action declared unconstitutional is the Center for Individual Rights, a pressure group dedicated exclusively to 'aggressively litigate and publicize a handful of carefully selected cases that advance the right of individuals to govern themselves according to the natural exercise of their own reason'. The Center provided the funding and legal expertise to bring the case of *Grutter* v. *Bollinger* to the Supreme Court in 2003, arguing that the Affirmative Action programme of the University of Michigan Law School was unconstitutional. The Court ruled against the Center but the fight will continue.

Submitting amicus briefs

Pressure groups may also make contributions to cases in which they do not play a direct role but which impact on issues that concern them. These contributions are called amicus curiae briefs, meaning 'friends of the court', and are a formal mechanism for courts to understand the views of people and groups beyond those directly involved in the case. Where a decision may have the effect of reinterpreting the

Constitution, wider input is considered appropriate. In the *Grutter* v. *Bollinger* case, more than 350 amicus briefs were submitted and the verdict mentioned their influence on the Court's decision. Other notable recent cases attracting large numbers of amicus briefs include *Lawrence* v. *Texas* (2003), which struck down laws that discriminate against gay men and lesbians, and *Hamdi* v. *Rumsfeld* (2004), which ruled that detainees arrested during the US invasion of Afghanistan at the Guantanamo Bay detention centre and held were entitled to legal representation.

Influencing the climate of legal opinion
The legal experts working for groups that bring test cases and submit amicus briefs often submit articles to scholarly legal journals arguing in favour of the causes they support. These journals, read by judges as well as other lawyers, play a role in shaping the climate of legal opinion and can be helpful to the legal campaigns mounted by their pressure groups.

The impact of pressure groups on the US political system

A continuing debate
As with other parts of the US political system, pressure groups are subject to debate about whether they serve to diffuse power, in a manner consistent with the designs of the Founding Fathers, or whether they tend to concentrate power. For decades, political scientists have debated with concern the impact of private groups, focusing in the nineteenth century on the activities of large companies that used their wealth to force smaller companies to sell up or go out of business. This led to the passing of anti-trust legislation, named after its sponsor, Senator Sherman, who argued, 'If we will not endure a king as a political power we should not endure a king over the production, transportation, and sale of any of the necessaries of life.' In modern times, the focus has transferred to pressure groups, with legislation being passed relating to lobbying and campaign finance aimed at ensuring that they did not become the 'kings' of political influence. How far have these measures succeeded?

A dangerous power elite?

On one side of the argument, it is claimed that efforts to ensure a balance of political power between all sections of society have been no more effective than efforts to ensure that major companies do not dominate the marketplace. Just as Microsoft dominates the software market, without being a monopoly, so a powerful, wealthy elite dominates political access without monopolising it.

According to this view, the wide range of opportunities to influence people in power can only be effectively exploited by pressure groups that have large memberships, effective lobbyists, effective lawyers and considerable wealth. Those most able to achieve all of these goals tend to be those who already dominate society in terms of group numbers or wealth. The less wealthy and minorities, by contrast, tend to lack the organisation, political connections and voting power to make themselves heard in the corridors of power. Consequently, the US political landscape, designed to promote maximum accountability of politicians, has the opposite effect, and provides a system that can be used by the already wealthy and powerful to entrench their privileges.

Critics of the current balance of power in the USA point to the 'K Street Project' and its role in allowing allies of the Republican Party to shape the work of government. The modern Republican Party has close links with a network of conservative groups including think-tanks, TV and radio stations, magazines, newspapers, campaign groups and policy strategists who work together to advance their political agenda. In 1995, after the party had taken control of the House of Representative, the majority whip launched a project (named after the street where the largest lobbying firms have their headquarters) to pressure Washington lobbying firms to hire Republicans in top positions, in return for access to influential officials. How can a system that operates in this way be seen as an open democracy, easily accessible to all, ask critics.

Healthy pluralism

On the other side of the argument, it is claimed that, even if it appears that one section of society is dominant, US society is so open, with multiple opportunities for everyone to be heard, that all groups may make a contribution to shaping their society.

According to this view, some of the most significant changes in recent times have been to the benefit of the kind of minority groups that elitist theorists argue are largely excluded from the corridors of power. For example, *Brown* v. *Board of Education* transformed the South, *Roe* v. *Wade* meant that vulnerable women no longer had to resort to back-street abortions, *Lawrence* v. *Texas* meant that laws discriminating against gays were declared unconstitutional, and, in 2004, gay marriage was permitted in Massachusetts. Political scientists who believe that the USA provides a healthy pluralist political system argue that none of these advances would have been possible if a small, wealthy, white, conservative elite controlled all meaningful power.

Furthermore, they claim, if the country goes through a period in which barriers develop to full participation, history demonstrates that these will be addressed through regulation. Hence the passage of the Federal Election Campaigns Acts (FECA) in the 1970s, when questionable relationships between the President and his donors were revealed by the Watergate scandal, and the passage of the Bipartisan Campaign Reform Act of 2002, when it was clear that FECA was proving ineffective (see Chapter 5 for more details). Similarly, when the Federal Regulation of Lobbying Act (1946) proved ineffective, it was replaced with the Lobbying Disclosure Act in 1995. Pressure groups, therefore, far from shaping the political landscape are forced to respond to it.

For those who believe that pressure groups enhance US democracy, their constructive contributions are emphasised, including:

- Proposing innovative policies.
- Providing expertise.
- Mobilising citizens who may not otherwise be aware of decisions that affect them.
- Complementing political parties in two ways: during periods when parties have lacked a coherent set of policies, pressure groups have taken the lead in driving the political agenda; during periods when parties have had a package of policies with a clear ideological direction, pressure groups have provided funds and volunteers to promote those policies, especially at elections.

Box 7.1 Comparing US and UK pressure groups

Multiple access points

Pressure groups in any liberal democracy aim to advance their agendas using whatever opportunities are afforded to them by the political system within which they operate. In the past, the most notable contrast between pressure groups in the USA and UK was the range of political institutions (access points) that could be influenced. At local, state and Federal levels, there are an abundance of access points in the USA, while in Britain most significant power has traditionally rested with the government at Westminster.

In recent decades, however, this contrast has become less marked. Since 1973, when the UK joined the European Union, a growing proportion of laws governing British society have been drafted by the European Commission in Brussels. Although these have to approved by the Council of Ministers, and may be amended, in general most of the initial proposals pass into law. This makes an effective European lobbying strategy increasingly important to pressure groups. Then, following devolution to Scotland and Wales in 1997, key decisions for those countries have been taken in Edinburgh and Wales but have had implications for the whole of the UK by setting a policy benchmark on issues such as smoking in public places.

Exploiting access points

Pressure groups in the UK have a long history of designing their strategies around the need to influence one key access point where the overwhelming majority of key decisions are made – the central government, based in Westminster. Even attempting to influence the legislature is unlikely to prove effective, for once a decision has been taken and announced as government policy, there is relatively little likelihood of it being challenged in Parliament. This is because the governing party almost always enjoys a parliamentary majority and MPs usually support their party. If a pressure group can influence policy before an announcement is made, it is almost certain that they will succeed in changing the law. The most effective pressure, therefore, is exerted by insider groups who enjoy the closest working relationships with ministers and senior civil servants, often because they went to the same elite school and/or university. Even outsider pressure groups, who do not enjoy this kind of access, tailor their strategies to force the government to respond to their agenda by creating a groundswell of public support.

Influencing the other, newer, access points requires different strategies. In the European Union, pressure is best exerted through associations of pressure groups from across Europe. The National Farmers Union, for example, is a member of the Committee of Professional Agricultural Organisations. Achieving objectives through these associations requires a willingness to compromise with many different interests. In continental Europe, where there is a political culture of coalition government, this approach is familiar; in Britain, which has a winner-takes-all political culture, this approach is alien and, coupled with a sceptical attitude towards the EU, has limited the influence British pressure groups have had on EU policy-making.

There is also little evidence that pressure groups have adapted to the opportunities arising from the establishment of devolved assemblies, especially the Scottish Parliament, which has law-making powers. Arrangements have been made to allow interested individuals and groups to be consulted about proposed legislation before it becomes a bill. This pre-legislative consultation is designed to be open and participatory, allowing access to the decision-making process. National pressure groups clearly have an interest in demonstrating to politicians at Westminster that successful policies in Scotland can be applied to the whole of Britain (as US pressure groups do with policy at state level), but this point does not appear to have been widely grasped. In this respect, UK pressure groups appear to be less adaptable than those in the USA, which have shown a remarkable ability to respond to changing circumstances (see Chapter 5).

In the USA there are no access points where a pressure group can have as dramatic an impact as insider groups do in the UK. Even presidential initiatives, influenced by those groups with close ties to the White House, rarely get through Congress without substantial amendments. This means that US groups tend to adopt one of two strategies to make the most of the access points available to them: specialising in making a major impact on one access point, or becoming large enough to make an impact on all of them.

Smaller specialist pressure groups may have a dramatic impact on society. As outlined above, in winning the case of *Brown* v. *Board of Education*, the NAACP Legal Defense Fund may have done more to reshape US society than any other single pressure-group initiative in modern times.

Larger pressure groups can become prominent participants in the political process, recruiting millions of members, building up huge funds, employing large teams of well-paid lobbyists in Washington DC and in state capitals, producing publications and actively marketing their message. It is this kind of prominence that creates the impression that they wield a disproportionate amount of influence in US politics and suggests that they are much more effective than their British counterparts. However, pressure-group effectiveness should be measured by achievement of goals, rather than size and visibility, and there is a case for arguing that insider groups in the UK and small specialist groups in the USA are every bit as effective as the largest US pressure groups.

✔ What you should have learnt from reading this chapter

- There are a number of parallels between pressure groups and political parties. In both cases, the Founding Fathers were extremely suspicious of them, fearing that they would be divisive and promote the interests of their supporters at the expense of the wider community.

- In both cases, these concerns appeared not to be well-founded for many decades. Pressure groups often brought together people of different classes and races in shared community-building activities, strengthening social bonds and educating citizens on democratic principles through the running of meetings. At a national level, pressure groups have historically developed links with both of the main parties.

- Pressure groups in the USA have always been effective at exploiting the opportunities presented by the political system, using different strategies to influence different access points.

- With the growth of two ideological parties, pressure groups have adapted, aligning themselves with the party most sympathetic to their agendas. The result is that, belatedly, they have developed into precisely the kind of 'factions' that the Founding Fathers feared.

🔎 Glossary of key terms

Access points Political institutions that decide public policy and how resources should be allocated.
Iron triangle A strong bond between a pressure group, government department and Congressional committee, all with shared political goals.
Lobbyists People with extensive political contacts who work full-time on

persuading decision-makers to support the interests of the groups for which they work.

Pluralism A political system in which a wide range of groups have an opportunity to make a significant impact on the political decision-making process.

Revolving door syndrome A tendency for people leaving elected office, or employment with a politician, to then work for a pressure group, using their knowledge and contacts to influence their former colleagues.

Likely examination questions

Issues that examiners may expect students to be able to effectively analyse include:

- Why, how and with what effectiveness pressure groups access specific points in the political system
- Understanding of methods used by pressure groups, such as professional lobbying
- The impact of pressure groups on the democratic system
- The effectiveness of legislation to limit the influence of pressure groups

Thus, examples of the kind of questions that could be asked include:
How important are professional lobbyists?
What tactics do US pressure groups use, and why are some groups more successful than others?

Where the question compares the US system with Britain's, the main issue to consider is the comparative effectiveness of pressure groups in the two countries.

Thus, an example of the kind of question that could be asked is:
'US pressure groups are more powerful than UK pressure groups.' Discuss.

Helpful websites

Pressure groups with a liberal political agenda:

www.naacp.org – website of the National Association for the Advancement of Coloured People, a leading African-American Civil Rights group.

www.now.org – website of the National Organisation of Women, which campaigns to bring about equality for all women.

www.aflcio.org – website of the AFL-CIO, the umbrella organisation for trade unions in the USA.

Pressure groups with a conservative agenda:

www.nra.org – website of the National Rifle Association, which campaigns against gun control.

www.cc.org – website of the Christian Coalition, which provides a vehicle for people of faith to be actively involved in shaping government policy.

www.nfib.com – website of the National Federation of Independent Businesses, which represents the interests of small companies.

 ## Suggestions for further reading

For an examination of the role of pressure groups in US society, arguing that they no longer play their traditional role at the heart of US life and that the foundations of society are threatened as a result, read *Bowling Alone* by Robert Putnam, available from Amazon.com.

For an alternative view, arguing that pressure groups have changed, but still play a valuable role in US society, read *Civic Engagement in American Democracy* by Theda Skocpol, which can also be purchased from Amazon.com, or any chapters of interest can be downloaded from the website of the publishers, the Brookings Insitution, at www.brookings.nap.edu.

PART III: TESTING THE LIMITS OF FEDERAL POWER – THE LEGISLATURE AND THE EXECUTIVE

Congress

Contents

Overview

On 8 April 2004, the National Security Advisor, Condoleezza Rice, appeared before the 9/11 Commission and was questioned about allegations that the Bush administration had ignored warnings about al Qaeda leading up to the 9/11 attacks. Specifically, she was pressed about the title of a confidential memo sent to the President a month before the attacks. 'I believe the title was "Bin Laden determined to attack inside the United States",' Ms Rice said.

The White House had objected to the creation of the Commission, resisted access to documents and witnesses and initially refused to allow Ms Rice to testify, arguing that historically national security advisors and presidential staff have not had to appear before Congress.

It was this kind of struggle between the three branches of government, with each challenging the others over the limits of their power, that the Founding Fathers envisaged when they designed a system of checks and balances to ensure that no individual or faction became too powerful.

In examining the work of Congress, this chapter will consider relationships between the legislature and the other branches of government and evaluate how well it fulfils its Constitutional roles.

Key issues to be covered in this chapter

- How Congress implements its constitutional responsibilities to limit the powers of the other two branches of the Federal government
- How Congress fulfils its roles in the governing of the USA
- The extent to which the operation of Congress matches the vision of the Founding Fathers

Congress and the Constitution

The most important branch of government

Had the Founding Fathers witnessed the dispute between Congress and the White House over the appearance of Condoleezza Rice before the 9/11 Commission, they may well have been pleased with the outcome. They may, however, have been disappointed that it was an example of Congress responding to presidential initiatives rather than the other way around.

After the USA gained its independence from Britain, with its King who they saw as largely unaccountable, the Founding Fathers were determined to design a system that would stop one person from holding too much power. One of the ways this was achieved was by taking almost all law-making responsibilities away from the executive branch of government and putting it into the hands of the legislative branch. This was expected to make Congress the most important and powerful branch of government, which is why its powers and responsibilities are outlined in the first article of the Constitution.

Limiting Congressional power

However, even in the hands of a group of people, rather than one individual, power can be abused and the Constitution included a range of restrictions on the power of Congress, including:

- Dividing power between two chambers (creating a bicameral legislature) that would have to agree on the precise wording of any bills before they could become law.
- Making the members of the lower chamber, the House of Representatives, accountable to 'the people' through elections held every two years. The voters (who did not include women, Native Americans of African-Americans) would be able to replace any representative who was abusing his power.
- Giving the power to deal with financial issues to the House of Representatives, who would face electoral defeat within two years if they imposed high taxes or did not use the people's money wisely.
- Giving states the power to each appoint two members of the upper chamber, the Senate, so that they could look after the interests of their state on equal terms regardless of their size or population.

- Giving Senators a six-year term of office, with one-third of them replaced every two years. Anticipating an event like 9/11, when a tide of emotion swept the country, the Founding Fathers set up a system that prevented one political group from gaining complete control of Congress.
- Giving Congress specific responsibilities, which were laid out in Article I, Section 8 of the Constitution. These powers, called **enumerated powers** because they are numbered from 1 to 18, can be categorised as five economic powers (raising taxes, borrowing money and so on), seven defence powers (declare war, provide a navy and so on) and six miscellaneous powers (naturalising citizens, establishing post offices and so on). The final enumerated power is known as the **'elastic clause'**, which gives Congress the right to make all 'necessary and proper' laws to carry out its responsibilities. It is called the 'elastic clause' because it allows Congress to stretch its powers to respond to situations the Founding Fathers could never have anticipated.
- To ensure that this final power was not abused, the Constitution gave the President the right to veto laws. Congress would be able to override a veto with a two-thirds majority, a very difficult hurdle to clear.
- The Constitution also limited the powers of Congress by laying down, in Section 9, specific restrictions on laws that could be passed. For example, no law can be passed that punishes a person without a jury trial, Congress may not pass laws favouring one state or region over another, and they were not allowed to place restrictions on the slave trade until 1808.

Constitutional amendments affecting Congress
This balance of powers and restraints has remained largely unchanged since the Constitution was ratified in June 1788. Only three significant changes have occurred since, namely:

1. The 17th Amendment, passed in 1913, so that Senators were directly elected by the people instead of by state legislatures.
2. The number of representatives in the House was set at 435 in 1929.

3. The 20th Amendment, passed in 1933, laid down that Congress would start its new session on January 3rd, after each Congressional election.

However, the use that Congress has made of its powers, and its relationships with the other branches of government, has changed substantially over the past two hundred years.

Congress and the presidency

Division of responsibilities

Considering the weight that the Founding Fathers placed on limiting the power of the executive branch, the role of scrutinising the presidency could be considered the most significant activity undertaken by Congress.

It is not surprising, therefore, that some of the scrutinising mechanisms available to Congress tend to attract nationwide publicity and controversy. This applies particularly to forms of scrutiny that are the constitutional responsibility of the Senate: **confirmation** of presidential appointments and ratification of treaties. This also applies to the form of scrutiny that is the constitutional responsibility of the House of Representatives: analysing the budget. However, other forms of day-to-day scrutiny, shared by both chambers, tends to go largely unnoticed.

Scrutinising presidential appointments

Once the President takes office, after winning an election, one of his first constitutional responsibilities is to appoint people to senior positions. These include the most important positions in the government departments and ambassadors. Over the following four years, until the next election, vacancies may arise in other important areas of government, such as judgeships on the Federal courts and the highest ranks of the armed forces, and the President is also responsible for appointing their replacements.

In each case, the Senate is constitutionally responsible for giving 'advice and consent' on each appointment. In practice, this means investigating the record of each person nominated by the President, holding hearings that give Senators an opportunity to question the candidate and anyone else who has a strong view on the appointment, and then taking a vote. If a majority of Senators vote in favour of the nominee, he/she is able to take up the position. If not, the President must choose someone else, who then has to go through the same process.

In the vast majority of cases, this process is completed without any controversy, although there are so many positions to be filled that it may take many months before an incoming President has a full team in place. Indeed, many hearings consist mainly of the Senators expressing their confidence that the nominee is supremely qualified to do an outstanding job (many people entering public service are giving up a better-paid job in the private sector) and congratulating them on their confirmation, even before a vote is taken. In a minority of high-profile cases, however, the confirmation process can be bitter and divisive:

- President Bush Snr had his first nomination for the post of Defense Secretary rejected, in 1989, when Senate investigations revealed evidence of womanising and excessive drinking.
- Similarly, in 1993, President Clinton had his first two nominations for the post of Attorney General rejected by the Senate, when it was controlled by his own party. It emerged in both cases that they had failed to pay social security taxes for domestic staff working for them. Cases like these are embarrassing for the President and unhelpful to his reputation, but it is political battles over appointments that do most to put the confirmation process into the headlines.
- In 1987, the Senate refused to confirm Robert Bork, a judge with extremely right-wing views who had been nominated to the Supreme Court by President Reagan. He failed to convince the Senators that he would protect the rights that vulnerable groups in society had won over the previous thirty years. Liberals across the USA were elated by his defeat while conservatives remain resentful that someone who shares their views was blocked from taking up a highly influential position.
- Four years later, in 1991, the public was transfixed by live television coverage of the confirmation hearings of Clarence Thomas, who was accused of sexual harassment. Added to this was the

suggestion that he harboured extreme right-wing views and was inadequately qualified to sit on the Supreme Court. Eventually, he was confirmed by a vote of 52–48, the narrowest margin of victory in the twentieth century.

- Between 2002 and 2005, since the election of George W. Bush, ten of his more controversial nominees to Federal courts were blocked by the minority Democratic Party in the Senate. They made use of a procedure, exclusive to the Senate, that allows a minority to stop a vote being called on anything that they feel very strongly about. This is called a **filibuster.** This blocking mechanism can only be overcome if sixty Senators vote to end the filibuster.

The ill-feeling generated by the Democrats' use of this tactic, which is traditionally saved for controversial legislation, was so intense that the majority Republican Party threatened to change the rules of the Senate to remove the right to filibuster confirmation hearings.

As these examples demonstrate, a majority of confirmation battles are over judicial appointments. As judges are appointed 'during good behaviour' until they retire, the President's choices can provide a vehicle through which they can use their power to influence policy for many years after leaving office. However, political disputes can also erupt over other appointments: after winning re-election in 2004, President Bush Jnr failed to get his nominee for the post of US Ambassador to the United Nations (UN), John Bolton, confirmed. Partly this was due to reports that he had a record of bullying staff he was responsible for, but mainly it was due to his reported hostility to the UN, which, it was argued, would hamper his diplomatic efforts when negotiating with other ambassadors.

In the case of John Bolton and one of the filibustered judges, Charles Pickering, the President used a device to get around the Senate's refusal to confirm his nominee. In both cases, he made recess appointments. Article II, Section 2 of the US Constitution says, 'The President shall have Power to fill up all Vacancies that may happen during the Recess of the Senate, by granting Commissions which shall expire at the End of their next Session.' This clause, written before the invention of modern transport systems, addressed the difficulties faced by Presidents in filling vacancies when the next meeting of the Senate could be weeks away. In the modern era it is used simply as a loophole.

The commission, or appointment, must be approved by the Senate by the end of the next session, or the position becomes vacant again. Charles Pickering's appointment to the Fifth Circuit Court of Appeals, in January 2004, expired when the next Congress convened one year later, at which point he withdrew from the process and retired. John Bolton's recess appointment enabled him to represent his country at the UN until January 2007, when he also resigned, accepting that he would not be confirmed by the Democrat-controlled Senate when it convened in January 2007.

Organisation of the executive branch
In addition to facing scrutiny over who can be appointed to key positions, Presidents are restricted in how they organise the government departments they control. It is Congress that is responsible for:

- Setting up Executive Departments, such as the Department of Defense, which have primary responsibility for running the government.
- Setting up Executive Agencies, such as the Federal Reserve Board, which are responsible for managing crucial areas of policy and have a greater degree of independence from the President than Executive Departments.
- Setting up Independent Regulatory Commissions, such as the Federal Elections Commission, which have an even greater degree of independence.

The organisation of these bodies can only be altered by an Act of Congress, giving the President extremely limited flexibility. When President Carter, for example, tried to transfer education programmes for ex-servicemen from the Veterans Administration to the Education Department, he was unable to gain sufficient support in Congress to make the change.

Presidents have more control over the Executive Office of the President (EOP), which they can reorganise whenever they choose. It was no surprise, therefore, that when it was proposed to set up an agency for Homeland Security after the attacks of 9/11, the President wanted it to be established as a part of the EOP. However, Congress insisted on establishing a new Executive Department, accountable to itself.

Scrutinising treaties

As each presidency unfolds, agreements will be concluded with other nations. The President is responsible for diplomatic negotiations but once a formal agreement (or treaty) is reached, it must receive the support of two-thirds – 67 votes – of the Senate. If the treaty receives the necessary level of support, sometimes with amendments, the President ratifies it and it becomes law. If the Senate and President cannot agree, however, the treaty does not come into effect.

When the Versailles Treaty, formally ending the First World War, was negotiated in 1919, it was largely based on proposals from President Wilson. Yet, when it was considered by the Senate it did not have the level of support it needed and the USA never ratified it. Since then, most treaties negotiated by US Presidents have gained the support of the Senate. A significant minority, however, have not:

- In 1979, President Carter negotiated the second Strategic Arms Limitation Treaty (SALT II) with the Soviet Union, which limited the manufacture of large nuclear missiles. Six months after the treaty was signed, but before the Senate had completed its consideration of the agreement, the Soviet Union invaded Afghanistan, relations between the two countries rapidly deteriorated and the treaty was never ratified. Despite this, both sides honoured the terms of the agreement.
- In 1996, President Clinton negotiated the Comprehensive Test Ban Treaty (CTBT), which banned testing of nuclear weapons as a way of stopping countries that did not already have such devices from being able to acquire them and test their effectiveness. The Senate did not vote on the treaty until 1999, as the President sought to build support for it, but when they did vote it fell far short of the two-thirds majority needed. Opponents argued that it risked eroding the USA's lead in nuclear weapons technology and would be impossible to monitor.

- In 1998, the Clinton administration signed the Kyoto Protocol, an international treaty to reduce greenhouse gas emissions and thereby reduce global warming. Even before the Kyoto Protocol was negotiated, however, the US Senate unanimously passed by a 95–0 vote the Byrd-Hagel Resolution, which made clear that the Senate did not believe that such a treaty would be in the best interests of the USA. Consequently, the treaty was never put to the Senate for its agreement.

As with presidential appointments, however, there is a loophole for Presidents who realise at an early stage that there is insufficient support in the Senate for a treaty being negotiated. An executive agreement can be signed between the President and a foreign head of state. These do not require the approval of the Senate, but the Supreme Court ruled in 1937, in *United States* v. *Belmont*, that such agreements have the same status in international law as a treaty. The United States is currently a party to nearly 900 treaties and more than 5,000 executive agreements.

Congress attempted to close this loophole in 1972, with the passage of the Case-Zablocki Act, which required the President to report on executive agreements within sixty days of negotiating them. The ability of Congress to do anything about them, however, was limited by a 1983 Supreme Court decision in *INS* v. *Chadha*, which ruled that the Act breached separation of powers.

Scrutinising presidential use of the armed forces
As well as negotiating with other nations, most Presidents since World War II have deployed US armed forces. Among the countries in which US troops have seen action over the past sixty years are:

- Korea
- Vietnam
- Grenada
- Libya
- Lebanon
- Panama
- Iraq
- Somalia

- Haiti
- Bosnia Herzegovina
- Kosovo
- Kuwait
- Afghanistan

Under the Constitution, only Congress can declare war. In none of these cases, however, was war declared. The President deployed America's armed forces in his capacity as Commander-in-Chief. That this could be done in Vietnam, in a conflict lasting over ten years, demonstrated that this was another area in which the President appeared able to avoid constitutional checks and balances. In 1973, at the end of the Vietnam War, the War Powers Act was passed to reassert Congressional control over armed conflict. It required the President to consult Congress whenever possible before using the armed forces and, in every case, to report to Congress within forty-eight hours of introducing troops to an area of conflict. Thereafter, if Congress does not declare war within sixty days, the troops have to be withdrawn. In practice, though, Congress has proved reluctant to exercise this right to challenge the President's actions for fear that it may undermine morale among the armed forces or signal division to an enemy.

Scrutinising presidential legislative proposals

These kinds of loopholes are not evident in domestic policy. Each January, usually around the 20th, the President makes his State of the Union Address, outlining the challenges facing the country and his policy proposals for dealing with them. Over the following months, he will put forward legislative proposals to change Federal laws to meet his objectives. The President cannot, however, introduce bills into Congress. He requires sympathetic members of the House of Representatives and of the Senate to introduce his bills into the two chambers.

The process that the bills then go through is outlined in detail below. Unlike the majority of bills, it is a convention that the President's proposals will not be blocked as they make their way though Congress. In common with all bills, however, they may be amended during their passage. Indeed, presidential proposals are more likely than most to be amended *because* they are virtually guaranteed to clear the many hurdles all bills face and therefore represent a prime opportunity to attach amendments that will benefit districts of individual Congressmen and Senators. (Members of the House of Representatives are known, confusingly, as Congressmen/Congresswomen; members of the Senate are known as Senators.)

By the time the President's proposals return to him, to be signed into law, they will certainly have been substantially changed and may have been transformed so dramatically that he finds himself forced to veto them. This situation can arise even when the two chambers of Congress are controlled by the same political party as the President, as demonstrated below by the case study of the Highways Bill.

Overriding vetoes

A bill does not become law unless it is signed by the President. If he finds a bill unacceptable, there are a number of responses at his disposal (see below). One option is to veto it, which is done by refusing to sign the bill and returning it to Congress with an explanation of his objections.

The bill will become law, however, if two-thirds of both chambers vote to override the veto. This is a very challenging hurdle to clear. During his two terms as President, Bill Clinton vetoed thirty-six bills and had his veto overridden just twice. In his first six years in office, despite making many threats, President George W. Bush only used the veto once and was not overturned.

Scrutinising presidential budgetary proposals

On the first Monday in February, the President follows up his State of the Union Address by sending up a detailed budget to Congress, outlining the costs of his proposals and precisely how he would like to see the Federal taxes for that year spent.

Article I, Section 7 of the Constitution makes the House of Representatives responsible for scrutinising 'all bills for raising revenue' first, although the Senate may do so later. The House and Senate both have budget committees that spend the next couple of months developing their own budget proposals, and amendments can be offered at each stage of the budget's passage through Congress.

The result is that most budgets become 'Christmas tree' bills, covered with presents for the voters of the 435 districts of the USA.

Congress does not only add to the President's proposals. Where there is strong disagreement, Congress may also cut proposals. Thus, in 2003, when President George W. Bush proposed tax cuts of $550 billion, members of his own party who were concerned about the growing budget deficit managed to reduce the amount in the final package to $350 billion.

Congressional investigations

When a major issue arises that suggests that the executive branch has been corrupt or incompetent, any Congressional committee may mount an investigation. Often, if the issue has attracted a great deal of media attention, a number of committees may mount simultaneous investigations.

The most famous example of Congress investigating corruption in the executive branch in modern times was the Watergate hearings, looking into a complex web of political scandals between 1972 and 1974 that ultimately led to the resignation of President Richard Nixon. Other similar investigations, such as the Iran-Contra hearings in 1987, which examined illegal sales of arms to Iran to raise funds for anti-government forces in Nicaragua, made much less impact.

In 1994, Congress added to its armoury, passing the **Independent Counsel** Law, which gives the House or Senate judiciary committees the right to require the Justice Department to investigate claims of criminal behaviour by senior members of the executive. This law has proved controversial because, although it is designed to effectively investigate abuse of power, there are no limits to the Independent Counsel's powers of investigation. In 1994, Kenneth Starr was appointed Independent Counsel to investigate investments made by President Clinton some years earlier. By 1998, Starr had widened his investigations to include allegations of sexual misconduct by the President, leading to impeachment proceedings (see below).

After Hurricane Katrina devastated the city of New Orleans, with heavy loss of life, in 2005, both the House of Representatives and the Senate investigated why the authorities failed to effectively protect the city's mainly African-American residents. No fewer than nine committees investigated the disaster and produced reports and recommendations:

- Senate Homeland Security and Government Affairs Committee
- Senate Environment and Public Works Committee
- Senate Commerce, Science, and Transportation Committee
- House Select Committee on Hurricane Katrina
- House Transportation and Infrastructure Committee
- House Energy and Commerce Committee
- House Science Committee
- House Government Reform Committee
- Government Accountability Office

Note that among these committees was one set up specifically for the purpose of investigating the consequences of the hurricane (highlighted). These are known as **select committees**. They study one specific issue and report their findings to the House of Representatives or the Senate.

Impeachment
In the event of there being evidence of wrongdoing by a senior member of the executive branch, or judicial branch, **impeachment** proceedings may begin.

If it is presented with evidence of 'Treason, Bribery or other High crimes and Misdemeanours' (Article II, Section 4 of the Constitution), it is the exclusive responsibility of the House of Representative to bring articles of impeachment (charges) against the accused person. These charges must have the support of a majority of Congressmen.

If a vote passes in the House, a trial takes place in the Senate. If the proceedings involve the President, then the Chief Justice of the Supreme Court acts as the judge. The House of Representatives, having bought the charges, acts as the prosecution. The accused person will have a team of defence lawyers. The Senate acts as the jury. If two-thirds (sixty-seven) of the Senate votes against the defendant, a guilty verdict is delivered and the person is removed from office.

As a result of the investigations carried out by Independent Counsel Kenneth Starr in December 1988, the House of Representatives charged (impeached) President Clinton with two counts of lying under oath (perjury) and obstructing justice. At the end of the trial, the Senate voted 55–45 in the President's favour on the perjury charge and 50–50 on the obstruction of justice charge, leading to his acquittal.

Two other Presidents have had impeachment proceedings brought against them. In 1868, President Andrew Johnson was acquitted by just one vote and in 1974 President Richard Nixon resigned before the trial could take place.

This form of scrutiny is, arguably, the most dramatic action that Congress can take against a President. It is also, however, the least frequently used and when considering its importance this should be taken into account. Its significance is greater in relation to the judiciary, as a number of judges have been successfully impeached.

Congress and the judiciary

Limited range of checks

As the Constitution provided the judicial branch with few constitutional powers, it faces few constitutional checks. However, it subsequently acquired the power of judicial review, enabling it to declare laws unconstitutional. Congress has developed two responses to the use of this power.

Modifying laws

When the Supreme Court declares a law unconstitutional, it gives detailed reasons for its decisions. Congress, often with the help of constitutional experts, may closely examine the Justices' opinions and then make minor, technical adjustments to their legislation to address the objections of the Court without significantly altering the purpose of the law.

In 2000, for example, the Supreme Court struck down a Nebraska law banning a particular type of abortion, 'partial birth abortion', on the grounds that the law did not make an exception for the procedure to take place if the mother's health was at risk. In 2003, Congress passed a partial birth abortion law that was almost identical to the Nebraska law. However, taking note of the Supreme Court's earlier ruling, it included a clause stating that this type of abortion was never medically essential therefore a health exception was not needed. This, inevitably became the subject of further legal challenges.

Initiating constitutional amendments

Supreme Court decisions can be overruled by a constitutional amendment. This has happened on two occasions.

In 1795, the 11th Amendment was passed in response to the Supreme Court's ruling in *Chisolm* v. *Georgia* that citizens could bring law suits against a state. There was a widespread view at the time that this could result in the states losing authority.

In 1913, the 16th Amendment was passed in response to a ruling that the Federal government did not have the constitutional right to levy income tax.

Impeachment

As with the executive branch, Congress has the right to remove judges from office for wrongdoing. Constitutionally, this power may not be used because a majority in Congress disagree with judicial decisions but there have been attempts to use it in this way. There were repeated calls, especially from the South, for Chief Justice Earl Warren to be impeached for exceeding his constitutional powers, after the ruling banning racial segregation. The only Supreme Court Justice to face an impeachment trial was Samuel Chase, who was acquitted in 1805. The unsuccessful proceedings were a blatant attempt by the President's party to intimidate their political opponents.

Eleven other Federal judges have been impeached, of which seven have been found guilty and removed from office. The most recent was Walter Nixon of the US District Court for Mississippi, who was removed from office in 1989 for a range of offences including lying to a grand jury.

Legislating: the process of passing laws

Limited government

The process for passing laws in Congress makes it much easier for initiatives to be blocked than for them to pass. Each year, as many as 10,000 bills may be introduced but often fewer than 500 become law.

Such a low rate of success could be seen as a sign of ineffectiveness. It could also be seen, however, as consistent with the constitutional values of limited government. The great fear of the Founding Fathers was that the national government would grow in power and, ultimately, become oppressive. Each law passed has the potential to add to the powers of those who pass and administer them, eventually realising the Founding Fathers' worst nightmares. Fewer laws ought to limit the growth and scope of government, reducing the risk of intrusion into people's lives. Furthermore, if only a few, essential, laws are passed, then the quality of the legislation ought to be high.

Critics of Congress, however, argue that the legislative process often has the opposite effect, with legislation that enhances the likelihood of being re-elected being prioritised over laws that would be of greatest value to the nation.

Types of laws

Legislative proposals introduced into Congress fall into one of five categories. The first two are proposed without any expectation that they will become law, but the other three types have a higher likelihood of passing:

1. Those that demonstrate the commitment of a member of Congress (usually to the voters) to a policy that has no realistic chance of being adopted. Often this serves to put on record the member's hard work for his/her district.
2. Those that serve to educate the public on an important area of public policy. Often these are sponsored by pressure groups, seeking to influence the public agenda. For example, the 'End Racial Profiling Bill', strongly supported by African-American Civil Rights organisations, has been repeatedly introduced to highlight the view that police officers continue to stop and search people on the basis of their race despite earlier legislation to end the practice.
3. Private bills that are used by Congressmen to highlight a specific concern of one of their constituents or remedy an injustice on the

part of the executive branch. Once commonplace, the number of these bills has declined significantly.

4. Joint resolutions, which go through the same processes as a bill but are often used to amend or correct errors in earlier bills.
5. Public bills, which cover major issues, usually with national significance.

Some public bills have a higher probability of becoming law than others:

- Presidential proposals, introduced on his behalf by Congressmen, are by no means guaranteed to survive their passage through the legislature. However, they tend to receive more publicity than most other bills and the President is able to use his high, nationwide-profile campaign for his proposals and to argue that members of Congress are failing to put the interests of the country ahead of their own local concerns.
- Reauthorisation bills provide funds for important public projects, such as maintaining the nation's transport systems, for a number of years before being reviewed. These bills are almost certain to pass, although they may encounter difficulties as they do so. A case study of one of these bills is presented below.

The Congressional timetable

Apart from the series of hurdles a bill has to clear before it becomes a law, the limited amount of time available to consider the annual avalanche of proposals is extremely limited.

- January: A session begins at noon on 3 January. The first few weeks may be spent working on any major bills left over from the previous session. Work on new proposals tends to wait until after the President's State of the Union Address, usually around 20 January, which largely shapes the political agenda for the year.
- February: Congress receives the President's budget on the first Monday of the month. Most of the month is spent reviewing this and rival budgetary proposals, except for the third week of February when Congress recesses for a week for President's Day. (During recesses, members of Congress have an opportunity to spend time in their districts.)

- March: Congress, ideally, completes work on the budget so that it is known how much money will be raised in taxes to fund any bills that become law that year. Other bills start their to make their way through Congress.
- April: Work on the bills continues but there will be a week-long recess for Easter. Most years the budget is still being debated by this time and work on other bills is held up as a result.
- May: Bills should be nearing completion, but often the work that should have been done in April takes place this month. Congress recesses for the last week of the month for Memorial Day. In an election year, Congressmen may have to face a primary election in their district around this time.
- June: Appropriations committees, which decide how much money each proposed project may have, start work.
- July: There will be a week-long recess for the 4 July Independence Day holiday. Outstanding work on bills and by the appropriations committees should be completed by the end of the month, although most years very few bills are as advanced as scheduled.
- August: Summer recess.
- September: The House and Senate should have each passed their versions of appropriations bills and will need to reconcile them, although it is almost unknown for the process to be completed this early. In election years, those who have survived their primaries are conscious that the first week of November is fast looming.
- October: Work to complete bills continues, except in election years, when all Congressmen and a third of the Senators return home to campaign.
- November–December: This should be time for members of Congress to spend a prolonged period in their districts. Most years, there is still a substantial amount of work to be done and work may continue up to Christmas Eve, with a recess for Thanksgiving in the third week of November.

The legislative process: first reading

Two magic numbers are required for a legislative proposal to become law: 218 and 60. These are the votes a bill must receive in the House of Representatives and the Senate for a bill to pass through both chambers of Congress, in identical form, to become law. Bills are almost always amended in both chambers, but the two versions have to be harmonised before being presented to the President for his signature. The following six sections will consider the various ways the magic numbers are reached and why, much of the time, they are not.

The first two stages of its passage are known as the first reading and only a small proportion of bills successfully survive this part of the process.

Stage 1: Introducing a bill Each bill is drafted by a member of Congress, with the support of his/her own staff, perhaps a pressure group, perhaps a White House staff member, or perhaps a lawyer from one of the Congressional committees. The member will attempt to attract co-sponsors to show that the bill has wide support. The member will also need to find a sympathetic member of the other chamber to introduce the bill.

In the House of Representatives, the bill has to be placed in a wooden box, known as the Hopper. In the Senate, it is given to the presiding officer's clerk. In each case, the bill will be given a number and name. Acronyms are popular, such as the Provide Tools Required to Intercept and Obstruct Terrorism (PATRIOT) Act of 2001.

Stage 2: Committee action All bills are sent to a committee for detailed consideration. In the House, the Speaker decides which committee to refer it to. The Speaker can make a range of choices about the future of a bill, and the decision is highly political. Bills can be:

- Referred to a single committee that deals with its subject-matter for consideration.
- Sent to two or more committees for concurrent referral, in which they work on the bill at the same time.
- Sent to two or more committees for sequential referral, in which first one, then the others, consider the bill.
- Split into several portions that are then sent to as many committees as appropriate in a split referral.
- Subject to a time limit to complete its passage.

The choices the Speaker makes significantly influences the likelihood of a bill passing. Referral to a single committee with no time limit reduces the number of hurdles a bill has to clear. It also indicates the

Speaker's support for the proposal. As everyone in the House with key decision-making powers owes their position to the Speaker, whom no one wants to alienate, this support increases the likelihood of bills negotiating obstacles in their way.

The equivalent stage in the Senate is much more straightforward. Bills are referred to committee by the staff of the presiding officer, with none of the political implications that accompany such decisions in the House.

When a bill reaches it designated committee, one of three things can happen.

- If it does not enjoy the support of the committee chairman, it can simply be ignored. This is known as **pigeonholing**, and a majority of bills get no further than this point.
- Alternatively, the chairman can bring the bill before the whole committee, or a subcommittee, for consideration. If a majority of the committee do not support the proposals, and vote against them, the bill will be killed.
- The third possibility is that the bill will be given careful, sympathetic, consideration. If this happens, then:
  - **Hearings** will be held, in which experts and pressure groups will testify on the advantages and disadvantages of the bill.
  - At the end of this process, the committee will **mark up** the bill, including any amendments they decide are appropriate.
  - The committee will then **report out** the bill to the whole chamber. Ideally, from the point of view of its sponsors, it will leave with a positive recommendation, but it can be reported out without a recommendation.

Committee chairmen: legislative tsars
With so much power residing in the hands of this small group of people, the position of committee chairman has always been controversial. One political scientist compared them to a 'toll bridge attendant who argues and bargains with each prospective customer; who lets his friend go free, who will not let his enemies pass at any price'.

Traditionally, chairmen were appointed on the basis of seniority. This had the advantage of rewarding experience and the consequent expertise that developed over time. It was challenged, however, because it was perceived to reward longevity over merit and, because chairmen were almost guaranteed re-election, was thought to lead to political complacency and abuse of power.

Two waves of Congressmen have challenged the seniority principle. In the 1974 mid-term elections, at the height of the Watergate scandal, the new young Democrats who swept the election on a promise to clean up government were not prepared to wait until they attained seniority before they made an impact and challenged the existing chairmen. The seniority system gradually re-established itself until, in the 1994 mid-terms, Republicans captured the House with their Contract with America campaign, which included a raft of proposals to reform Congress.

The then Speaker, Newt Gingrich, selected the Congressmen who he believed to be most committed to the Contract as committee chairmen, in consultation with the House Republican Steering Committee, which contained the other leading members of the party such as the majority leader. His decision required the **ratification** of all the other Republicans in the House, organised into the Republican Conference.

In many cases, he found the most senior Republican on each committee to be acceptable, but anyone who had been too accommodating to Democrats was passed over and the chairmanship given to a more committed conservative, including the chairmanship of the powerful Appropriations Committee. The Speaker also has the power to reorganise the committees, which may include eliminating or adding some.

This wave of Republicans also imposed a rule on themselves that committee chairmen can serve no longer than six years. The only exception to this rule is the House Rules Committee, whose chairman 'serves at the pleasure' of the Speaker.

The term-limits imposed in 1994 took effect after the 2000 election. Retirements, followed by replacements, meant that some of the chairmen had not yet served six years at that point, but fourteen out of twenty House chairmen were forced to step down. As before, the Speaker allowed the most senior Republican on each committee to become the next chairman in most instances, but in some cases, such as the powerful Ways and Means Committee, installed a Congressman who did not have seniority.

This arrangement highlighted three advantages of the old seniority system that were not widely recognised at the time. First, since chairmanships are usually the pinnacle of a Congressman's career, they often leave the House once they lose their position. Of the fourteen who were term-limited in 2000, nine left the House within two years. Opponents of the system argue that it leads to the unnecessary loss of talent. Second, because of the possibility of leap-frogging more senior members, ambitious Congressmen mount behind-the-scenes campaigns for chairmanships that can last for up to two years before a term-limit comes into effect, which is a distraction from their primary commitments and divisive within the party. Third, since 1994 the senior House Republicans, who choose the chairmen, have all been committed conservatives on the right of their party. This power of patronage has tended to shift the centre of gravity among House Republicans.

Pork-barrel politics and logrolling

Clearly, it is advantageous to a bill if the Speaker and other key members of Congress support its aims and objectives. They may also find a bill attractive, however, if it provides Federal funds for projects in their districts. Many bills, therefore, have such proposals added to them to aid their passage. This is known in political circles as **pork-barrel politics**. An example of how this works can be illustrated by the experience of Congressman Bill Young, who represents the 10th District of Florida. He had been bypassed in 1994 as committee chairman for not having a sufficiently conservative voting record. He was somewhat less moderate in the following years and was rewarded with the chairmanship of the Appropriations Committee in 1998. In the 108th Congress, between 2002 and 2004, he saw $80 million allocated to his district for military projects and another $30 million allocated to his state, Florida, to rebuild eroded beaches. In the previous Congress, he secured $116 million for Florida projects.

Sponsors of bills also have to be sensitive to the needs of less influential members of Congress. This may involve agreeing to support bills brought forward by other members in return for votes. This is known as **logrolling**.

The legislative process: second reading

Stage 3: Floor action This stage, like the first, sees a significant difference in procedure between the House and the Senate. In the House, the powerful Rules Committee makes two decisions that have a critical impact on a bill:

- When to schedule a bill for debate. The later in the year that a bill is scheduled, the less likely it is to complete its passage before running out of time.
- Which rule a bill should be debated under. The three options are:
  - Open rule, which permits amendments to a bill. Under this rule, a bill may be amended out of all recognition.
  - Modified open rule, which permits amendments to specified parts of a bill.
  - Closed rule, which allows no amendments.

In the Senate, there is a tradition of unlimited debate. The Senate Rules Committee therefore plays a much more minor role than in the House. However, a bill may be subject to a **filibuster** on the floor of the Senate, a blocking mechanism in which a single Senator, or a group working together, can stop a vote from being called. If this process continues for long enough, with all other work being held up, supporters of a bill may withdraw it, in which case it dies.

A filibuster can only be ended if by a **cloture motion.** Until 1975, it took a two-thirds majority, or sixty-seven votes, to win a cloture motion. After a rule change, the number needed was reduced to three-fifths, or sixty votes (one of the magic numbers), but even this figure is hard to attain.

Once a debate has taken place in both chambers, all members of Congress have an opportunity to vote on the House and Senate versions of the bill, which may be, by this time, quite different. In the both cases, a simple majority is required, which is 218 in the House (the other magic number) and 51 in the Senate. If this threshold is not met in one of the chambers, the bill dies. If it clears this hurdle, however, it still faces the challenge of reconciling the two versions.

The legislative process: reconciling two versions of a bill

Stage 4: Conference committee Both the House and the Senate appoint representatives to negotiate an agreed version of a bill. Usually these are the people who have played the pivotal role of shepherding the bill through their respective committees and much of the negotiating is carried out by phone and e-mail between the specialist staff they employ. Periodically, the two sides becomes deadlocked, in which case the bill will die. Usually, however, a bill that has reached this stage has enough support for the conferees to find a way to compromise with each other.

The agreed version is then sent back to the two chambers for their approval. Sometimes one of the chambers finds the compromises made on their behalf unacceptable and votes against it. In this case, further negotiations take place in the Conference Committee, but it is possible that even at this late stage one of the chambers will kill the bill. If, as is usual, both chambers vote for it, the bill will have been approved by Congress.

Presidential signature

A bill cannot become law until it has been signed by the President. At this stage, any delays in the bill's passage through Congress becomes crucial.

If the bill is sent to the President shortly before the end of the Congressional year, when Congress is about to adjourn, it will die if the President fails to sign it within ten days. The President does not need to publicly reject the bill, he can ignore it and allow it to quietly expire. This is known as the pocket veto.

If, on the other hand, a bill is sent to the President while Congress is in session, and he fails to sign it within ten days, it becomes law.

Most bills, however, culminate in a much more public fashion. If the President strongly objects to a bill he will veto it, in which case he will return it to Congress with an explanation of why he has refused to sign it. If the bill has enough support in Congress they can override a veto with a two-thirds majority in both chambers, at which point it becomes law.

If the President signs a bill, he usually does so in a public ceremony that gives him an opportunity to take a significant share of the credit for the benefits the new law will bring. In a rare case, in 2002 the Bi-partisan Campaign Reform Bill was signed behind closed doors, indicating the President's dissatisfaction with a law he described as 'far from perfect'. More typically, in 2001 the No Child Left Behind Act, was signed in a classroom in Ohio, with the President surrounded by the Act's most senior Congressional supporters, alongside students and teachers, to demonstrate how many groups had faith in its ability to transform America's education system.

Box 8.1 outlines the passage of a specific piece of legislation to demonstrate how this process works in practice.

Representation: promoting the interests of constituents

Visibility in the district

There is almost 5,000 miles between Washington DC and the most distant state of Hawaii. There may be as much as 3,600 miles

---

Box 8.1 Legislation case study: the 2005 Transport Equity Act

The start

The 108th Congress began work in January 2003, with Republicans having increased their majority in the House of Representatives and having narrowly won control of the Senate in the mid-term elections the previous November.

One of their major tasks would be to pass a new Highways Bill. Transport requires long-term planning and, in recent decades, the President has proposed transport legislation about once every five years. The last bill had been passed in 1998 and was due to expire on 30 September 2003.

Key players

1. **The President** and his administration, who unveiled their bill in May 2003, proposing $247 billion for transport-related projects.
2. **Pressure groups** that could benefit from these projects or be affected by them, including:
   - The Highways lobby, such as the American Road & Transportation Builders Association, the Associated General Contractors of America and the National Stone, Sand and Gravel Association, representing companies who would construct any new roads and bridges authorised by the legislation.

- State and city transport officials, such as the National Governors Association and the American Public Transportation Association, aiming to ensure that a significant proportion of the money would be allocated to developing public transport.
- Environmentalists, concerned that new roads would mean more car journeys, leading to more pollution.
3. **Members of Congress** in both the House of Representatives and the Senate, whose re-election prospects would be helped if their districts and states benefited from new roads and bridges, and the jobs that would be created by them.

The political climate

Transport has to compete with other political priorities for resources. The President's budget of $247 billion for the bill was a lot less than transport lobbyists and key members of Congress had hoped for. The Senate proposed the allocation of $311 billion for transport. The House of Representatives proposed $375 billion.

Two factors suggested that it would be difficult to pass a bill that would cost a lot more than the President had proposed:

- Because of the terrorist attacks of 2001, spending on security was a priority, and in the spring of 2003 the war and reconstruction in Iraq were clearly at the top of President Bush's concerns.
- The obvious way of raising more money for transport would be to raise fuel taxes, but the President had promised in his election campaign not to increase taxes. George W. Bush was keenly aware that his father had broken a similar pledge in 1990, which had cost him re-election.

On the other hand, two other factors suggested that the President could be persuaded not to veto a bill costing more than he had proposed:

- The economy was performing poorly and unemployment was rising. Large construction projects can both boost the local economy and create jobs. They are also often seen as reducing traffic congestion and deaths.
- In 1982, President Reagan had raised fuel taxes to fund transportation and was subsequently re-elected, demonstrating that not all tax increases are electorally damaging.

It was clear from the outset, therefore, that the shape of the bill would be determined by battle between those seeking to boost spending on transport and those whose priority was to restrain overall spending.

The campaign to boost spending

- **Strengths**
    - A wide range of groups supported the bill. Even before the bill was published, a group of more than 200 lobbyists from highways pressure groups, business leaders and trade unions pooled their efforts in a day of action to persuade Congress of the case for investing in transport on a huge scale.
    - Members of the House of Representatives, needing to impress their constituents before the next election in 2004, were drafting proposals for projects in their districts. Within weeks, nearly 5,200 requests, known as earmarks, had been made (an average of twelve projects per member), worth about $300 billion.
    - Tom DeLay, the President's principal ally in the House of Representatives, was leading a movement to ensure that all states benefited from highway construction projects to the value of at least ninety-five cents for every dollar they paid into the highways fund. This would mean that his state, Texas, would see an increase in Federal transport funds. To achieve this goal he would, in all probability, have to compromise with representatives in other states, who were demanding a large increase in highways.
- **Weaknesses**
    - The White House remained adamant that it opposed tax increases in any form, and in July 2003 the Treasury Secretary announced that he would recommend that the President veto legislation containing any such proposals.
    - Congressional leaders, as well as the President, were hostile to the proposals put forward by the two authorising committee chairmen. They were convinced that their slim majority in both houses would be threatened if they did anything to damage George W. Bush's popularity. House majority leader, Tom DeLay, let it be known at an early stage that he would block a full debate on the floor of the House of any bill that emerged from the Committee process including raising fuel taxes. At one stage DeLay even threatened to use his power to re-write the bill and bypass the committee chairmen.
    - The committee chairmen, who were responsible for guiding the bill through Congress in the face of strong opposition from the President, were relatively inexperienced. In the House the bill was sent to the Transportation and Infrastructure Committee chaired by the relatively inexperienced Alaska Congressman, Don Young (Republican). Consideration of the bill was shared

by three committees in the Senate but the key committee was the Environment and Public Works Committee, chaired by Oklahoma Senator, James Inhofe (Republican), also quite inexperienced in the role.

- Raising extra money for the highways bill would not come from the two committees with responsibility for guiding the bill through Congress. The money would only be raised if the Senate Finance Committee and the House Ways and Means Committee agreed to the necessary tax-raising measures. Early in the process, the two most senior members of the Senate Finance Committee expressed their opposition to funding the level of expenditure proposed by the authorising committees.
- If the extra money could not be found, groups supporting road and bridge construction would find themselves in competition with those supporting public transport for the available resources. In that situation, the strong alliance in support of the bill could be replaced by in-fighting, putting in doubt the future of the bill.

Committee stage

If the budgetary process had followed the traditional timetable, the finance committees would have decided on any amendments to the President's tax-raising proposals in the spring. The appropriations committees would then decide in September how those taxes should be spent, giving enough time for the original authorising committees to make any necessary changes to bills. However, by September 2003, there had been no meaningful progress on the bill.

As the 1998 Highways Act expired, with the new bill not completed, Congress had to pass a **continuing resolution** to ensure that spending on transportation continued at existing levels. This resolution gave Congress until the end of February 2004 to complete work on the bill.

In an effort to put pressure on its opponents, the coalition of interest groups supporting the legislation launched 'rolling thunder', a campaign to build support for the proposals through the autumn. They held receptions to honour law-makers who had pledged their support for increased funding for transport, as well as placing advertisements in political publications, websites and on radio. However, the campaign petered out and, significantly, supporters of public transport improvements played a minor role, suggesting that the alliance in support of the bill was weakening.

Without agreement having been reached on funding, the bill returned to the authorising committees in the House and Senate, to begin work on the principles of the bill, in November 2003. However, reaching decisions without knowing how much money would be available to spend was difficult and the bill made little progress before Congress adjourned for Thanksgiving and Christmas.

Meanwhile, problems for supporters of the bill continued to mount:

- Attacks by environmentalists. Builders and local authorities formed an alliance with a majority of Republicans to streamline the process for planning, construction and environmental monitoring. Environmentalists and groups committed to preserving historic sites formed an alliance with the majority of Democrats to fight what they saw as part of a larger effort by President Bush and his allies to dismantle the environmental protection mechanisms created over recent decades.
- Attacks by the media. The bill attracted growing attention for including projects that were seen as wasting public money. The project that attracted most criticism was a proposed 'Bridge to Nowhere' in the district of the Transportation Committee chairman, Don Young, which would link an island community of about 50 residents with a town of under 8,000 inhabitants at the cost of about $200 million.
- A sharp improvement in the economy undermined one of the main arguments in support of higher spending, that it stimulates the economy. In their defence, the bill's supporters pointed out that the economic upturn was not producing many jobs.
- A growing concern about the size of the Federal deficit. The President had come to power promising to cut taxes and had done so. After the events of 9/11, defence expenditure had risen. This combination of events was seen as unavoidable at first, and had not been a controversial issue in 2002–3, but by early 2004 the budget deficit was projected at $521 billion and concern, especially among Republicans whom the President would be relying on for re-election, was rising.

Despite these difficulties, supporters of the bill still had cause for optimism:

- History – congressmen and pressure groups had overcome similar, and even more formidable, challenges during the passage of previous Highways Bills in the 1980s and 1990s.
- 'Pork' – in election years, Congressmen are desperate to demonstrate to their constituents that their time in Washington has

produced practical benefits. Few things are more practical than projects that create jobs and make travel easier and safer.

- A general understanding that transport planners needed an agreement so that they knew how much money they had to spend and what they would be allowed to spend it on.

Proposals to break the deadlock

In February 2004, the Senate completed work on its version of the bill, providing $318 billion for transportation over six years. The White House immediately announced that it would veto such a bill.

In the House of Representatives, attempts to avert a presidential veto led to discussions of two compromises, both based on the idea that the most difficult tax-raising decisions could be dealt with after the elections of November 2004:

1. A two-year bill. This would provide enough additional funding for transport to keep Congressmen happy while postponing discussions on possible tax increases until after the presidential elections, which would, possibly, keep George W. Bush happy. Transport pressure groups, extremely unhappy with a plan that would continue to make long-term planning difficult, again mounted a concerted campaign against this compromise and in support of the Senate's version of the bill.

2. A bill providing $275 billion for transport over six years. Crucially, this compromise contained a provision to review funding levels after two years, after the presidential elections and, possibly, when the economy was generating higher tax revenues, which could provide more money for transport.

The White House also compromised, raising the spending ceiling it would accept to $256 billion.

While these discussions were taking place, another continuing resolution had to be passed, lasting until 30 April, 2004.

In late March 2004, the House Transportation and Infrastructure Committee approved the compromise $275 billion bill ($100 billion less than they had originally authorised) and reported it out for floor debate.

Floor debate

In both the Senate and the House of Representatives there was little meaningful debate on the two versions of the bill. There was some criticism of wasteful spending, reflecting media coverage over previous weeks, and some concern about the effect on the budget deficit. The main priority for most members, however, was the valuable projects that they would be able to present to their constituents in time for the election in November.

In the Senate, the bill was passed 76–21. In the House, the bill was passed 375–65.

The margin of victory was significant. If a bill is vetoed by the President, the Constitution allows Congress to override the veto if two-thirds of both chambers vote to do so. The vote margins were well over the number required.

Conference Committee
With the second continuing resolution due to expire on 30 April 2004, a committee of leaders from the two chambers began work to produce an agreed bill from:

- The Senate version, 1,412 pages, costing $318 billion.
- The House version, 984 pages, costing $275 billion.

All members would have preferred a final version closer to the Senate bill, but they needed an agreement the President would sign before Congress ended its work ahead of the election campaign – which would be in full flow by the autumn.

Even though they appeared to have enough support to override a veto, a majority of the Conference Committee members were Republican and preferred not to have a public confrontation with a Republican President, causing him political embarrassment. Unable to break the impasse, Congress passed another continuing resolution lasting until 30 September, in the hope that a compromise could be reached before Congress broke up for the election campaign. Yet, even with all the 'pork' that both the President and Congressmen would have to boast about on the campaign trail, no agreement was reached and another continuing resolution was passed to maintain funding at the levels of the previous bill until 31 May 2005, more than two years after work first began on the bill.

Meanwhile, states seeking funds for major new transport projects turned to their citizens to pay for them. In twelve states, including California, Colorado and Arizona, when voters went to the polls in November 2004 to vote in the presidential and Congressional elections, they also had the opportunity to vote for tax increases to fund road and rail projects.

109th Congress
When the 109th Congress started work in January 2005, any bills from the previous Congress were supposed to be reintroduced

and started again from scratch. However, work on the Highways Bill began where the previous Congress had finished. During the election campaign, the budget deficit had not been a major issue and the President was prepared to make further compromises on the cost of the Highways Bill.

When he announced his budget on 7 February, President Bush gave his support to a $284 billion, six-year bill, an increase of £28 billion over the amount he had been prepared to accept before the election. In the House, Transportation and Infrastructure Committee Chairman, Don Young, reintroduced the bill, now numbered HR3, which would allow Congress to review the level of spending if the economy improved. In the Senate, the Environment and Public Works Committee Chairman, James Inhofe, reintroduced the bill with plans for spending $295 on Highways. The President threatened to veto any bill that emerged with either a cost in excess of $284 billion or a provision to increase spending at a later date.

The new House version of the bill was passed on 10 March by a vote of 417–9. The Senate passed its version of the bill on 11 May by a vote of 89–11. With insufficient time to resolve their differences before the sixth continuing resolution expired at the end of May, another extension had to be agreed, lasting until 30 June 2005.

Hard bargaining through June and July (requiring a seventh continuing resolution) resulted in a compromise figure of $286.5 billion, which the White House was prepared to accept. President Bush signed the bill, officially entitled the Transportation Equity Act, into law on 10 August 2005, almost two years after the previous bill had expired. The signing ceremony took place at one of the largest factories of the Caterpillar Corporation, which makes construction machinery, in Montgomery, Illinois. The event symbolised the jobs that would be created for ordinary workers around the country.

Even at that point, however, controversy continued to surround the bill. In November 2005, when Republicans in Congress were proposing budget cuts of $50 billion over the following five years, the media contrasted consequent cuts in welfare programmes with the 'pork' that members of Congress had benefited from. The criticisms were so intense that Congress took the rare step of eliminating the money set aside in the Highways Bill for the 'Bridge to Nowhere'. The money was not saved, however: it was instead given to the state of Alaska to be spent as it saw fit on the original proposal or any other transportation project.

Box 8.2 Passage of the 2005 Transport Equity Act

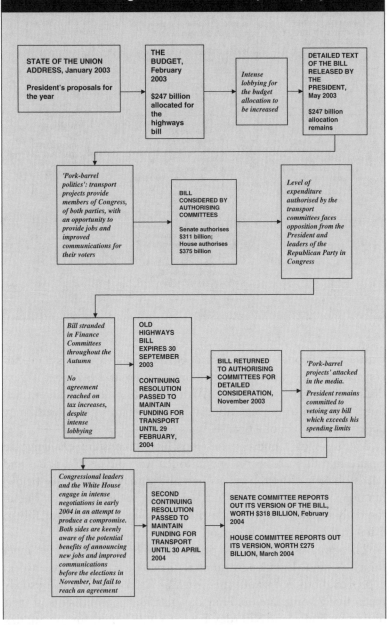

STATE OF THE UNION ADDRESS, January 2003

President's proposals for the year

THE BUDGET, February 2003

$247 billion allocated for the highways bill

Intense lobbying for the budget allocation to be increased

DETAILED TEXT OF THE BILL RELEASED BY THE PRESIDENT, May 2003

$247 billion allocation remains

'Pork-barrel politics': transport projects provide members of Congress, of both parties, with an opportunity to provide jobs and improved communications for their voters

BILL CONSIDERED BY AUTHORISING COMMITTEES

Senate authorises $311 billion; House authorises $375 billion

Level of expenditure authorised by the transport committees faces opposition from the President and leaders of the Republican Party in Congress

Bill stranded in Finance Committees throughout the Autumn

No agreement reached on tax increases, despite intense lobbying

OLD HIGHWAYS BILL EXPIRES 30 SEPTEMBER 2003

CONTINUING RESOLUTION PASSED TO MAINTAIN FUNDING FOR TRANSPORT UNTIL 29 FEBRUARY, 2004

BILL RETURNED TO AUTHORISING COMMITTEES FOR DETAILED CONSIDERATION, November 2003

'Pork-barrel projects' attacked in the media.

President remains committed to vetoing any bill which exceeds his spending limits

Congressional leaders and the White House engage in intense negotiations in early 2004 in an attempt to produce a compromise. Both sides are keenly aware of the potential benefits of announcing new jobs and improved communications before the elections in November, but fail to reach an agreement

SECOND CONTINUING RESOLUTION PASSED TO MAINTAIN FUNDING FOR TRANSPORT UNTIL 30 APRIL 2004

SENATE COMMITTEE REPORTS OUT ITS VERSION OF THE BILL, WORTH $318 BILLION, February 2004

HOUSE COMMITTEE REPORTS OUT ITS VERSION, WORTH £275 BILLION, March 2004

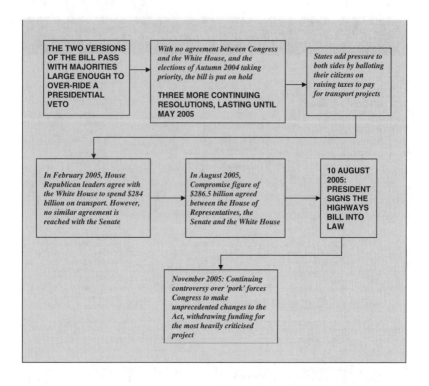

between the capital and the district of many other Congressmen. For constituents, the work of their Congressmen and Senators is very distant in a geographical sense. With all the technicalities and procedures required to get legislation through Congress, their work may appear distant in a practical sense as well.

Members of Congress therefore face a constant challenge to ensure that they are seen to be in touch with the people, issues and needs of their district. This is done in a variety of ways (see below) but none is more important than being seen in the district, sharing in the daily activities of their constituents as well as being available to listen to their concerns in person.

The Congressional year is organised to help Congressmen meet this challenge. Most Congressmen return to their districts most weekends. For those in distant states, such as California, this will usually mean flying home late on Thursday, fulfilling commitments in their district on Friday and Saturday, having a little family time on Sunday and taking the 3,000-mile flight back to Washington DC on Monday morning. The week-long recesses give Congressmen an opportunity to also spend time in their districts during the working week with reasonable frequency, giving them an opportunity to engage with a different range of people and activities, perhaps in schools and local businesses. Clearly, therefore, the apparent lack of activity in Washington DC (outlined in the section 'Types of laws', above) does not reflect laziness on the part of members of Congress.

Accessibility to constituents

Apart from appearances in the district, members of Congress have a variety of methods of making themselves accessible to their constituents:

- District office: All members of Congress have at least one office in their district that constituents can contact or visit with enquiries or concerns. In larger districts, such as that of Congressman Earl Pomeroy, which covers the whole of sparsely populated North Dakota, more than one office may be required. He has one in the state capital, Bismarck, and another 188 miles away in Fargo. Similarly, Senator John Cornyn, who represents the whole of the massive state of Texas, has seven offices in different parts of the state. All of the staff in these offices are likely to have requests for his time and attention when he returns home.

- Washington DC office: All members also have an office in, or near, the Capitol building, which serves as a base for the specialist policy staff they use to support their work in committee or on the floor of the chamber. Up to a dozen people work in these offices, of which three or more devote their time exclusively to dealing with constituent affairs. This includes giving tours of the building to constituents visiting Washington, often without prior arrangement.

- Post: The need to keep constituents informed of their work in Washington DC has meant that members of Congress have long been entitled to free postage. These franking privileges may only be used for keeping constituents informed on issues or Congressional business and may not be used for anything relating to election campaigns. Despite this, members use them a great deal more in election years than in other years.

- Websites: Traditional communications have been supplemented by modern information technology. All members have their own websites, which can be accessed directly or through the House and Senate websites. Generally, member sites cover where they stand on key issues, speeches they have made, how they have voted, photos of events they have attended and how they can be contacted. Overall, member sites seek to convey an understanding of how hard they work in their constituents' interests.
- E-mail: Members' offices can also be contacted by e-mail. Any member of staff may receive up to 300 e-mails each day from constituents, lobbyists, Congressional staff and others, but those from constituents are almost always given priority.
- C-Span: The work of Congress, in committee and on the floor, as well as major speeches and press conferences, are carried live on Congress's dedicated broadcasting service, which has three television channels and a radio station. Much of the daily work of Congress makes dull viewing but Congressional staff report that whenever a speech is made or a vote taken, at least two or three phone calls will be received from constituents with an enquiry or an opinion on the member's actions, demonstrating that a significant minority of constituents are keeping an eye on their representatives' work. It is estimated that whatever impression the constituent takes away from their phonecall to the office will be shared with, on average, twenty friends, relatives, neighbours or work colleagues, so these frequent contacts are significant.

Bringing home the bacon

For all the efforts made by members to ensure their visibility and accessibility to constituents, they know that at election time they will mainly be judged by the number of projects, funded by the Federal government, that are authorised by Congress.

Congressmen know they will be judged by voters every two years and are particularly prone to indulge in pork-barrel politics. Senators, facing re-election every six years, are widely perceived to be more thoughtful representatives but, as the Highways Bill case study (Box 8.1) demonstrates, they also recognise the value of being seen to provide for their states. Overall, this an area in which all members excel.

Political parties in Congress

Ideological commitment

The legislative and representative roles of members of Congress may create the impression that local affairs and winning re-election are the only factors that influence Congressional behaviour. This would be misleading. A majority of politicians first stood for election because they had a view of how their society should be run and, in many cases, were strongly opposed to the policies of the other main party. This kind of ideological conflict has always been played out in the corridors of Congress but has grown in intensity since the Republican Party seized control of the legislature in 1994 with a conservative agenda.

Concentration of power in the hands of the House leaders

As demonstrated by the committee stage of the Highways Bill (see Box 8.1), important legislative proposals make little progress unless they are acceptable to the House leadership.

In 2003, key details of the $400 billion Medicare Bill (providing healthcare for the elderly) were decided in private meetings between Speaker Hastert and leaders of the main pressure group representing people over fifty-five years of age, the AARP. The House and Senate committees were completely bypassed. Then, when the bill completed its passage through the House, the Speaker held open the voting period for an unprecedented three hours, until the leadership had rounded up the Republican votes they needed.

Non-cooperation between the parties in committee

Because Republican Party leaders exerted so much control over legislation, committee chairmen worked closely with them and often ignored the views of the Democrats on their committee. In July 2003, relations between the two sides on the House Ways and Means committee reached such a low point that the Democrats staged a protest in the committee room at the lack of consultation on major bills, and the chairman called the police to have them removed.

Although this incident was an extreme example of non-cooperation, an atmosphere of partisanship dominated Congress and deeply affected its day-to-day work from the mid-1990s.

Increased use of the closed rule

Democrats found it as difficult to influence bills supported by the Republican leadership on the floor of the House as they have in committee. This is because of the vastly increased use of the closed rule (see above), which does not allow amendments to be proposed during floor debates. Just 15 per cent of bills were passed under the closed rule in the late 1970s; by 2003, the figure had risen to 76 per cent.

Increased use of Senate amendments and filibusters

In retaliation, the Democrats made increasing use of the mechanisms enabling a minority to block bills they are unable to influence.

One method was to propose multiple amendments in the Senate, which has a tradition of unrestricted floor debate, thereby slowing down the progress of a bill. In the early 1990s, around 1,500 amendments were proposed per year; a decade later, the number had risen to more than 2,600. The other method was to filibuster a bill. In the same period, filibusters have risen from 24 per year to 58 per year.

Cycles of co-operation and confrontation

This level of hostility between the parties has occurred before, notably during the Great Depression of the 1930s. There have also been periods of cross-party co-operation, notably over the issue of race in the 1950s, when conservatives in both parties blocked Civil Rights measures. After gaining control of Congress in the mid-term elections of 2006, the leaders of the Democratic Party committed themselves to acting in a more bi-partisan manner. In both environments, however, ideology has been a driving factor in the operation of Congress, as the major issues of the day have either drawn the parties together or driven them apart.

Evaluating the effectiveness of Congress

Congress in the system of checks and balances

The Founding Fathers expected Congress to play a pivotal role in keeping the other branches of government within their constitutional boundaries. To what extent has this happened?

In relation to the presidency, Congress has not, as intended, taken primary responsibility for initiating policy. It was expected that Congressional leadership in this area would lead to the sharing of power by a large group of people, accountable to the voters, rather than a single person controlling affairs. In practice, responding rapidly to events, as well as formulating a coherent programme of policies, is done more effectively by a small group of people with an identifiable leader. This role has, therefore, largely passed to the executive branch.

This development has made Congress's role as a check on the actions of the executive all the more important and, as the section on 'Congress and the Presidency' (above) demonstrates, Congress has a wide range of weapons in it armoury, some of which it uses frequently and aggressively.

In relation to the judiciary, the Constitution did not provide Congress with mechanisms to balance the power of judicial review, which was acquired through the case of *Marbury* v. *Madison* (1803). However, Congress has demonstrated a determination to challenge judicial power in whatever ways it can, primarily through technical amendments to laws that have been declared unconstitutional.

Congress limiting the scope of government

As well as expecting Congress to play the central role in limiting the powers of the other Federal branches of government, the Founding Fathers intended to limit the overall scope of the national government, including the influence of Congress itself. To what extent has this happened?

The more legislation that was passed, the more responsibilities government would acquire (if only to administer its own laws), from which greater power would develop, potentially at the expense of liberty. It would be reasonable to infer, therefore, that the Founding Fathers would have approved of all the hurdles in the way of legislating.

However, slowly but surely, the scope of the Federal government has increased, with Washington playing a growing role in a range of policies traditionally thought of as the preserve of the states (see Chapter 4).

Congress and legislating

Today, most Americans judge Congress not by what the Founding Fathers would have expected but by its efficiency in meeting their needs through effective representation and legislation. When weighing up these roles, there are positive and negative factors to consider:

- Members of Congress are viewed as effective representatives of their constituents. Between elections, they invariably secure projects that produce both jobs and improved services for their constituents.
- Congress as a whole is often viewed as inefficient, especially when passing legislation. The Highways Bill, which should have been completed by September 2003, was not completed until August 2005.
- Congress is often viewed as irresponsible. The apparent lack of concern for the Federal deficit and the determination to secure lucrative contracts for their districts results in spending decisions that are widely seen as wasteful.

These factors lead many Americans to reach two, contradictory, conclusions:

- Most believe that their representative is doing an excellent job. With so much Federal money being brought into the district, it is rare for members of Congress to be defeated at elections unless they have become embroiled in scandal.
- Most view Congress, as a whole, as doing a poor job. Public esteem for Congress has steadily declined over the past two decades, with polls showing more than 70 per cent of Americans disapproving of the way that Congress is doing its job.

Congressional authority

The public perception that Congress is inefficient and often irresponsible has a subtle, but highly significant, impact on its place in the system of checks and balances.

Despite the range of restrictions that Congress actively imposes on the executive branch, there has long been a sense that power has tended to drift away from the Capitol towards the White House, a trend which intensifies at times of crisis. In part, this is due to the executive having taken over responsibility for deciding national political priorities. In part, this is due to a widespread belief that Presidents are more likely than Congress to act in the national interest and take decisive action. It was striking that public esteem for Congress has risen, and that it has been particularly effective in imposing its will, whenever respect for the presidency has fallen, such as during the Watergate crisis in the 1970s and when it was revealed that President Clinton had become involved with an intern in the 1990s. Conversely, in the aftermath of the 9/11 attacks in 2001, the standing of the President rose dramatically and Congress adopted a highly deferential role.

Ultimately, therefore, the effectiveness of Congress depends on its credibility with the American public, and if it is to arrest (or even reverse) to flow of power to the presidency it will have to consider reforms that address the perceptions of irresponsibility and inefficiency.

Box 8.3 Comparing Congress and the UK Parliament

Key differences
The two legislatures carry out similar functions, but the way in which they operate is affected by significant differences between them:

- **Separation of powers v. fusion** Congress is separately elected from the presidency, and separately accountable, while in the UK the Prime Minister is drawn from the largest party in Parliament.
- **Elected v. unelected upper chamber** Congress is composed of two elected chambers while, in Parliament, the House of Lords is unelected.
- **Resources** Members of Congress have a number of staff in their district or state and a larger team in the Washington office, including legislative and committee specialists, a press officer, an appointments secretary and case workers to deal with issues relevant to the district, under the direction of a chief of staff. In addition, when working in committee, members may rely on the

research and advice of hundreds of specialist staff. They also have the resources of the Library of Congress, with more than 130 million items, and the resources of the Congressional Research Service, which has researchers who are experts in a wide variety of policy areas and provide comprehensive reports within hours of a request. Members of Parliament, by contrast, are allocated staff allowances of around £70,000 per year, which can fund no more than two full-time staff and one part-time worker to deal with case work, appointments and research. Committees are staffed by a clerk, with limited expert assistance, and the House of Commons library provides an efficient, prompt service to MPs but lacks equivalent resources to the Congressional Research Service.

Scrutiny

Separation of powers means that most people who enter Congress expect to build their career there. Presidents do sometimes invite members of Congress to fill important positions in the executive branch but the short period of office of Presidents (at most eight years), combined with the power that can be wielded as a committee chairman, means that this may not be an attractive option. When scrutinising the executive branch, therefore, most members of Congress do not have to consider the effect on their careers of potentially embarrassing their own party. Of course, factors such as party loyalty and shared ideological goals may affect their scrutiny if the same party controls both Congress and the White House, but since the Second World War these two institutions have been controlled by rival parties most of the time. Furthermore, the resources available to Congress means that it is able to mount detailed examinations of the executive branch whenever it is inclined to do so, as illustrated by the work of the 9/11 Commission outlined in the introduction to this chapter.

Ambitious Members of Parliament, by comparison, expect to build careers as ministers or shadow ministers in positions that are in the gift of their party leaders. The governing party *always* has a majority in the legislature (albeit not always an overall one), which, in principle, has responsibility to hold it to account. Aside from the factors of party loyalty and shared ideological goals, this dependence on the very people they are supposed to be scrutinising inevitably inhibits the process. Moreover, the mechanisms available to MPs to scrutinise the executive lack teeth and are poorly resourced. Questions to ministers, and the Prime Minister, are short, and half of the questions come from supporters of the government who may be more interested in ingratiating themselves with senior members of their party than in holding them to account. Select committees often attempt to adopt a bi-partisan approach (except when an election is imminent), but their membership is heavily influenced by party whips and they have limited resources to carry out in-depth research into issues they are investigating.

Legislating

The factors that influence the relationship between the legislature's scrutiny of the work of the executive also apply to their approach to legislative proposals from the two heads of government.

Presidential bills are almost certain to be substantially modified by Congress. Government bills in the UK have to be sensitive to the views of the parliamentary party, and those that are not – such as the Education Bill of 2006 – may be in jeopardy. Aside from this caveat, however, government bills will usually pass through Parliament unscathed.

Representation

Legislatures may be judged on how effectively they fulfil their representative role in two ways.

They may be judged by the extent to which they reflect the population they are supposed to represent. Both the USA and UK are diverse societies led by politicians who have historically tended to be white, male and Protestant. This is no longer as true as it once was in Congress. In the 109th Congress, starting in 2005, of the 435 Congressmen and 100 Senators, there were 43 African-Americans (all Democrats) but only one of these, Barak Obama, was a Senator. There were 24 Hispanics, 1 Native American and 4 Asians. There were 68 women, of which 14 were Senators. In Parliament, there were 15 minority ethnic MPs in a chamber of 645 after the 2005 general election. The House of Lords, with 728 members, does not keep figures on ethnicity but in 2004 the campaign group Operation Black Vote identified 24 non-white peers. At the same time, there were 126 women in the Commons and 134 in the Lords. The devolved assemblies in Scotland and Wales do better at attracting female representation than the 'mother of parliaments': 40 per cent of the Scottish Parliament and 50 per cent of the Welsh Assembly after their 2004 elections.

Alternatively, legislatures may be judged by their responsiveness to the needs and wishes of the voters. In this respect, one difference between the two systems is immediately apparent. Senators face re-election every six years while their counterparts in the UK are unelected. Supporters of the House of Lords point out that their appointed membership is more diverse than either the Commons or their US equivalents in the Senate. Furthermore, appointing a range of people who have a distinguished record of service in their field creates a centre of expertise that makes a significant contribution to the roles of scrutiny and legislation. Critics respond that a lack of accountability is a relic of a past age and that all of the contributions made by the Lords can also be made by an elected body, such as the Senate, which boasts a range of vastly experienced people, not least a former First Lady. Besides, in the final analysis, Peers cannot block government legislation, regardless of its faults.

When comparing the House of Commons and the House of Representatives, the dependence of MPs on their party leaders for career development again becomes a factor. If there is a tension between the demands of constituents and decisions made by the party leadership, there is no guarantee that local issues will prevail. The only Independent MP in the Commons won as a result of a campaign by local residents who felt let down by the lack of support from their previous (government) MP to save their local hospital from closure. It is hard to imagine a similar situation arising in a Congressional district. Facing election every two years, Congressmen expect to be judged mainly by their record of providing Federal resources to their district. As a result, even if the population profile of a district changes, making it more sympathetic to the other main party, an incumbent Congressman can be confident of re-election if he or she has a strong record of 'bringing home the bacon'.

Overall effectiveness

Independence from the executive, together with the resourses to mount potent investigations, has earned Congress the title of the most powerful legislative body in the world. Certainly, when compared to Parliament, it is highly effective at scrutinising the work of the Executive and legislative proposals. It also appears to fulfil its representative role more effectively. In sum, therefore, it appears to deserve the accolade.

☑ **What you should have learnt from reading this chapter**

- Congress, intended by the Founding Fathers to be the most important branch of the national government, was given a wide range of constitutional responsibilities.

- It has proved effective at fulfilling one of the most important roles: scrutinising the work of the executive branch and limiting the scope of presidential action, especially in domestic affairs.

- However, it has allowed the President to take primary responsibility for shaping the legislative agenda. With hindsight, this was inevitable: it was never realistic that a legislature, which is a forum for rival views, would be suited to providing clear national leadership.

- Furthermore, with all of the hurdles that a bill has to clear before becoming law, Congress as an institution is widely perceived as inefficient.

- Despite this, individual members of Congress are generally held in high esteem by their voters, as they are accessible and are often effective at securing Federal funds for their constituencies.

- Therefore, while at first glance Congress has appeared not to have lived up to the expectations of the Founding Fathers or of today's Americans, it is quietly effective at fulfilling some of its most important constitutional roles, with little public recognition.

Glossary of key terms

Cloture motion A vote to end a filibuster, requiring three-fifths of the Senate (sixty votes).

Confirmation A process, culminating in a majority vote, agreeing (or refusing) to appoint a person nominated by the President to an executive or judicial post.

Elastic clause The constitutional clause providing Congress with the right to take any 'necessary and proper' steps to meet its constitutional responsibilities.

Enumerated powers Specific powers granted to Congress by the Constitution.

Filibuster A device available to Senators enabling them to block a vote on a measure by prolonging a debate.

Hearing A session of a Congressional committee, usually in public, to explore details of a matter the committee is considering, with experts or people with an interest in the issue.

Impeachment A term applied to the process of investigating, accusing, trying and convicting a high-ranking government official, although properly it applies to the formal accusation made by the House of Representatives.

Independent Counsel A special prosecutor appointed to investigate allegations of misconduct by high-ranking government officials.

Logrolling The trading of votes between members of Congress, in which some agree to support a measure, usually benefiting a colleague's district, in return for reciprocal support for measures benefiting their own district.

Mark up The process by which a Congressional committee amends and/or approves a bill before releasing it to be voted on by the whole chamber.

Pigeonholing A decision by a committee chairman not to consider a bill, thereby killing it.

Pork-barrel politics A term applied to members of Congress agreeing to amendments added to appropriations (spending) bills that benefit each other's districts.

Ratification A process, culminating in a two-thirds majority vote, agreeing (or refusing) to confirm a treaty entered into by the President.

Report out When a Congressional committee has given its approval to a bill, it will report its reasons for supporting it to the whole chamber.

Select committee A committee established to consider a specific issue (such as the impact of Hurricane Katrina) and report to its chamber, after which it is usually dissolved.

? Likely examination questions

Issues examiners may expect students to be able to effectively analyse include:

- The powers of Congress and each of its two chambers
- The role of Congress in the system of checks and balances
- The operation of Congress (legislative, scrutiny and representation) and its power centres
- The effectiveness of Congress in fulfilling its roles

Thus, examples of the kind of questions that could be asked include:
How powerful are Congressional committee chairmen?
Assess the power and significance of Congress.

Where the question compares the US system with Britain's, issues tend to focus on the comparative powers of the two institutions, especially in relation to the powers of their respective executives.

Thus, an example of the kind of question that could be asked is:
Compare and contrast the effectiveness of the US Congress and the UK Parliament in controlling the executive.

Helpful websites

www.house.gov and www.senate.gov – the official websites of the House of Representatives and the Senate, containing information about the legislative proposals being considered and providing links to the websites of all of the Congressmen and Senators.

www.cq.com – the website of the respected political journal *Congressional*

Quarterly, provides a free subscription to its Midday Update, which is sent to subscribers' e-mail inbox each day that Congress is sitting. It provides concise comments on the latest developments in Congress, as well as news and gossip about forthcoming electoral contests.

www.hillnews.com and www.rollcall.com – the websites of the two daily newspapers that serve Congress, *The Hill* and *Roll Call,* which are also available online.

 ## Suggestions for further reading

For an accessible, but detailed, account of the workings of Congress, including advice to Americans on how to make use of Congressional services, read *Congress for Dummies* by David Silverberg. The book, written by a former managing editor of *The Hill,* does not live down to its title.

The Presidency – Domestic Affairs

Contents

Overview

On 16 December 2005, the *New York Times* revealed that President George W. Bush had secretly authorised the monitoring of telephone calls of Americans without a court-approved warrant. The White House, however, was unapologetic. The Bush administration had come to power believing that the previous President had allowed the powers of the office to be eroded and they were determined to restore executive authority. This determination was strengthened by the terrorist attacks of September 2001. 'After 9/11 the President felt it was incumbent on him to use every ounce of authority available to him to protect the American people,' argued one advisor.

Others interpreted the Constitution differently. Amidst a tide of outrage at the revelations, one Senator accused the President of assuming 'unchecked power, reserved only for Kings and potentates'. Furthermore, their criticisms related not only to domestic eavesdropping but to holding prisoners, defined by the President as 'enemy combatants', without charge and refusal by the White House to provide documents for investigations. They argued that so much unsupervised power in the hands of a small team of people was precisely what the Founding Fathers sought to avoid when they wrote the Constitution.

This chapter will consider the extent to which, in relation to domestic affairs, this fear of unchecked executive power is justified.

Key issues to be covered in this chapter

- The President's constitutional responsibilities in domestic affairs and how they have evolved
- How Presidents fulfil their domestic roles in the governing of the USA
- The extent to which the domestic operation of the President matches the vision of the Founding Fathers

The presidency and the Constitution

Giving the Executive a secondary role

Keeping the executive branch in check was, for the Founding Fathers, central to their constitutional design. After the War of Independence, there was such a determination to avoid a tyrannical leader emerging that the central government had no executive branch at all. The need for more effective co-ordination of national affairs led to the setting up in 1787 of the Constitutional Convention which drafted the current Constitution.

While the need for a stronger government was evident, the Founders remained fearful of giving too much power to its leader. Thus, they gave primacy to the legislature, with a range of specified powers in the, symbolically significant, Article I of the document. The executive, reduced to secondary consideration in Article II, would be responsible for carrying out the wishes of Congress and representing the nation in foreign affairs. Considering these concerns, it is surprising that the Constitution is quite vague about the precise powers of the President, especially in domestic affairs.

Qualifications for the Presidency

Section 1, the first and most detailed part of Article II of the Constitution, covers who may become President (and Vice President) and the process of election. The key qualifications are that a candidate must:

- Have been born in the USA.
- Be at least thirty-five years old.
- Have been resident in the USA for the previous fourteen years at the time of standing for the position.
- Have not served as President for more than one term. This qualification was added in the 22nd Amendment in 1951.

Powers of the President

Section 2 of the Article outlines the few presidential powers, in both domestic and foreign affairs, specifically identified in the Constitution. In domestic affairs, these are:

- Authorisation (but not the requirement) to form a **cabinet** of the heads of departments of state.

- Pardoning people convicted of crimes, except in cases of impeachment.
- Temporarily filling vacancies in the Federal government when the Senate, whose responsibility it is to confirm nominees, is not in session.

Duties of the President

Section 3 of the Article outlines the duties of the President. In domestic terms, these are, again, extremely limited. They are:

- Delivering the annual State of the Union Address.
- Proposing legislation.

Executive Power

With such a limited range of defined powers and duties, the key constitutional sentence is found in the beginning of Article II: 'The Executive Power shall be invested in a President of the United States of America.'

This vague wording has always been open to a wide range of interpretations and, in the event of the checks on presidential power proving inadequate, created the potential for the development of a powerful executive.

From this, a range of Presidential roles have emerged. The sections below outline how they operate in the modern USA and evaluates whether, in practice, the President is the most powerful person in the world or the limited, highly restricted figure envisaged by the Founding Fathers.

The President's role as chief executive of the government

The benchmark of presidential success

Unless the USA is at war, Presidents take office knowing that they have been elected on the basis of their policies to strengthen the economy and the nation's social fabric. Central to the success of a presidency, therefore, is the effective management of the executive branch of government, which means:

- Implementation of existing Federal laws.

- Initiation of new laws and programmes to address the needs and development of the nation.
- Management of the economy.

In order to manage the executive branch effectively, however, each President faces a number of challenges, including:

- Assembling a suitable team to lead the departments that administer government policy.
- Exerting effective political control over the civil servants who implement policy.
- Maintaining effective political focus on his political agenda when the next presidential election is looming.

Furthermore, Presidents have a limited period in which to establish their reputations as effective chief executives. Since F. D. Roosevelt became President in 1933, rapidly implementing a range of measures to address the effects of the economic depression, it has become customary for commentators to evaluate the effectiveness of the President after one hundred days in office.

Choosing the Cabinet

On the day that a President takes office, his team has to ensure the smooth operation of government, even before taking any steps to implement his political agenda. Thus, between winning an election in the first week of November and inauguration in the third week of the following January, a top priority is selecting people to run the fifteen government departments. This means appointing people who can ensure that the President's political priorities are implemented within their departments, work together with other departmental heads whenever co-ordination of policy is necessary and support the President with policy proposals that support his goals.

In this crucial task, however, the President has less freedom of choice than the head of government in many other countries, including Britain. The restrictions include the following:

- The President cannot adjust the number of departments, or their responsibilities, to help promote his policy priorities. This can only be done by Congress.

- By convention, the head of each department has a background that is compatible with the responsibilities of the department.
- By convention, the heads of department (who make up the Cabinet) are expected to be broadly representative of the population of the country. Presidents may use the 'egg formula' as one of the factors in considering candidates, to ensure that each **e**thnic group, both **g**enders and all **g**eographical regions are represented in the Cabinet. This is particularly important when a state governor becomes President, as was the case with both Bill Clinton (Arkansas) and George W. Bush (Texas). It would be inappropriate for the national government to be run almost exclusively by the President's close associates from his home state.
- By convention, powerful pressure groups that have an interest in the affairs of a department are consulted in the appointment of its head.

Once the President has found potential appointees to his Cabinet, he still faces a number of obstacles:

- Persuading candidates to move to Washington DC. A President will be in office for a maximum of eight years, which may mean a candidate leaving a well-established career and uprooting a family for a limited period.
- Persuading candidates to take a pay cut. In 2006, the pay of a head of department was $175,700, considerably less than the earnings of senior managers in the private sector.
- The Senate has to confirm the appointees before they can take office. In most cases, this is routine but, as outlined in Chapter 7, confirmation is certainly not guaranteed.

These factors were evident in President George W. Bush's appointee as Commerce Secretary in 2004. Carlos Gutierrez was born in Cuba and had made his home in Miami, Florida. He rose through the ranks of the Kellog Company, becoming chief executive officer. In the year before accepting the position of Commerce Secretary he earned $7.4 million.

In a variety of ways, Gutierrez helped the Cabinet reflect the diverse nature of US society: he was a member of the Hispanic community, with links to the South, who brought a wealth of business experience and had the backing of business pressure groups.

Working with the Cabinet

As the appointment of Secretary Gutierrez demonstrates, the President is able to find people of the highest calibre to head departments despite all the restrictions he faces. When bringing department heads together to form an advisory body, however, Presidents have not found Cabinets helpful on the whole. There has been a general pattern of Cabinet meetings diminishing in frequency the longer a President remains in office. Both President Carter and President Reagan held thirty-six Cabinet meetings in their first year but just six and twelve respectively four years later.

A range of factors limit the usefulness of Cabinets:

- The fact that heads of department, the Cabinet secretaries, are usually policy specialists means that they may have little to contribute to discussions on unrelated policy areas. The result can be meetings in which there is little meaningful discussion, which hardly aids the President's decision-making.

- Some of the heads of department may not be close colleagues of the President. They are even less likely to have a close relationship with each other. As a result, there may not be a deep level of trust within the group. Presidents tend to be wary of discussing sensitive or confidential issues with a group that does not have close bonds.

- Once appointed to head a department, there is an understandable tendency for each member of the Cabinet to develop strong ties to the career officials within their department, as well as other people they work with most closely, such as Congressional committees and pressure groups. In part, this is due to the dynamics of the working environment, which can forge strong bonds and make the White House (and its political priorities) seem remote. In part, this is due to the long-term planning that takes place in departments appearing to be at odds with the short-term needs of a President who will be in office for two terms at most. Additionally, Cabinet members often adopt longstanding rivalries between departments, such as that between the Department of State (which tends to seek diplomatic solutions to international disputes) and the Department of Defense (which tends towards military solutions to disputes). In the first term of President George W. Bush, Secretary of State Colin

Powell was frequently at loggerheads with the Defense Secretary, Donald Rumsfeld. Consequently, over time there is a growing tendency for the Cabinet to become divided, as each member becomes increasingly committed to their own departmental priorities rather than a shared agenda.

- Friction between departments also arises due to competition for funds for their programmes.
- Cabinet secretaries are accountable not only to the President but also to Congress. For example, in response to more than one hundred traffic deaths caused by failures in tyres in the late 1990s, Congress passed a law requiring the Department of Transport to issue new rules that would lead to early detection of safety hazards in tyres and vehicles. With each department having to respond to such instructions and to account for its performance to different Congressional committees, their distinctive, separate, priorities tend to be emphasised.

A consequence of these shortcomings is that policy-making is often the result of bi-lateral meetings between the President and the most influential 'top tier' Cabinet members: Defense, State, Treasury and Justice.

Notwithstanding these limitations, since George Washington instituted regular meetings with his four Cabinet secretaries, all Presidents have found it beneficial to bring the Cabinet together periodically. The benefits to the administration include:

- Embodying the presidential platform – for Clinton, the Cabinet represented his campaign theme of inclusivity; for George W. Bush, the cabinet represented his campaign theme of compassionate conservatism.
- Presenting an image of being 'in touch' – having representatives from all sectors of American society creates an image of a government that understands all sectors of American society.
- Presenting an image of open, collective government – Cabinet meetings are always accompanied by a photo opportunity, which counters the sense that most key decisions are taken by a small group of advisors who have never been subject to Senate ratification.
- Although Cabinets have a reputation for limited debate on government policy, there are points in the calendar when the President

will usually call the secretaries together to discuss major initiatives that affect all departments, such as when the annual budget is being submitted to Congress.

- At other times, even in the absence of useful policy-making discussions, Cabinet meetings provide an opportunity for information exchange, a check on the progress of legislation, an opportunity for secretaries to meet each other and an opportunity for the 'second tier' secretaries to meet the President. All this can help build team spirit, which can be significant if the administration goes through a period of political turbulence.

Overall, therefore, while Cabinet secretaries, collectively and individually, make some contribution to Presidents, they tend to be a less useful source of support for the head of government in the USA than in many other countries. This can have a significant impact on a presidency.

Of particular concern to a President is the difficulty that Cabinet secretaries may have in advancing his political agenda. With about 1.9 million civilian employees, working in offices spread throughout the land, the departments are notoriously difficult to control. Former House Speaker, Newt Gingrich, described the dynamics of government departments in these terms: 'The leader comes into the room and says, "We are going to march North" and the bureaucracy all applaud. Then the leader leaves the room and the bureaucracy says, "Yeah, well, this 'march north' thing is terrific, but this year, to be practical, we have to keep marching south. But what we'll do is, we'll hire a consultant to study marching north, so that next year we can begin to think about whether or not we can do it." ' Even more of a concern is the tendency of some members in each Cabinet to be persuaded to support the existing priorities of their departments, which may not be compatible with the President's priorities.

Considering that the work of government departments touches the daily lives of every American, from regulations on airbags in cars to how much water should be allowed for a clean flush of a toilet, a presidency can be substantially undermined if there is a lack of effective political control exerted over each department, or a lack of co-ordination and co-operation between departments. In short, ineffective leadership of departments and poor co-operation between departments can prove to be one of the greatest 'checks' on a presidency. Finding ways to exert control over the departments, therefore, has been one of the greatest challenges that Presidents face.

Regulatory commissions, independent agencies and government corporations

This challenge is even made even greater by other parts of the Federal government that have, by law, a significant measure of independence from the White House or have the effect of complicating the organisational pattern of government.

The executive branch of government includes **independent regulatory commissions**. These are agencies, established by Congress and independent of the President, with responsibility for regulating important aspects of society. They are empowered to establish rules for the policy area they regulate, which have the force of law, and to enforce their rules. All are run by boards of commissioners, consisting of five or seven members, who are appointed by the President. Their independence from the President is established by long terms of office that end at different times. Thus, at any one time, some of them will not owe their allegiance to the current President. In addition, a maximum of four members of a seven-person board of Commissioners, or three members of a five-person board, may be of the same party, so that even if one political party controls the White House over an extended period (for example, when President Reagan was succeeded by George Bush Snr), the views of the opposition party must be considered by the Commission. Finally, they cannot be removed by the President if they become a political irritant. In the case of *Rathbun* v. *United States* (1935), the Supreme Court ruled that commissioners could only be removed from office for failing to fulfil their obligations or for abusing their powers. The most visible commissions are the Federal Reserve, the Central Bank of the USA, which oversees the financial sector and sets interest rates, and the Federal Elections Commission, which administers and enforces campaign finance legislation.

The Federal Reserve illustrates how difficult it can be for Presidents to effectively control their administrations. Whenever there is an economic slowdown the President is invariably held responsible, yet the main tool for manipulating economic growth is controlled by the independent Federal Reserve, which does not consider presidential political fortunes when setting interest rates. Conversely, one of the reasons that Al Gore did not win the presidency in 2000, despite having been a leading member of the Clinton administration that had presided over eight unbroken years of economic growth, was that many Americans credited their increasing prosperity to the Federal Reserve.

The executive branch of government also includes **independent agencies**. These are responsible for specific areas of policy and are, in most respects, organised like the fifteen main government departments, headed by people responsible to the President. As such, the President has more control over these bodies than he does over the independent regulatory commissions, but they tend to complicate the organisation of government and lines of responsibility. For example, the Environmental Protection Agency has responsibilities that overlap with, and sometimes clash with, the Department of the Interior, which is responsible for managing inland waterways, forests and national parks, and the Department of Agriculture, which describes itself as 'the nation's largest conservation agency'.

The Environmental Protection Agency (EPA) illustrates how such bodies come into being. In response to the growing public demand for cleaner water, air and land, it was agreed by Congress and the White House that the Federal government was not structured to make a co-ordinated attack on the pollutants that harm human health and degrade the environment. The EPA was thus established to repair the damage already done to the natural environment and to provide guidance on making a cleaner environment a reality.

The executive branch also includes **government corporations**, which are public services administered as business enterprises, such as the United States Postal Service and the national passenger rail service, Amtrak. Inevitably, the President plays a minimal role in the daily functions of these organisations but public perception of the effectiveness of his administration may be significantly affected by the late delivery of the mail or the late arrival of a train.

Exerting control over the Federal bureaucracy: the spoils system

Considering the importance of effective political control of the executive branch, it is unsurprising that, since George Washington,

Presidents have appointed political sympathisers to jobs in the government. The third President, Thomas Jefferson, fired hundreds of Federal employees who supported his predecessor's party and replaced them with his own supporters. By the time that the seventh President, Andrew Jackson, took office, the size of the Federal government had grown substantially and he replaced more than a thousand Federal employees. The practice was defended at the time on the grounds that 'to the victor goes the spoils', since when appointment of political supporters has been known as the **spoils system**.

In 1881, President Garfield was assassinated by a man who had been passed over when the 'spoils' were handed out. This led to a reorganisation of government, with most positions held by permanent civil servants, appointed on merit, although about 3 per cent of positions continue to be filled on the basis of political affiliation, rather than merit. Each presidential election year, Congress publishes a list of these jobs in a book referred to by Washington insiders as the 'plum book'.

There are three categories of political appointees put in place to try to ensure that the President's agenda is implemented:

- At the top level – that is, the most senior people who run the departments and agencies that comprise the executive branch – appointees are nominated by the President but have to be confirmed by the Senate.
- 'Schedule C' appointees work alongside permanent senior managers, formulating and implementing specific areas of policy.
- 'Buddy system' appointees are offered mid-level posts by people in 'Schedule C' positions.

Directing and co-ordinating the Federal bureaucracy: the Executive Office of the Presidency

Even with political appointees in place to monitor the implementation of presidential priorities, there is a need for providing co-ordination and direction to an executive branch that has become larger and more complex each decade.

This was apparent by the mid-1930s, with President F. D. Roosevelt and his advisors struggling to managed all of the new agencies created to overcome the effects of the economic depression. He set up a committee, generally known as the Brownlow Committee, which reported that 'the president needs help' and recommended that a new team of advisors be ' installed in the White House itself, directly accessible to the president' to co-ordinate day-to-day matters. In response, Congress passed the Reorganization Act of 1939, creating the **Executive Office of the President (EOP)**.

As the size of government increased, and society became more complex, the EOP grew. Its most important elements are:

- The White House staff: The TV drama, *The West Wing*, was based on this group of people, who form the President's closest and most trusted advisors. Often these ties have been forged well before the President even considered running for the position. For example, Karl Rove, who is credited with masterminding the 2000 and 2004 election victories, first met George W. Bush in 1973. These advisors have the tasks of:
  - Providing information and analysis of the key issues facing the administration.
  - Providing guidance in specialist policy areas.
  - Evaluating the political and legal significance of presidential decisions.
  - Writing speeches and presenting the President's views to the outside world.
  - Liaising with Congress to gain support for the President's programmes.
  - Filtering who, and what, gets access to the President.
  - Above all, monitoring the work of executive departments and agencies to ensure that they are carrying out the President's political agenda.

This arrangement has both advantages and disadvantages for the President. It is, of course, beneficial for the head of government to have complete confidence in his closest advisors and to be certain that they are doing everything in their power to ensure that the administration's political agenda is being implemented. Furthermore, because power in Washington DC is often measured by access to the President, the White House staff can use their privileged positions to exert considerable pressure on his behalf. However, such is the reverence attached to the position of

President that even longstanding close friends can find it difficult to present unpleasant news or voice criticism. This can lead to presidential isolation, a problem exacerbated if only a very small group of advisers have direct access to the President, as was the case with President Nixon and President Reagan.

- The Office of Management and Budget (OMB): This is the largest agency within the EOP and, after the White House staff, the most important. It prepares the budget the President proposes to Congress each year, with the amount allocated to each policy area reflecting the President's priorities. In the same way, it reviews all policy proposals produced by the executive departments and agencies to ensure that they are consistent with the President's goals. The OMB is of such importance that the post of director is subject to Senate confirmation.

- The Council of Economic Advisors: While the OMB tends to focus on short-term economic policy, the Council of Economic Advisors concentrates on long-term economic planning and aids the executive departments and agencies with their long-term plans.

- National Security Council (NSC): The NSC is responsible for co-ordinating foreign and military policy. Given the longstanding rivalry between the State Department and the Department of Defense, as well traditional mutual suspicion between the two main intelligence services, the CIA and the FBI, some Presidents have found themselves heavily dependent on the advice from their National Security Advisors, notably George W. Bush in the after-math of the attacks of 9/11.

Each President has added or abolished other agencies within the EOP in accordance with his priorities. President Johnson, for example, set up an Office of Economic Opportunity to support his Great Society programme (see Chapter 4), but it was abolished by his successor, President Nixon, who wanted to chart a different course in domestic affairs. President George W. Bush set up the Office of Faith-Based and Community Initiatives because he wished to see religious groups playing a greater role in resolving the nation's social problems.

It is a measure of the value that Presidents place on the support provided by the EOP that when the government was reorganised to improve domestic security in the aftermath of 9/11, George W. Bush tried to persuade Congress that the new agency should be part of the EOP, rather than a separate department, and only changed his mind when it became evident that his appeal would not be heeded.

Making the Federal Bureaucracy accountable

Despite having the spoils system and the Executive Office of the President at their disposal, Presidents have continued to feel that the **Federal Bureaucracy** has failed to implement their policies as they wished. Consequently, they have tried a number of strategies to make civil servants more responsive and more accountable for their actions.

- President Nixon introduced Management by Objectives, which attempted to identify the goals of Federal programmes and thereby evaluate which were successful.
- President Carter introduced Zero-Based Budgeting, which attempted to force departments and agencies to justify the value of their programmes each year.
- President Clinton introduced Reinventing Government, which aimed to reduce the number of government regulations, cut the size and cost of government and improve the quality of government services.

While each of these initiatives has been credited as going some way towards helping Presidents implement their political agenda, all are regarded as having had far less impact than intended.

The progress of President George W. Bush's Management Agenda illustrates why it is so difficult to hold the Federal bureaucracy to account. Proposals to increase accountability included:

- Grading Federal departments and agencies on the results they achieved, with the White House defining 'success'.
- Increased White House oversight of regulations issued, to ensure that they were consistent with the President's aims.
- The introduction of performance-related pay to make it easier to reward or fire employees according to the administration's goals.
- 'Competitive sourcing', which would force Federal workers to compete against private contractors to run programmes.

- Creating a 'sunset' process, which would require Federal pro-grammes to justify their existence every ten years.

They were immediately criticised by civil servants and independent commentators, who argued that:

- It is not realistic to change the entire focus of government every time a new President is elected.
- It is the responsibility of the civil service to execute the laws already in place, not only those passed by the latest administration, and an evaluation system which fails to recognise this is inevitably flawed.
- A framework to make it easier for political appointees to overrule, marginalise or fire career employees who are perceived not to be fully behind the President's agenda undermines the independence and effectiveness of the civil service.
- The overall result is a Federal bureaucracy that loses the ability to raise concerns about waste, fraud and abuse of power for fear of being victimised by political appointees (critics pointed, in partic-ular, to reductions in protection for employees who publicise adverse consequences of the administration's programmes) and too many decisions being taken by people lacking in technical expertise.

All administrations are sensitive to the charge that their reforms of the bureaucracy are leading to its politicisation and undermining its inde-pendence and effectiveness. While this does not stop the reforms, inevitably it blunts their impact.

Conclusion

Overall, therefore, the President faces a range of challenges that limit how effectively he can impose his will on the branch of government that he leads, including:

- An inability to reorganise the executive branch to meet the needs of his agenda.
- A lack of control over key instruments for implementing policy, such as the Federal Reserve.
- Term-limits that cause all political forces to concentrate their attention on the next President once the mid-terms are over.

- The sheer size of the Federal bureaucracy, combined with the complexity of a highly developed economy, which makes it difficult to control.

Thus, despite the spoils system and the Executive Office of the President, which should help him exert control over the executive branch, the Federal bureaucracy has emerged as a check on presidential power to supplement those which the Founding Fathers designed.

The President's role as chief legislator

The State of the Union Address

It is expected that the legislative agenda for the Federal government will be set by the President. As the only person elected by the whole nation, the President is expected to present a programme for government that meets the nation's needs, and when Congress assembles in January, little meaningful business is done until the President has outlined his priorities for the year.

This is done in the **State of the Union Message**, an address to both houses of Congress, which takes place around 20 January. The President identifies the key issues the administration believes need to be addressed and outlines the bills the White House will send to Congress to resolve these issues.

On the first Monday in February, the President's budget is delivered to the House of Representatives, which, constitutionally, is responsible for scrutinising all revenue bills first. This will contain the President's judgements of the cost of his legislative proposals and of the level of taxation needed to fund them.

Negotiating with Congress

There is an old saying that 'The President proposes; Congress disposes'. By convention, bills drafted by the executive branch will be allowed to clear all of the hurdles that Congress puts in the way of legislative proposals. However, both houses of Congress can, and will, amend bills written by the executive branch, sometimes to the extent that they are no longer acceptable to the President.

Unacceptable modifications come in two forms. Congress may delete key provisions that weaken the bill to such an extent that it will not be able to fulfil its purpose even if it passes. Members of Congress may also add provisions to the bill, known as 'riders' or 'earmarks', which benefit their districts. This can lead to presidential initiatives becoming 'Christmas tree' bills, covered with presents for the constituents of the most influential members of Congress at huge expense to the taxpayer.

In order to avoid either of these outcomes, the White House needs to actively engage with key members of Congress. This may mean:

- Working closely with Congressional leaders and committee chairmen on which proposed amendments may be acceptable.
- Invitations to the White House (a rare occurrence for less senior members of Congress) or an offer for the President to visit a Congressman's district.
- When the concern is that a key provision may be stripped from a bill, to offer Federal investment in the district of an undecided member.

This kind of negotiation, as a bill makes its way through Congress, is illustrated in greater detail in Chapter 8, which also outlines the impact of other key players such as pressure groups.

The power of veto

Part of the negotiation process is the threat that the President will use his constitutional power to **veto** an entire bill if it no longer meets his key requirements. This is quite a powerful weapon, as Congress will be reluctant to force a veto if there is a perception that the electorate feels they are jeopardising the national interest for their local interests. The fact that the President has a national platform on which to put forward his viewpoint, such as his weekly radio address, while members of Congress have no similar mouthpiece, gives the President a distinct advantage in such a situation. Furthermore, as it takes a two-thirds majority of both houses of Congress to override a presidential veto, only rarely is Congress able to gather sufficient votes to force through legislation that does not have the President's support.

On the other hand, the veto is a blunt weapon, eliminating the benefits of a bill as well as its disadvantages. In the past, Presidents have had the means of ignoring those parts of bills of which they disapproved. It used to be possible for Presidents to impound (not spend) money for any programme Congress had funded but which the President did not support. President Nixon impounded as much as $13 billion for social programmes that he did not favour in a single year. This power was removed by the Congressional Budget and Impoundment Control Act (1974). It also became possible for the President to veto only those parts of a bill with which he disagreed, a line-item veto, as a result of an act passed in 1997. Just one year later, however, the power to veto only parts of a bill was declared unconstitutional by the Supreme Court on the grounds that it effectively gave the President the power to draft legislation, which breaches the constitutional principle of separation of powers.

Making effective use of this blunt weapon requires political skill and judgement. If threats are made too often, there is a risk of the President appearing to bully Congress, rather than engage in constructive negotiation. As a result, it could come to be seen as an empty threat, undermining the President's standing. Moreover, the actual use of the veto also carries risks in that the public perception that nothing is being achieved in Washington DC can affect the President's reputation, as well as that of Congress.

Executive Orders
In one respect, however, Presidents have considerable freedom of legislative manoeuvre. Once a law is passed, Presidents have the power to issue rules and regulations that clarify the law or aid its implementation. The precise limits of this power are difficult to establish. The desegregation of the US armed forces in 1948, for example, was made by Executive Order 9981. However, when the same President, Harry S. Truman, placed all of the nation's steel producers under Federal control during the Korean War, in Executive Order 10340, he was overruled by the Supreme Court in *Youngstown Sheet & Tube Co. v. Sawyer* (1952), on the grounds that this amounted to creating new legislation.

Conclusion
The presidential role of chief legislator appears to work largely as the Founding Fathers intended. At the heart of their constitutional design was an intention to limit the power of the executive branch to both devise and implement policy, which, in their view, was a recipe for

tyranny. The separation of powers that they devised has remained intact, with most breaches, such as impoundment and the line-item veto, being eliminated.

One development, however, has been unexpected. The Founding Fathers anticipated that the people's representatives in the House would restrain the growth of government, under pressure from the voters to keep Federal taxes to a minimum. In practice, the chief legislator and Congress have tended to work together to establish an ever-expanding range of Federal programmes, which facilitate the President's agenda and provide Federally-funded resources to the districts, leading to a dramatic growth of government.

The President's role as head of state

Pomp and ceremony

The President has a range of ceremonial duties that, in most countries, are not carried out by the most senior politician. As head of state, he hosts visiting dignitaries such as kings and queens, as well as presiding over a range of formal events, such as giving awards and medals, lighting the national Christmas tree and throwing out the first ball of the Major League baseball season.

Some of these traditions may seem quirky, especially to foreigners. Every Thanksgiving, the President pardons a turkey that is then guaranteed to live the remainder of its natural life without facing the possibility of becoming the centrepiece of a Thanksgiving meal.

A political instrument

The President's duties as a head of state make him much more than just a politician. He is a living symbol of the nation, representing the collective image of the USA. The aura that develops around the head of state is enhanced by the lifestyle of the President. The White House is designed to serve the needs and desires of the President: his personal aircraft, *Air Force One*, is the most expensive, sophisticated, best-protected civilian aircraft in the world, and the people around him treat him with reverence.

When a President has to wrestle with the bureaucracy in order to implement a programme, or has to negotiate with Congress in order to pass legislation, the immense authority and influence that comes with being head of state can help to advance his political agenda, especially if it clear that the President reflects the hopes, fears and mood of the nation. Congress can become more receptive to the President's proposals, aware that they may be seen as putting local interests before that of the nation. The Federal bureaucracy may also be more responsive to his leadership, aware that policies that have the clear support of the nation have a greater likelihood of remaining in place over many years, beyond the term of office of the incumbent President.

Using the prestige of head of state as a political weapon

If used with delicacy and skill, the President's standing as the symbol of the nation and its interests can be used as a powerful political weapon.

At a low point in his presidency, in 1995, Bill Clinton faced a hostile Congress with a Republican majority and the two sides could not agree on a budget. Eventually, the government had to be closed down for lack of money, resulting in millions of Americans being unable to use public services on which they were dependent. Inevitably, both sides blamed each other but, by arguing that he was defending the interests of the most vulnerable in society and that he was willing to accept electoral unpopularity by doing what was in the best interests of the nation, President Clinton was able to deflect blame onto his opponents, who were seen as putting their narrow political views ahead of the needs of the nation.

Similarly, at a low point in the presidency of George W. Bush, in the summer of 2001, he faced widespread criticism as a President who spent far too much time on his ranch in Texas or playing golf, and not enough time leading the nation. After the events of 9/11, however, his standing as the leader of the nation's interests soared and for the two years he was able to implement his political agenda almost without opposition.

The risk of this political weapon backfiring

If a President fails to recognise how much of his authority comes from his status as head of state, or lacks the political judgement on how best to use it to his political advantage, his entire political programme and even the powers of the office can be damaged.

When it became apparent, during the Watergate scandal, that President Nixon had been party to breaking the law while in office, he resigned rather than face impeachment. In addition, Congress looked more closely at the powers of the presidency, and how they had been used, which led the passage of a number of laws limiting those powers, including the Case-Zablocki Act of 1972, the War Powers Act of 1973 (see Chapter 8) and the Congressional Budget and Impoundment Control Act of 1974 (see above).

Similarly, when President Clinton's affair with a White House intern was revealed, the impeachment proceedings that followed harmed the international standing of the USA, damaged the reputation of the whole administration, contributed to the defeat of Al Gore in the 2000 presidential election and, politically, paralysed the domestic policy agenda of the President for the remainder of his second term.

The dangers of misusing the status of head of state is illustrated by the transformation of President George W. Bush from leader of a wholly united nation in the autumn of 2001 to being the focus of the bitter, divisive, presidential election campaign of 2004. In 2002, President Bush actively campaigned for Republican candidates during the Congressional elections, repeatedly questioning the patriotism of Democrats and arguing that a Republican majority in Congress was essential to prevailing in the 'War on Terror'. Democrats, who had voted for the President's measures over the previous year and prided themselves on their patriotism, were outraged at the President using his prestige in this way.

Conclusion

In combining the positions of head of government and head of state in one person, the Founding Fathers created a position with the potential to develop in political power by skillfully appearing to rise above politics and present a policy agenda as being in the national interest. This, in turn, can undermine the effectiveness of the system of checks and balances.

However, not all Presidents have had the political skill to effectively exploit this potential loophole in the constitutional design, and others have discovered that if the position is not treated with proper respect then substantial damage can be inflicted on their administration.

The President's role as party leader

Striking a difficult balance

As the most prominent member of his party, the President is effectively (although not officially) the leader of his party. He is, as a result, under pressure to use his position to help the party's political prospects and to reward his supporters for helping him to win office. For the head of state, however, to behave in a partisan way is generally considered inappropriate and, as illustrated above, can be highly divisive.

Building political support

In the exercise of political power, a President is able to accomplish a great deal more if he has supporters in a majority of the other branches of government. In his first six years in office, with a supportive Republican majority in the House of Representatives, President George W. Bush was only once forced to use his veto and succeeded in passing a majority of his main policies through Congress. It was not surprising, therefore, that he campaigned as hard as he did for Republican candidates during the 2002 mid-term elections.

The President can also encourage active support for the party by rewarding those who help the party, especially during elections, with appointment to political office.

The President also has an unmatched ability to raise campaign funds. Ahead of the 2006 mid-term elections, with the prominent Pennsylvania Senator Rick Santorum facing a strong challenge, President George W. Bush attended a fund-raising event that raised $1.7 million, followed by another nine months later that raised $700,000.

Above all, if the President's policies are popular, the whole party can be relied upon to rally around to provide support to turn proposals into policies that are implemented. These, in turn, can have a coat-tails effect that leads to electoral success for the party around the country.

Conclusion

The role of party leader is an awkward one for Presidents. Used effectively, it can add to the likelihood of the successful implementation of the President's agenda. Against this, however, Presidents have to be aware that if they appear to be using their position for party advantage, there is a risk of squandering the political advantages that come with the prestige of being head of state.

The Vice President

'Not worth a bucket of warm spit.'

Jack Garner, who served as Vice President to F. D. Roosevelt between 1933 and 1941, is credited with saying that the position was 'Not worth a bucket of warm piss', although the quote was adjusted a little by reporters. He was not the first Vice President to dismiss the importance of the office. John Adams, the first Vice President, said, 'My country has in its wisdom contrived for me the most insignificant office that ever the invention of man contrived or his imagination conceived.'

These complaints arise from the fact that the Vice President has only two roles outlined in the Constitution, one of which has little practical importance much of the time. The Vice President is officially the presiding officer of the Senate, although on most occasions this role is carried out by a Senator and the Vice President breaks a tied vote in the Senate. The other role is to take over the presidency if the President dies in office or is unable to carry out his duties.

This second role is very important, as both John Adams and Jack Garner would have recognised. Indeed, had an attempt on the life of President F. D. Roosevelt in Miami in 1933 been successful, Jack Garner would have become President. Furthermore, because all Vice Presidents are 'a heartbeat away from the presidency', the position is quite a strong launch pad for a presidential election campaign. However, for those who were never elevated to the top office, their role and importance in the White House has depended entirely on the discretion of the President, hence the complaints.

A position of growing importance

Despite the limitations of the vice presidency, it has grown in stature since the Second World War for a variety of reasons:

- The Vice President has played a significant role in winning elections by 'balancing the ticket' and compensating for perceived weaknesses in the presidential candidate.

- As the role of the Federal government has grown, the Vice President has been given increasingly high-profile roles to support the President in running the executive branch.
- Some Vice Presidents have played important advisory roles to the President, such as Al Gore on environmental policy in relation to President Clinton.
- Some Vice Presidents have played an important role in liaising with the party and colleagues in Congress, such as Dick Cheney in relation to George W. Bush.
- Of the eleven most recent Vice Presidents, four have gone on to be President and three more were chosen as their party's presidential candidates.

Overall, therefore, while the importance of the position remains at the discretion of the President, it is increasingly recognised as a post that can be used to assist in the execution of domestic policy.

Evaluating the domestic powers of the President

Negotiator-in-Chief?

President Harry Truman described his role in the following terms: 'I sit here all day trying to persuade people to do the things they ought to have sense enough to do without my persuading them. That's all the powers of the President amount to.' It is this frustration at the limitations on presidential power that has led the position to be described, at various times, as 'persuader-in-chief', 'bargainer-in-chief' or 'negotiator-in-chief'. Is this a true reflection of the powers of the presidency, or a reflection of one man's irritation during a period of personal frustration?

The frustrations of the presidency

Presidents certainly face a range of restrictions that make Truman's frustration understandable:

- Assembling a policy-making team of people who fulfill the requirements to run the executive departments and agencies is almost an impossible challenge.
- The smooth running of the executive branch in a way that meets the policy requirements of the President is hindered by the fact

that he cannot reorganise the branch in a way that suits him: this can only be done by Congress.

- Some of the most important agencies, such as the Federal Reserve, are headed by people beyond the control of the President.
- The President has limited ability to influence the passage of legislation, which is the primary way that proposals become policy.
- Even if policy is passed which meets the President's needs and wishes, he may have difficulty getting it implemented by a Federal Bureaucracy that is often reluctant to overhaul programmes it may have been developing over an extended period for an administration that will not be in office for more than eight years.

Comparatively few heads of government around the world face such a formidable range of limitations.

The instruments of presidential power

Given the priorities of the Founding Fathers – to put obstacles in the way of an over-mighty executive – the difficulties faced by Presidents in wielding power are to be expected. However, the Founding Fathers also wanted to put in place a government that could be effective. Thus, the President has at his disposal a range of instruments, both official and informal, that can help him to achieve his policy goals:

- Even if the Cabinet, as a body, has shortcomings as a policy-making instrument, it nevertheless contains influential 'top tier' members in whom the President usually has great confidence and who help him formulate policy on a bi-lateral basis.
- Since 1939, the President has had the support of the Executive Office of the Presidency (EOP) co-ordinating the executive branch and monitoring the implementation of presidential priorities.
- The spoils system enables the President to appoint to the Federal bureaucracy political sympathisers to help supervise the implementation of policy.
- The President is able to use his power of veto and, equally importantly, the *threat* of a veto to put pressure on Congress to pass legislation in a form he will find acceptable.
- The President is also able to use the discretion available to him over how and where Federal resources are spent to forge alliances in Congress in support of his proposals.

- In recent years, he has made increasing use of the Vice President to bolster party support for his policies.
- Above all, some Presidents have made skilful use of their prestige, as head of state, to undermine those opposing their policy agendas by creating an impression that opponents are motivated by ideological considerations, or even narrow self-interest, while he represents the interests of the nation.

The influence of foreign policy

Before reaching a definitive conclusion on the extent of the US President's domestic powers, the political benefits of leading the world's sole super-power (some would argue mega-power) have to be considered. In much the same way as the President's position head of state can act as a catalyst to his effectiveness in his formal political roles, so too can his foreign-policy responsibilities. How this works in practice is explored in the next chapter.

··

✔ What you should have learnt from reading this chapter

- It was the intention of the Founding Fathers that the executive branch would not be allowed to develop into a powerful leader, reminiscent of a monarch, but would play the secondary role of implementing the wishes of Congress.

- A range of constitutional checks and balances were put in place to ensure that the powers of the President were restricted.

- In addition, as the USA grew in size and the government grew in scope, a cumbersome bureaucracy emerged that all Presidents have found difficult to control, further limiting their ability to impose their will on the nation. Hence the frustrations of some Presidents who felt that they were reduced to being 'negotiator-in-chief'.

- However, by giving the President the role of head of state, the Founding Fathers provided the executive branch with a powerful political tool, the immense authority of being the living symbol of the nation, which means that the presidential political agenda can be presented as being in the national interest.

- Taken together with the foreign-policy powers of the executive branch, covered in the next chapter, does this mean that the President is 'the most powerful person in the world'?

🔍 Glossary of key terms

Cabinet An advisory group that may be called upon to aid presidential decision-making, consisting of the heads of the executive departments and some members of the Executive Office of the Presidency.

Executive Office of the Presidency (EOP) A cluster of agencies to provide the President with advice and help in the running of the executive branch.

Federal Bureaucracy The civil service with responsibility for implementing Federal laws.

Government corporations Businesses, such as the Postal Service, that are government-owned.

Independent agencies Similar to the fifteen executive departments, with responsibility for devising and implementing specific areas of policy, but on a smaller scale.

Independent regulatory commissions Agencies, established by Congress and independent of the President, with responsibility for regulating important aspects of society.

Spoils system The award of government jobs to political supporters.

State of the Union Message An annual speech to Congress, in which the President sets out his political and legislative priorities for the year ahead.

Veto The constitutional power of a President to block a bill that has passed through Congress by refusing to sign it into law.

❓ Likely examination questions

See 'likely examination questions' at the end of Chapter 10 (page 332).

🖥 Helpful websites

www.whitehouse.gov – the official website of the President.

Every aspect of the presidency is the subject of such intense interest that the best way to keep up with the latest political developments is to view the websites of any of the most influential news organisations in the USA, such as *The New York Times* (www.nytimes.com), *The Washington Post*, (www.washingtonpost.com), or CNN (www.cnn.com).

Suggestions for further reading

The greatest insight into the challenges facing Presidents and their responses are found in their autobiographies, such as *My Life* by Bill Clinton and *An American Life* by Ronald Reagan.

The Presidency – Foreign Affairs

Contents

Overview

On 26 March 2003, during the second Gulf War, US forces were attacked by the Iraqi army during an intense sandstorm. The Iraqis, believing that the storm had rendered them invisible, sought to use their experience of local conditions to compensate for the technological superiority of the Americans. However, using satellites and thermal imaging, the US troops were able to track them as easily as on a clear day and within hours the Iraqi forces were destroyed.

This one-sided engagement is the result of decades of defence-spending at a level that dwarfs other countries. By some estimates, the USA spends more on defence than every other country in the world combined, and expenditure is projected to keep rising to $439 billion in 2009. In addition, the USA is also immensely powerful economically, with a Gross National Product (GNP) on a par with the whole of the European Union. The US economy is so large that the GNP of California alone is equivalent to that of the world's fifth-largest economy.

Yet the Constitution of the USA was written for a nation that was many weeks' travel from the major powers of Europe and Asia, and the Founding Fathers anticipated that their country would have minimal involvement with the affairs of other countries. This is reflected in limited checks and balances being placed on the President in foreign affairs.

This chapter examines whether the emergence of the USA as the world's sole super-power has put too much unfettered power in the hands of one person, contrary to the spirit of the Constitution, and, if so, what effect this has had on the overall political design of the Founding Fathers.

Key issues to be covered in this chapter

- The President's constitutional responsibilities in foreign affairs and how they have evolved
- How Presidents fulfil their foreign roles in the governing of the USA
- The impact of foreign policy on the domestic powers of Presidents
- The extent to which the combined foreign and domestic operation of the President matches the vision of the Founding Fathers

The presidency and the Constitution

Giving the executive freedom of manoeuvre

For the Founding Fathers, keeping the executive branch in check, so that it could not threaten the freedoms of the American people, was the highest priority. They did not appear to place as high a priority on keeping the executive branch in check in foreign affairs.

When the Constitution was being written, the newly created nation was surrounded by territory controlled by the powerful imperial countries of Europe. The British controlled Canada to the north. The Spanish controlled the land to the south, in what is now Florida. The French claimed sovereignty over all the land to the west of the Mississippi River, from Canada to the Mexican border. All of these European powers had a record of constantly seeking to add to their territorial possessions and posed a genuine threat to the fledgling USA, if it appeared unable to effectively defend itself. When negotiating with them on behalf of nation, therefore, the President was provided with the diplomatic and military powers to respond to whatever situation arose.

Coupled with these concerns was a certain level of complacency that, provided local threats could be neutralised, there was little likelihood of the USA becoming entangled in world affairs. In an age of sail ships, the Atlantic Ocean provided a 3,000-mile-wide buffer between the USA and Europe, which could take weeks to cross. To the west, the USA did not even have access to the Pacific Ocean, and then there was another 4,000 miles or more to the Far East. Thus, the Constitution gave the President the powers of being chief diplomat, responsible for the conduct of relations with other countries, and Commander-in-Chief of the armed forces.

The Constitution also placed a number of congressional checks on how the President used these powers:

- All treaties require ratification by two-thirds of the Senate.
- Senior diplomats and senior appointees to the armed forces have to be confirmed, by a simple majority, by the Senate before they can take up their positions.
- While the President has the power to deploy and use the armed forces in minor engagements, the Constitution made Congress alone responsible for declaring war.

However, while in domestic affairs the constitutional emphasis was on giving primary responsibility for policy to Congress, in foreign affairs the balance of powers emphasises responsibility upon the executive branch for policy, providing a freedom of manoeuvre that has had far-reaching implications for the power of the President in both foreign *and* domestic affairs.

Making full use of freedom of manoeuvre

The executive was given greater freedom in foreign affairs despite the expectation of the Founding Fathers that even people of the highest integrity could be tempted to expand the power at their disposal, justifying it on the basis that they could govern more effectively in the public interest.

Just fourteen years after the adoption of the Constitution, events illustrated the importance of effective checks on executive power. In 1803, President Jefferson bought the land claimed by France in an arrangement known as the Louisiana Purchase. For $15 million, the USA acquired land that doubled the size of its territory and was eventually made into thirteen new states. The President knew that the transaction tested the boundaries of his constitutional powers. He wrote, 'The Constitution has made no provision for our holding foreign territory, still less for incorporating foreign nations into our Union. The Executive . . . have done an act beyond the Constitution.' However, the fact that Congress failed to challenge him and went on to ratify and pay for the arrangement meant that the expansion of presidential powers in foreign affairs had begun.

The Supreme Court demonstrated a similar unwillingness to challenge the President in his capacity as Commander-in-Chief. When the Civil War broke out in 1861, President Lincoln assumed emergency powers, including the suppression of publications (violating the 1st Amendment) and detentions without trials (violating the 6th Amendment). He argued that the only concern was whether the government would be 'not *too* strong for the liberties of its people [but] strong *enough* to maintain its own existence, in great emergencies'. The Supreme Court made one attempt to challenge these powers, in the case of *ex parte Merryman* (1861), which ruled that detention without trial was unconstitutional, but the army ignored the decision and followed the orders of the President instead. The Chief Justice was forced to recognise that while he had 'exercised all the power which the constitution and laws confer on me' at a time of national emergency, the President's use of his military powers represents 'a force too strong for me to overcome'.

Indeed, faced with the reality that they could not impose their will on the Commander-in-Chief, the judiciary went further and effectively gave its blessing to the expansion of presidential powers. In the Prize Cases of 1863, the owners of four ships that had been captured and sold as prizes of war took the President to court, arguing that such actions were only allowed at wartime and since Congress had not formally declared war the government's actions were unconstitutional. The Supreme Court ruled that if the USA finds itself defending its national interests by force, it is effectively at war even if there has been no official declaration by Congress. Thus, the most significant constitutional check on the President's use of the military was substantially diluted.

US Presidents have also used a device for evading the principal check on their powers as chief diplomat. Executive Agreements are formal agreements between the USA and the leaders of another country that have the same status in international law as a treaty. However, unlike treaties, which require ratification by two-thirds of the Senate, Executive Agreements can be negotiated and implemented without Congressional scrutiny.

Should a President wish to have Congressional support for an Executive Agreement that is unlikely to receive two-thirds support in the Senate, there is the option of negotiating a Congressional-Executive Agreement, which is ratified by a simple majority in both houses of Congress. Again, it has been open to question whether this device is constitutional, but the Supreme Court upheld its validity in *Missouri v. Holland* in 1820.

Manifest destiny

The Founding Fathers were well aware of the risks of giving the executive too much unchecked power in diplomatic and military affairs. Throughout history, national leaders had bolstered their standing among their people or enhanced their powers by precipitating international crises during which any challenge could be portrayed as unpatriotic and from which they could emerge as national heroes. During the national debate on whether or not to ratify the Constitution, its principal author warned, in *The Federalist* No. 41, that 'The liberties of Rome proved the final victim to her military triumphs, and that the liberties of Europe, as far as they ever existed, have with few exceptions been the price of her military establishments.' Why, then, did they provide so few effective checks on the President in foreign affairs?

A significant factor was a widespread belief in the USA that it was their nation's destiny, ordained by God, to eventually expand to control the whole of North and Central America, and possibly even South America as well. This belief, known as manifest destiny, was compatible with giving the President the means to respond rapidly to any situation that provided an opportunity to fulfil the nation's territorial destiny, including military conquest.

The goals of US foreign policy

Conflicting objectives

The influence of manifest destiny in US attitudes towards its neighbours would suggest that aggressive expansionism would dominate its foreign policy.

Similarly, one of the legacies of having been ruled from London was that the USA's main commercial links were with the UK. Future prosperity would mean building new markets for American exports. However, with the fierce commercial rivalries between the major European powers, and their control over much of the New World, advancing American commercial interests had the potential to spark conflict.

However, in the USA there was another highly influential view of the country's role in the world that ran counter to the views that were likely to cause American involvement in complex international engagements. For those who believed that US foreign policy should be consistent with the ideals of the first settlers who came to North America, Christian refugees, the primary objective should be to demonstrate their nation's moral superiority by conducting foreign affairs in a way that distinguished America from the greedy self-interest of the European countries their forebears had escaped from. Rather, insofar as the USA engaged with far-flung places, policy should be driven by the promotion of freedom and democracy around the world.

Thus, from the outset, there was a potential for US foreign policy to veer between aggressive self-interest, a reluctance to engage with the rest of the world and a highly moralistic approach to relationships with other nations.

National interest

In the nineteenth-century, US policy was dominated by a determination to expand its territory and assert its influence over the rest of the continent. The expansion of its territory was accomplished through wars, treaties and purchases, including:

* Fighting a war against Britain in 1812, in an unsuccessful attempt to end restrictions on the ports its trading ships could use and to capture territory in Canada.
* Forcing Spain, in 1819, to relinquish control over Florida by threatening to invade the area.
* Starting wars, in the 1830s, with the Native American nations, leading to their expulsion from what is now Oklahoma.
* Gaining control over the north-west of the country, by a treaty with Britain, again after a threat of war, in 1846.
* Acquiring a huge sweep of land, from Texas to California, following the defeat of Mexico in a war between 1846 and 1848, and a purchase of land by the USA in 1853.
* Purchasing Alaska from Russia, for $7.2 million, in 1867.

The process of asserting its influence over the parts of the continent it did not control began with the announcement of the Monroe Doctrine in 1823. President Monroe warned the major European powers not to interfere in the American continent. Any unwelcome interventions, in which the USA perceived its 'rights are invaded or seriously menaced', would lead to 'preparations for our defence'.

In the name of protecting small nations in the region from European powers, the USA took control of Cuba, the Philippines, Puerto Rico and Hawaii. When, in 1903, Columbia refused permission for the United States to build a canal linking the Atlantic and Pacific oceans, a local revolution was sponsored that led to the creation of the nation of Panama. This new country then allowed the canal to be constructed and controlled by the USA.

This kind of direct intervention in the affairs of other countries clearly went further than the terms of the Monroe Doctrine and was justified, in retrospect, by the Roosevelt Corollary in 1904. President Theodore Roosevelt asserted the right of the USA to ensure that the continent remained 'stable, orderly and prosperous' in the event of 'wrongdoing or impotence' amongst its neighbours, which required the USA to exercise 'international police powers'.

In the period before the start of the First World War, Presidents tended to use the growing economic power of the USA to shape its relations with other countries, starting with President Taft, who introduced the idea of dollar diplomacy, promoting American investments to help ensure economic and political stability while strengthening diplomatic ties. Military intervention became a strategy of last resort. With the eruption of war in Europe, however, and attacks on US ships, mainly by the German navy, avoiding military intervention became impossible and the USA entered the war on 6 April 1917.

Promoting freedom and democracy

The immense loss of life during the First World War caused people all around the world to review how international relations were managed. President Woodrow Wilson's peace proposals reflected this mood and, arguably, ushered in a shift in emphasis towards a more moralistic foreign policy. He wanted a new approach to international relations based on:

- Open, honest diplomatic relationships between countries, rather than the secret negotiations that had led to the hostility and insecurity that had sparked the war.
- Free trade, which forged links between countries, rather than the rival economic fortresses that the imperial powers had tried to build at the end of the nineteenth century.
- Restoring land to countries that had lost territory as a result of war, thereby reducing resentment that could, in time, lead to further conflict.
- Self-determination, in which people would be able to live in the same country as others of the same culture and language, and be

able to have sovereignty over their own affairs. This would mean the dismantling of empires, first within Europe and later around the world.

- A 'general association of nations' with the power to arbitrate between nations during an international dispute and the means to protect nations threatened by more powerful, aggressive, countries.

Some, but not all, of these proposals were included in the Versailles Treaty, which formally brought the First World War to an end, and even those that were incorporated were often diluted. The response of the Senate, which had to ratify the treaty before the USA could participate in the new international arrangements it introduced (such as the League of Nations), was to reject the shift towards a moralistic approach to foreign policy and shift towards isolating their nation from future disastrous international entanglements. By a margin of 53–38, the Senate voted against ratification.

This tension between Presidents seeking to build greater stability in international affairs and promote American values, and Congresses inclined to isolationism, continued in the inter-war years.

The USA played a leading role in defusing escalating tension between France and Germany in 1923, over the payment of reparations. The Dawes Plan, named after the US Vice President who led the negotiations, helped stabilise the German economy with US loans, which allowed reparations payments to be made. Six years later, the USA persuaded the other victors of the First World War to accept a longer-term plan for ensuring that Germany could cope with the economic impact of reparations. The Young Plan, again named after the American who led the negotiations, came into effect in 1930. Meanwhile, Presidents kept a close eye on the emergence of totalitarian dictators in the Soviet Union, Germany and Italy. All three were regarded as regimes committed to the destruction of democratic liberties, and through the 1930s US foreign policy was increasingly aligned with European democracies, culminating in the Lend-Lease Act of 1941, in which military resources were provided to countries at war with Nazi Germany. Congress, on the other hand, passed three Neutrality Acts between 1935 and 1937, in an attempt to ensure that the USA would not once again be drawn into any war that erupted in Europe.

The attack on Pearl Harbor, on 7 December 1941, demonstrated how unrealistic a policy of isolationism was in an age of long-range weapons, and when the Second World War was over, the influence of isolationists receded. Between 1945 and 1989, when the regimes of Eastern Europe collapsed, foreign policy was dominated by a global battle for supremacy between the values of liberty and democracy, underpinned by a capitalist economy, and the values of economic and social equality, underpinned by a centrally-controlled economy. Led by the USA and the Soviet Union, the struggle to promote each ideology and undermine the other led to levels of hostility that fell just short of war between the two super-powers and often led to proxy wars between their allies around the world.

The US approach to the post-war world was based on the Truman Doctrine. In 1947, the President committed the USA to supporting through economic or military assistance all nations around the world who were resisting the advance of Communism. This led to the Marshall Plan, a huge economic aid programme for Western Europe in the aftermath of the Second World War to promote economic and political stability, military intervention in Korea in the 1950s, Vietnam in the 1960s and support for resistance fighters in Afghanistan after an invasion by the Soviet Union in 1979. This was accompanied by an arms race in which weapons became ever more sophisticated and potent in case the rivalry between the two sides ever erupted into direct conflict.

The intensity of this **Cold War** fluctuated. In 1963, the deployment by the Soviet Union of ballistic missiles in Cuba, just ninety miles from the mainland of the USA, almost sparked a nuclear conflict. In the 1970s, however, there was a period of détente, when the two sides engaged in diplomacy to reduce tensions and slow the pace of the arms race. The Cold War only came to an end, however, with the collapse of Communist governments in Eastern Europe and the Soviet Union being dissolved in 1991.

What was seen as the triumph of American values shaped US foreign policy in the years immediately following the Cold War. In 1991, President Bush Snr proclaimed a new world order based on the principles of liberal democracy, free trade and the renunciation of military aggression to further foreign-policy objectives. His speech followed the success of a coalition of thirty-four countries, under US leadership, in ejecting the Iraqi army from Kuwait, which had been invaded the previous year. The prospect of the world coming together to ensure stability by protecting the weak from the powerful appeared a realistic prospect, and in the 1990s the USA intervened in a number of countries to bring an end to military aggression, including Somalia (1992), Haiti (1994), Bosnia (1995) and Kosovo (1999).

Conflicting historical perspectives on twentieth-century foreign policy

Some historians strongly dispute any suggestion that US foreign policy since the First World War was motivated by idealism. They argue that the support offered by the USA – from loans to Germany in the 1920s to the Marshall Plan of the 1950s – required countries that benefited from economic aid to open themselves up to free trade with the USA, thereby providing markets for American products.

It is also argued that military assistance to resist the advance of Communism was not a defensive measure, as suggested by President Truman, but part of an aggressive strategy to ensure US global dominance that started with the dropping of atomic bombs on Hiroshima and Nagasaki to demonstrate America's military superiority. Even the war that restored independence to Kuwait in 1991 is seen by critics as a thin veil for US control of Middle East oil fields, on which its economy depends.

Other historians argue that US policy has never been driven exclusively by either self-interest or idealism, but by a fusion of both, with one element carrying more weight than the other at different times.

The foreign policy of George W. Bush

Does the foreign policy of President George W. Bush fall into the category of self-interest, idealism or a fusion of both?

As candidate for the Presidency, George W. Bush was quite clear about his priorities: he would put America first, engaging only in foreign-policy initiatives he believed to be in the national interest. That would mean not seeking Senate ratification of the Kyoto Protocol on climate change, which, he believed, would damage the US economy while offering only questionable benefits to the environment; withdrawal of support for the International Criminal Court as it had the potential to infringe the sovereignty of the US judicial system (this policy was implemented when the ICC was established in May 2002); withdrawal from the Anti-Ballistic Missile Treaty, which limited the ability of the USA to build a missile defence system (this policy was implemented in June 2002); and an intention to avoid brokering peace deals around the world, such as the Israeli–Palestinian conflict, unless it was clearly in the interests of the USA to do so. To some observers, this appeared reminiscent of the isolationism that dominated Congressional policy in the 1930s.

This policy was, however, transformed into interventionism on 11 September 2001, when airliners were flown into the World Trade Center in New York City and the **Pentagon** in Washington DC, with the loss of more than 3,000 lives. What was the thinking that underpinned the new approach?

Policy has centred on al Qaeda as the main threat to the USA. For the first time since the end of the Cold War, this has meant fighting an enemy that represents both a physical danger and a set of ideas that seek to capture the hearts and minds of millions of people around the world. In response, the administration of President George W. Bush has adopted a two-pronged strategy that defends US territory while promoting the values of freedom and, especially, democracy around the world. The National Security Strategy for 2002 declared that policy 'will be based on a distinctly American internationalism that reflects the union of our values and national interests'.

A pressure group that has been particularly influential in developing this new policy is the Project for the New American Century. From its establishment in 1997, it argued that foreign policy should be based on 'a military that is strong and ready to meet both present and future challenges' and 'a foreign policy that boldly and purposefully promotes American principles abroad'. Another particularly strong influence on President George W. Bush has been a book entitled *The Case for Democracy*, by a former Soviet dissident who became a minister in the Israeli government, Natan Sharansky. This argues that terrorism flourishes in societies that are not free and that the promotion of democracy is central to success in a 'War on Terror'.

Based on these ideas, US foreign policy has moved away from co-existence with authoritarian or totalitarian regimes that had previously been cultivated in the name of stable international relations.

Instead, pressure has been put on allies to introduce democratic reforms, and the most undemocratic, aggressive governments, which support terrorist groups, have faced concerted US efforts to replace them with democracies. Fostering democracy as a precondition for peace has also led to a reversal of the President's original policy of avoiding interventions in distant conflicts, such as that between the Israelis and Palestinians. One key element in the President's original policy did not change: US decisions would not be subject to agreement from international organisations such as the United Nations or even dependent on support from traditional allies, such as France. Once a course of action had been decided upon, the United States would welcome support from a 'coalition of the willing' but would not be constrained by friend or foe.

The intended impact of these policies, combined with operations to directly attack terrorist groups, was to reshape environments in which terrorism thrives so that they become environments in which democracy leads to a more peaceful world. In his State of the Union Address on 29 January 2002, President George W. Bush identified North Korea, Iran and Iraq as the three nations offering no prospect of democratic reform, who were willing to support terrorist groups and were implacably opposed to the USA and its interests, describing them as 'an axis of evil'. Although there was no evidence of a direct link between these nations and the group that attacked the USA on 9/11, the logic of the relationship between tyranny and terrorism made them legitimate targets in the eyes of the President. Just over a year later, a US-led coalition invaded Iraq and deposed its dictator, Saddam Hussein.

The policy of 'American internationalism' has the potential to involve the USA in a number of simultaneous conflicts around the world. This, in turn, has led to a thorough review of the armed forces and intelligence services. The military has been expected to adapt its tactics to rely on agile, smaller forces, rapid deployment and precision strikes. In 2003, the successful invasion of Iraq used less than half as many troops as were needed to expel Iraqi forces from Kuwait in 1991. The intelligence services have been under pressure to detect further terrorist attacks while in their planning stage, which has meant a return to infiltrating small, tightly-knit units, a form of spying that had been largely neglected during the Cold War, when the most useful information was provided by satellites and sophisticated monitoring equipment.

The effectiveness of these policies has been a matter of fierce worldwide debate since the President's 'axis of evil' speech. Critics argue that the core principle of US policy, that free societies are more likely to be peaceful, is flawed. Democracies are as likely to fight to defend their vital interests as non-democracies. Further, countries do not make the transition from dictatorship to democracy in one step. It takes time and there is evidence that partial democracies are the most belligerent and unstable form of government. One of America's closest allies, Pakistan, is often held up as proof of this point.

Further, critics argue that while the US military is devastatingly effective in battle, it has never been skilled at winning the hearts and minds of the people in the territory it has won. The new high-tech forces may not have adequate manpower to be an effective occupation force. Almost any action taken to subdue any resistance, such as raiding a home, alienates the local population. In the case of Iraq, the armed forces arrived with inadequate 'cultural intelligence': with few US students graduating with a university degree in Arabic (just six in 2002), the military had too few people it could call upon to promote mutual understanding, leading to avoidable misunderstandings such as the assumption that a household with photos of Saddam Hussein still supported their former ruler because the soldiers could not read the captions denouncing him. The consequent growth in hostility between the Iraqis and the US forces has led to incidents such as the abuse of prisoners at Abu Ghraib in 2003.

Above all, there is a concern that these policies have the potential to spark further conflict. The logic of a successful operation to replace a dictatorship with a democracy is that it is worth repeating, and for countries labelled as an 'axis of evil' there is an obvious incentive to build up their defences with the most powerful weapons at their disposal to ward off a potential US attack.

A survey of world opinion, conducted in 2004 by the renowned Pew Research Centre, suggests that the prestige and moral authority of the USA has diminished since the adoption of 'American internationalism'.

Supporters of the policy, however, argue that although it takes time for the seeds of democratic reform to grow and flourish (especially in parts of the world that have not been fertile territory for democracy in the past), there have already been signs of an 'Arab spring'. They argue that the Middle East has witnessed, on Arab news networks, Afghans participating in free elections for the first time in their history and Iraqis voting despite the threat of car bombs, and that tentative steps towards peace and democracy have been seen in other parts of the region. Libya, in 2004, gave up its weapons of mass destruction; in 2005, Egypt and Saudi Arabia held elections that were more free than any that had preceded them; and Syria was forced by a mass movement to withdraw its army from Lebanon. One of Lebanon's prominent leaders who made no secret of his initial opposition to the US invasion of Iraq said, 'But when I saw the Iraqi people voting, eight million of them, it was the start of a new Arab world. The Berlin Wall has fallen. We can see it.'

Additionally, it is argued, the policy has been more pragmatic and flexible than some critics have recognised. The USA has always made it clear that it does not intend to use military force against North Korea, and in June 2006 the Secretary of State announced that the USA would be prepared to engage Iran in negotiations in return for a suspension of a programme that could lead to the building of a nuclear bomb.

The instruments of US foreign policy

Formulating policy
The development of US foreign policy is the product of the political priorities of the President and the advice/guidance/pressure of three key institutions that have responsibility for implementing decisions.

The State Department
Originally known as the Department of Foreign Affairs, the **State Department** is responsible for 'the conduct of foreign relations, to promote the long-range security and well-being of the United States'. It fulfils its functions by:

- Keeping the President informed about international developments.
- Maintaining diplomatic relations with foreign governments.

- Negotiating treaties.
- Protecting the interests of Americans abroad.

As an organisation that often spends years carefully cultivating rela-tionships with foreign governments, which it is loathe to abandon, the State Department is often perceived by Presidents as one of the parts of the Federal bureaucracy least responsive to an incoming adminis-tration's goals (see Chapter 9). This is particularly true of decisions to resolve diplomatic disputes by use of armed force. In the planning stage of the invasion of Iraq, for example, although the Department was led by a former general, it strongly advised delaying military action until all diplomatic avenues had been exhausted and support for American intervention had been built up around the world.

The Department of Defense
The largest of all the departments that make up the executive branch of government, with about 800,000 civilian employees and more than a million military personnel, the Department of Defense is often referred to as the Pentagon, after the shape of its Headquarters in Arlington, Virginia. Its primary role is to assist the President in car-rying out his duties as Commander-in-Chief. This gives it a very different relationship with the White House, as a military culture tends to be highly responsive to orders issued by their Commander-in-Chief, which, in turn often results in the Secretary of Defense having disproportionate influence on the President and intruding into the responsibilities of the Department of State. Certainly, during the first term of President George W. Bush, when these two departments offered conflicting advice the Pentagon usually prevailed.

Intelligence agencies
When weighing up the most appropriate course of action in relation to foreign nations, the President will need to take into account assess-ments of the intentions and likely actions of both allies and enemies. For this, he depends on the intelligence services. The most famous of these is the Central Intelligence Agency (CIA) but this is not the only, nor even the largest, intelligence service.

Fifteen Federal agencies belong to the 'intelligence community'. Eight of these, representing more than 80 per cent of the annual budget of £40 billion, fall under the responsibility of the Department of Defense. The work of the different agencies has frequently either overlapped, creating rivalry, or left gaps, leading to mutual blame. Most notably, the CIA failed to recognise the imminent collapse of Communist regimes in Eastern Europe in the late 1980s and, despite having a significant amount of information, none of the agencies were able to anticipate and intercept the attacks of 9/11.

To prevent further attacks and to make accurate judgements on interventions to promote the goal of spreading democracy, there was widespread agreement in political circles that the intelligence community's command structure needed to be reformed. In 2004, Congress passed the Intelligence Reform and Terrorism Prevention Act, which created the post of Director of National Intelligence with responsibility to co-ordinate the work of all intelligence agencies. Whether the new arrangement will be an improvement will not become clear for many years.

The impact of foreign policy on domestic affairs

Is the system of checks and balances working?

James Madison, the principal architect of the US Constitution, observed that since the days of the Roman Empire, countries that became world powers have suffered a loss of domestic liberty as a direct result of the concentrated power at the disposal of national leaders, combined with the immense stature of bringing greater glory to their countries.

Clearly, some Presidents have made skilful use of the prestige that accompanies the position of head of state, to advance their political agendas by creating an impression that they are motivated by interests of the nation (see chapter 9). Has the development of the USA into the world's sole super-power, led by the President, had a similar effect on the powers of the President, serving as a catalyst to bolster his position in domestic as well as foreign affairs, and thereby exposing a major flaw in the constitutional design?

Disregarding the Constitution at times of national crisis

There is certainly substantial evidence that when defence of the nation has been at the top of the political agenda, Presidents have been able and willing to evade the restrictions imposed by the Constitution, including the following examples:

- President Lincoln, during the Civil War, blockaded Southern ports despite no declaration of war having been made, suspended habeas corpus, spent money without Congressional authorisation and imprisoned 18,000 suspected Confederate sympathisers without trial.
- President F. D. Roosevelt, during the Second World War, issued Executive Order 9066, which resulted in 120,000 Japanese-Americans being held in internment camps for up to three years. The policy was upheld by the Supreme Court in *Korematsu* v. *United States* (1944), which ruled that the detentions were justified by military necessity. (Subsequently, in 1988, Congress issued a formal apology and authorised the payment of reparations for the infringements of their rights.)
- President Truman, during the Korean War, seized control of the steel industry to secure the necessary raw materials for the armaments industry. The decision was challenged and overturned by the Supreme Court in *Youngstown Sheet & Tube Co.* v. *Sawyer* (1952), which ruled that even in a national emergency the President could only use exceptional powers if authorised by Congress.
- President Johnson was able to escalate US involvement in the Vietnam War from 16,000 men in 1963, when he took office, to 500,000 in 1968 when he left office, without war being declared.
- President Nixon, during the Vietnam War, authorised secret military operations into Cambodia and Laos, run directly from the White House, after Congress had expressly rejected his plans. Some commentators link the ability of the administration to circumvent the law with its decision to take a similar approach to domestic politics and authorise a break-in at Democratic headquarters in the Watergate Building in Washington, to steal documents and install wiretaps on phones.
- The administration of Ronald Reagan, in the 1980s, secretly sold weapons to Iran in violation of international sanctions, in an attempt to increase its influence with a hostile regime. The

proceeds of the sales were then secretly channelled to anti-Communist forces in Nicaragua seeking to overthrow the government, again in violation of international law.

Strengthening Constitutional safeguards in foreign affairs

The combination of the executive branch fighting a full-scale war in Vietnam, without a formal declaration of war, and President Nixon's flagrant disregard of the constitutional constraints in both foreign and domestic affairs, led Congress in the mid-1970s to strengthen its checks on the President. New laws included:

- The Case-Zablocki Act (1972), which required the President to report on Executive Agreements within sixty days of negotiating them. However, as a result of a 1983 Supreme Court decision, *INS* v. *Chadha*, Congress cannot simply overrule an Executive Agreement it does not support but must negotiate with the President on any amendments it wishes make.
- The War Powers Act (1973) requires the President to consult with Congress prior to the start of any hostilities, inform Congress of developments until US armed forces are withdrawn and to remove US armed forces within sixty days if Congress has not declared war or passed a resolution authorising the use of force. In practice, Congress has been reluctant to invoke the resolution and force a withdrawal, as to do so may be seen as undermining the armed forces.

Both laws were intended to 'fulfill the intent of the framers of the Constitution of the United States' in ensuring that Congress should be fully consulted on foreign policy in order to properly carry out its duties as a check on executive power. Neither was very effective and they were resented by all Presidents, of both parties, as undermining their ability to act decisively in an international crisis.

The impact of foreign policy on domestic affairs in the presidency of George W. Bush

When George W. Bush became President, he was convinced that there had been an erosion of executive powers, with Congress having overstepped its constitutional boundaries, and that it was a priority to restore the balance. In the aftermath of the attacks of 9/11, it appeared that he had the opportunity to enhance presidential power at home as well as abroad.

A month after the attacks, Congress overwhelmingly passed a resolution giving the President its support in whatever military and diplomatic measures he thought necessary to defend the country. The President, bolstered by record levels of public support, took full advantage of the opportunity in:

- Taking the nation to war in Afghanistan and Iraq.
- Pushing through the PATRIOT Act, which extended the powers of law enforcement agencies.
- Imprisoning 'enemy combatants', including US citizens, without charge or legal representation.
- Removing or withholding government information from official websites.
- Authorising electronic surveillance on US citizens without a warrant, disregarding the Foreign Intelligence Surveillance Act (1978), which outlines procedures for such measures.
- Authorising secret 'rendition' of people suspected of involvement in terrorism, which involved transferring suspects to countries where torture is permitted during interrogations.
- Attempting to obstruct a bill (introduced when the practice of secret rendition was revealed) banning 'cruel, inhuman and degrading treatment' of detainees and, when this was unsuccessful, making it clear that 'the executive branch shall construe it in a manner consistent with the constitutional authority of the commander in chief'.

As the consequences of some of these actions became clear, however, such as the steady loss of US forces in Iraq, the President's public support fell and his assertions of executive power began to be challenged:

- Congress questioned the cost of the operation in Iraq and whether it was appropriate for the Department of Defense to be in charge of reconstruction after the war.
- The Supreme Court, in the case of *Hamdi* v. *Rumsfeld* (2004), ruled that a man held without charge as an enemy combatant was entitled to challenge his detention and declared that 'a state of war

is not a blank cheque for the president when it comes to the rights of the nation's citizens'.

Thus, over his two terms of office, President George W. Bush has learned that his ability to use his foreign policy powers to extend presidential authority has been largely dependent on the public mood and perceptions of how effective his foreign policy has been.

Evaluating the powers of the President

The most powerful person in the world?

Keeping the executive branch in check was, for the Founding Fathers, central to their constitutional design and, as Chapter 9 demonstrates, in domestic affairs they imposed constraints that Presidents have found intensely frustrating.

When the stature that comes with being both head of state and Commander-in-Chief are added to the equation, is the limited role of being 'negotiator-in-chief' transformed into being 'the most powerful person in the world'?

A loophole in the Constitution?

The Founding Fathers recognised that foreign-policy powers could act as a catalyst to the President's domestic powers and that this could significantly affect the balance of the Constitution. Against this risk, they chose to put the President in a position to fulfil their nation's 'manifest destiny' of dominating the continent of America. Thus, they knowingly left a loophole in their design that a skilful politician could exploit.

They had no way of knowing how dominant in world affairs their nation would become, and how large this loophole would grow as a consequence; but with the hopes they harboured for the future, they must have expected a powerful figure to emerge. Consequently, as leader of by far the most powerful nation on earth, the US President is permitted to dominate both domestic and international affairs at times of international crisis by a Constitution drawn up to protect against precisely such a situation.

The effectiveness of the constitutional design

Do the powers of the President therefore demonstrate that the Constitution of the USA is fundamentally flawed, unable to fulfil its objectives? Experience suggests not. The more effectively the loophole available to the President is exploited, the more it generates anxiety that the President's powers have become excessive, putting the nation's liberties at risk. This, in turn, has always provoked a reaction from the other branches of government – the States, the opposition political party, pressure groups and the wider electorate. Just as being the head of state and having immense foreign-policy powers acts as a catalyst to the overall power of the President, so the political culture described in the first chapter of this book acts as a catalyst to the forces that check and balance the power of the President.

Box 10.1 Comparing the heads of government of the USA and UK

Contrasting constitutional frameworks
Despite constitutional constraints, the President of the USA has emerged as an immensely powerful figure. This is particularly true in foreign affairs but, if the White House is occupied by a skilful politician, it can also apply to domestic matters. How does this compare to the powers available to the leader of the UK, where there are far fewer constitutional constraints?

Party loyalty: the benefits of a parliamentary system of government
The British Prime Minister heads a government that can, in most cases, rely on the support of the legislature. This means that Prime Ministers do not have to contend with the restrictive checks on their powers that can prove so frustrating to US Presidents.

There have been instances of a government not having a majority in Parliament: the Labour governments of Harold Wilson and James Callaghan in the 1970s had to make deals with some of the opposition parties, and the Conservative government of John Major lost its overall majority when a group of rebellious MPs were expelled from the Parliamentary party in 1994. However, these periods have not been typical, and the longest-serving Prime Ministers in modern times, Margaret Thatcher and Tony Blair, both enjoyed election victories that delivered large Parliamentary majorities.

This is a significant advantage in implementing the Prime Minister's political agenda, because:

- A loyal legislature is responsible for passing the government's legislative proposals.
- It is also responsible for scrutinising the day-to-day work of the government.
- MPs with reservations about an aspect of government policy will be forcefully reminded that they owe their electoral success to the party's leader.
- MPs in the governing party are also acutely aware that political promotion is dependent on the Prime Minister's patronage.

This combination of factors, none of which is available to the President of the USA, usually ensure that Parliament puts the interests of the government first, ahead of rival interests of constituents or the conscience of MPs. In contrast, Presidents have to contend with a legislature that may not be controlled by their own party and, even when it is, has a constitutional duty to act as a check on his powers.

Furthermore, although commentators often focus on the personal rivalries of the UK Cabinet, it is a much more cohesive decision-making tool than its US equivalent. This is because, in the UK, it is composed of people who have built their careers in the legislature, often having fought alongside one another in Parliamentary and electoral battles for the party's interests. Thus, Prime Ministers benefit from contributions of experienced politicians committed to the party's agenda and demand their full support for implementing a programme for which they have collective responsibility. Presidents, by comparison, do not have such close ties with their Cabinets, some of whom may not be senior politicians.

In foreign affairs, however, while Presidents face the constraints of having key appointments confirmed and treaties ratified, they have almost as much freedom of manoeuvre as Prime Ministers and much more formidable military and economic weapons at their disposal.

Importing the advantages of a presidential system of government

Among the advantages that a President used to have over a Prime Minister were two instruments to help him manage the complex machinery of government. The Executive Office of the President helps co-ordinate policy and the spoils system enables him to insert sympathetic eyes and ears into the government that which are supposed to carry out his programme.

In recent years, similar instruments have been made available to Prime Ministers. In the past, Prime Ministers relied on government departments for information and strategies in order to formulate policy. Now, the Prime Minister has a dedicated office that development long-term strategic plans, offers short-term policy advice, communicates with Parliament, develops relationships with the media and maintains links with the Prime Minister's party. Like the US President, this puts the Prime Minister in a position to challenge, and even overrule, policies prepared by government departments and gives the Prime Minister the opportunity to have a much higher political profile than any other politician in the party. Also, like the US President, in recent years Prime Ministers have appointed growing numbers of special advisors to the civil service to strengthen government control.

Party disloyalty: the drawbacks of a Parliamentary system of government

While the support of a Parliamentary majority, and an operational Cabinet, frees Prime Ministers from substantial checks on their powers, these assets can become liabilities if they lose the support of their political parties.

In the event that a perception grows within a political party that the current Prime Minister is heading towards electoral defeat, reservations about policy and legislative proposals will surface and support can ebb away. Under those circumstances, the Prime Minister's continued leadership of the party can be challenged. That was how Margaret Thatcher lost power in 1990 and John Major faced a serious challenge to his leadership in 1995.

A President, by comparison, is directly elected and cannot be removed by the party even in the event of becoming an electoral liability. When President Clinton, for example, was the focus of a Republican landslide in the 1994 mid-term elections, there was no question of him relinquishing his position. The nearest comparable situation would be a challenge to the President during the primaries during a re-election campaign, as happened to President Carter in 1980.

Party and power: a double-edged sword

Thus, backed by a united party, the powers of Prime Ministers are almost unchecked. At the height of their powers, prime ministerial power clearly exceeds presidential power.

Without a united party behind them, however, Prime Ministers are vulnerable in ways that Presidents are not. At the depths of political unpopularity, Prime Ministers may well find themselves unceremoniously removed from power. A President suffering similar levels of unpopularity is insulated from party pressures due to being directly elected. Further, as head of state, Presidents are able to distance themselves from partisan politics and present themselves to the population as defenders of the nation's interest, willing to accept unpopularity in order to do whatever is best for the country. Prime Ministers have no similar card to play.

Conclusion
Thus, the absence of constitutional constraints in the UK allows the Prime Minister to wield immense domestic power, if the political conditions are favourable. Only in exceptional circumstances, such as the months following 9/11, are comparable powers available to the President of the USA in domestic affairs, and such circumstances rarely last long.

At times of adverse political circumstances, however, the situation is reversed. A Prime Minister is more likely to be deposed during an extended period of unpopularity than is a President. Likewise, in foreign affairs, where the sheer scale of the US economy and armed forces make the President's influence unparalleled by any other world leader, the powers available to the leader of the USA outweighs that of the leader of the UK.

What you should have learnt from reading this chapter

- Despite the determination of the Founding Fathers to limit the power of the President, the executive was given substantial freedom of manoeuvre in foreign affairs.

- This power has been used to expand the territory of the USA and promote 'American values' around the world, both of which have led to recurrent armed conflict.

- By the twenty-first century, the USA had grown to be the world's dominant economic and military power.

- The concentration of such awesome power in the hands of one man adds to the prestige and authority that comes with being head of state (see Chapter 9) and would appear to undermine the whole system of checks and balances designed by the Founding Fathers.

- However, experience suggests that when Americans feel that their President is using these powers in ways that threaten the nation's liberties, there will be a reaction leading to the imposition of new restrictions, whether it be the War Powers Act of 1973 or the Supreme Court's ruling of *Hamdan* v. *Rumsfeld* (2006), which gave all prisoners captured during anti-terrorism operations the same legal protections as conventional prisoners of war.

- Thus, while being the head of state and having immense foreign-policy powers acts as a catalyst to the overall power of the President, so the political culture of challenging concentrations of power acts as a catalyst to the forces that check and balance the power of the President.

Glossary of key terms

Cold War A term describing the tension between capitalist nations, led by the USA, and Communist nations, led by the Soviet Union, which never erupted into direct conflict.
Pentagon A term applied, after the shape of its headquarters, to the Department of Defense, which is responsible for the armed forces of the USA.
State Department The department responsible for diplomatic relations between the USA and other countries.

Likely examination questions

Issues examiners may expect students to be able to effectively analyse include:

- The powers of the President and the effectiveness of the checks on his actions: imperial v. imperilled presidency
- The role of the Federal bureaucracy in aiding or hindering the President's agenda
- The importance of the Cabinet and/or Executive Office of the Presidency
- The importance of the Vice President

Thus, examples of the kind of questions that could be asked include:
'Presidents have only the power to persuade.' Discuss.
How important is the Executive Office of the President?

Where the question compares the US system with Britain's, issues tend to focus on the comparative powers of the two executives, especially in relation to the powers they wield and the constraints they face.

Thus, an example of the kind of question that could be asked is:

Compare and contrast the powers of UK Prime Ministers and US Presidents.

Helpful websites

www.whitehouse.gov – the official website of the President.

Every aspect of the presidency is the subject of such intense interest that the best way to keep up with the latest political developments is to view the websites of any of the most influential news organisations in the USA, such as *The New York Times* (www.nytimes.com), *The Washington Post* (www.washingtonpost.com) or CNN (www.cnn.com).

Suggestions for further reading

The greatest insight into the challenges facing Presidents and their responses are found in their autobiographies, such as *My Life* by Bill Clinton and *An American Life*, by Ronald Reagan.

Index

Bold indicates that the term is defined